DR. B.R. AMBEDKAR

Man of Millennium for Social Justice

Dr. C.P. Sharma

CENTRUM PRESS
NEW DELHI-110002 (INDIA)

CENTRUM PRESS
H.O.: 4360/4, Ansari Road, Daryaganj,
New Delhi-110002 (India)
Tel: 23278000, 23261597, 23255577, 23286875
B.O.: No. 1015, Ist Main Road, BSK IIIrd Stage,
IIIrd Phase, IIIrd Block, Bangalore-560085 (INDIA)
Tel: 080-41723429
Email: centrumpress@gmail.com
Visit us at: www.centrumpress.com

Dr. B.R. Ambedkar: Man of Millennium for Social Justice

First Edition, 2011

ISBN 978-93-80836-45-4

PRINTED IN INDIA

Printed at Mehra Offset Press, Delhi

Contents

Preface

Social justice was Babasaheb's passion. He believed that political democracy cannot last unless there lies at its base social democracy. He was anguished that "in politics we will have equality and in social and economic life we will have inequality" and wondered "how long shall we continue to deny equality in our social and economic life"?

He warned that if this contradiction was not removed at the earliest, "those who suffer from inequality will blow up the structure of democracy which this Constituent Assembly has so laboriously built up". We have not yet heeded Ambedkar's warning. Unfortunately, we have got used to this life of contradictions. Wide disparities in wealth and income persist and may be accentuated in the wake of unregulated globalization. Social justice, the signature tune of our Constitution, still eludes us.

Babasaheb was not in favour of hero worship and the personality cult that flourishes in our country. In the Constituent Assembly he underlined these dangers because, in his prophetic words, "In India, Bhakti or what may be called the path of devotion or hero-worship, plays a part in its politics unequalled in magnitude by the part it plays in the politics of any other country in the world. Bhakti in religion may be a road to salvation of the soul. But in politics, Bhakti or hero-worship is a sure road to degradation and to eventual dictatorship."

The book, which provides a rare opportunity to debate and discuss the contribution of Dr. Ambedkar in nation-building, will be great interest to all sections of people.

—Dr. C.P. Sharma

1

Brahmins versus Sudras

The thesis that the Sudras were Kshatriyas and that if they became the fourth *Varna* it was because they were degraded to that position does not wholly solve the problem. It only raises another problem. This problem is why were the Sudras degraded?

The problem is new. It has never been raised before. The existing literature on the subject cannot, therefore, be expected to contain an answer. The question is raised by me for the first time. As it is a question on which my theory of the Sudras rests, the burden of giving a satisfactory answer must rest on me. I believe, I can give a satisfactory answer to this question. My answer is that the degradation of the Sudras is the result of a violent conflict between the Sudras and the Brahmins. Fortunately for me, there is abundant evidence of it.

There is direct evidence of a violent conflict between the Sudra king, Sudas and Vashishtha, the Brahmin rishi. The facts relating to this conflict however are stated in a very confused manner.

In the narration which follows, I have made an attempt to state them in a neat and an orderly fashion. To understand the nature of the conflict, it is necessary first to understand the relations between Vashishtha and Vishvamitra.

Vashishtha and Vishvamitra were enemies and were enemies first and enemies last. There was no incident to which one of them was a party in which the other did not know himself as an opponent. As evidence of their enmity, I will refer to some of the episodes. The first one is that of Satyavrata otherwise called Trishanku. The story as told in the Harivamsha is as follows:

> *"Meanwhile Vashishtha, from the relation subsisting between the king (Satyavrata's father) and himself, as disciple and spiritual preceptor, governed the city of Ayodhya, the country, and the interior apartments of the royal palace. But Satyavrata, whether thorough folly or the force of destiny, cherished constantly an increased indignation against Vashishtha, who for a (proper) reason had not interposed to prevent his exclusion from the royal power by his father. "The formulae of the marriage ceremonial are only binding,' said Satyavrata, 'when the seventh step has been taken, and this had not been done when I seized the damsel; still Vashishtha, who knows the precepts of the law, does not come to my aid.' Thus Satyavrata was incensed in his mind against Vashishtha, who, however had acted from a sense of what was right. Nor did Satyavrata understand (the propriety of) that silent penance imposed upon him by his father... When he had supported this arduous rite, (he supposed that) he had redeemed his family position. The venerable muni Vashishtha did not, however, (as has been said), prevent his father from setting him aside, but resolved to install his son as king. When the powerful prince Satyavrata had endured the penance for twelve years, he beheld, when he was without flesh to eat, the milch cow of Vashishtha which yielded all objects of desire, and under the influence of anger, delusion, and exhaustion, distressed by hunger, and failing in the ten duties he slew... and both partook of her flesh himself, and gave it to Vishvamitra's sons to eat. Vashishtha hearing of this, became incensed against him and imposed on him the name of Trishanku as he had committed three sins. On his return home, Vishvamitra was gratified by the support which his wife had received, and offered Trishanku the choice of a boon. When this proposal was made, Trishanku chose his boon of ascending bodily to heaven. All apprehension from the twelve years' drought being now at an end, the muni (Vishvamitra) installed Trishanku in his father's kingdom and offered sacrifice*

on his behalf. The mighty Kaushika then, in spite of the resitance of the gods and of Vashishtha exalted the king alive to heaven."

The next episode in which they appear on opposite sides is that of Harishchandra, the son of Trishanku. The story is told in the Vishnu Purana and in the Markandeya Purana. The following account is given The story runs:

"On one occasion, when hunting, the king heard a sound of female lamentation which proceeded, it appears, from the sciences who were becoming mastered by the austerely fervid sage Vishvamitra, in a way they had never been before by anyone else; and were consequently crying out in alarm at his superiority. For the fulfilment of his duty as a Kshatriya to defend the weak, and inspired by the god Ganesha, who had entered into him, Harishchandra exclaimed "What sinner is this who is binding fire in the hem of his garment, while I, his lord, am present, resplendent with force and fiery vigour? He shall today enter on his long sleep, pierced in all his limbs by arrows, which, by their discharge from my bow, illuminate all the quarters of the firmament.' Vishvamitra was provoked by this address. In consequence of his wrath the Sciences instantly perished, and Harishchandra, trembling like the leaf of an ashvattha tree, submissively represented that he had merely done his duty as a king, which he defined as consisting in the bestowal of gifts on eminent Brahmins and other persons of slender means, the protection of the timid, and war against enemies. Vishvamitra hereupon demands a gift as a Brahmin intent upon receiving one. The king offers him whatsoever he may ask: Gold, his own son, wife, body, life, kingdom, good fortune. The saint first requires the present for the Rajasuya sacrifice. On this being promised, and still more offered, he asks for the empire of the whole earth, including everything but Harishchandra himself, his wife, and son, and his virtue which follows its possessor wherever he goes. Harishchandra joyfully agrees. Vishvamitra then requires him to strip off all his ornaments, to clothe himself in the bark of trees, and to quit the kingdom with his wife

Shaivya and his son. When he is departing, the sage stops him and demands payment of his yet unpaid sacrificial fee. The king replies that he has only the persons of his wife, his son and himself left. Vishvamitra insists that he must nevertheless pay, and that unfulfilled promises of gifts to Brahmins bring destruction. The unfortunate prince, after being threatened with a curse, engages to make the payment in a month; and commences his journey with a wife unused to such fatigues, amid the universal lamentations of his subjects. While he lingers, listening to their affectionate remonstrances against his desertion of his kingdom, Vishvamitra comes up, and being incensed at the delay and the king's apparent hesitation, strikes the queen with his staff, as she is dragged on by her husband. Harishchandra then proceeded with his wife and *little son to Benares, imagining that the divine city, as the special property of Shiva, could not be possessed by any mortal. Here he found the relentless Vishvamitra waiting for him, and ready to press his demand for the payment of his sacrificial gift, even before the expiration of the full period of grace. In this extremity, Shaivya the queen suggests with a sobbing voice that her husband should sell her. On hearing this proposal Harishchandra swoons, then recovers, utters lamentations and swoons again, and his wife seeing his sad condition, swoons also. While they are in a state of unconsciousness their famished child exclaims in distress. 'O, father, give me bread;* O, *mother, mother, give me food; hunger overpowers me and my tongue is parched.' At this moment Vishvamitra returns, and after recalling Harishchandra to consciousness by sprinkling water over him, again urges payment of the present The king again swoons, and is again restored. The sage threatens to curse him if his engagement is not fulfilled by sunset. Being now pressed by his wife, the king agrees to sell her, adding, however. If my voice can utter such a wicked word, I do what the most inhuman wretches cannot perpetrate.' He then goes into the city, and in self-accusing language offers his queen for sale as a slave. A rich old Brahmin offers to buy her at a price corresponding to her value, to do his household work. Seeing his mother dragged away the child ran after her, his eyes dimmed with tears, and crying 'mother.' The Brahmin purchaser kicked him when he came up; but he would not let his mother go, and continued crying 'mother, mother.' The queen then said to the Brahmin, 'Be so kind, my master, as to buy also this child, as without him I shall prove to thee but a useless purchase. Be thus merciful to me in my wretchedness, unite me with my son, like a cow to her calf.' The Brahmin agrees: Take this money and give me the boy.' After the Brahmin had gone out of sight with his purchases. Vishvamitra again appeared and renewed his demands: and when the afflicted Harishchandra offered him the small sum he had obtained by the sale of his wife and son, he angrily replied. If, miserable Kshatriya, thou thinkest this a sacrificial gift befitting my deserts, thou shall soon behold the transcendent power of my ardent austrere-fervour of my terrible majesty, and of my holy study,' Harishchandra promises an additional gift, and Vishvamitra allows him the remaining quarter of the day for its liquidation. On the terrified and afflicted prince offering himself for sale, in order to gain the means of meeting this cruel demand, Dharma (Righteousness) appears in the form of a hideous and offensive chandala, and agrees to buy him at his own price, large or small. Harishchatidra declines such a degrading survitude, and declares that he would rather be consumed by the fire of his persecutor's curse than submit to such a fate. Vishvamitra, however, again comes on the scene, asks why he does not accept the large sum offered by the Chandala, and when he pleads in excuse his descent 'from the solar race, threatens to fulminate a curse against him if he does not accept that method of meeting his liability. Harishchandra implores that he may be spared this extreme of degradation, and offers to become Vishvamitra's slave in payment of the residue of his debt; whereupon the sage rejoins, if thou art my slave, then I sell thee as such to the Chandala for a hundred millions of money.' The Chandala, delighted pays down the money, and carries off Harishchandra bound, beaten, confused, and afflicted, to his own place of abode. Harishchandra is sent by the Chandala to steal grave clothes in a cemetery and is told that he will receive two-sixths of the value for his hire; three-sixths going to his master, and one-sixth to the king. In this horrid spot, and in this degrading occupation he spent in great misery twelve months, which seemed to him like a hundred years. He then falls asleep and has a series of dreams suggested by the life he had been leading. After he awoke, his wife came to the cemetery to perform the obsequies of their son, who had died from the bite of a seipent At first, the husband and wife did not recognise each other, from the change in appearance which had been wrought upon them both by their miseries. Harishchandra, however, soon discovered from the tenor of her lamentations that it is his wife, and falls into a swoon; as the queen does also when she recognises her husband. When consciousness returns they both break out into lamentations, the father bewailing in a touching strain the loss of his son, and the wife, the degradation of the king. She then falls on his neck, embraces him and asks 'whether all this is a dream, or a reality, as she is utterly bewildered'; and adds, that "if it be a reality, then righteousness is unavailing to those who practise it." After hesitating to devote himself to death on his son's funeral pyre without receiving his master' leave. Harishchandra resolves to do so, braving all the consequences and consoling himself with the hopeful anticipation. If I have given gifts and offered sacrifices and gratified my religious teachers, then may I be reunited with my son and with thee (my wife) in another world.' The queen determines to die in the same manner. When Harishchandra, after placing his son's body on the funeral pyre, is meditating on the Lord Hari Narayana Krishna, the supreme spirit, all the gods arrive, headed by Dharma (Righteousness), and accompanied by Vishvamitra. Dharma entreats the king to desist from his rash intention; and Indra announces to him that, he, his wife, and son have conquered heaven by their good works. Ambrosia, the antidote of death, and flowers are rained by the gods from the sky; and the king's son is restored to life and the bloom of youth. The king adorned with celestial clothing and garlands, and the queen, embrace their son. Harishchandra, however, declares that he cannot go to heaven till he has received his master the Chandala's permission, and has paid him a ransom. Dharma then reveals to the king that it was he himself who had miraculously assumed the form of a Chandala. The king next objects that he cannot depart unless his faithful subjects, who are sharers in his merits, are allowed to accompany him to heaven, at least for one day. This request is granted by Indra; and after Vishvamitra has inaugurated Rohitashva the king's son to be his successor. Harishchandra, his friends and followers, all ascend in company to heaven. Even after this great consummation, however, Vashishtha, the family priest of Harishchandra, hearing, at the end of a twelve years' abode in the waters of the Ganges, an account of all that has occurred, becomes vehemendy incensed at the humiliation inflicted on the excellent monarch, whose virtues and devotion to the gods and Brahmins he celebrates, declares that his indignation had not been so greatly roused even when his own hundred sons had been slain by Vishvamitra, and in the following words dooms the latter to be transformed into a crane: 'Wherefore that wicked man, enemy of the Brahmins, smitten by my curse, shall be expelled from the society of intelligent beings, and losing his understanding shall be transformed into a Baka.' Vishvamitra reciprocates the curse, and changes Vashishtha into a bird of the species called Ari. In their new shapes the two have a furious fight, the Ari being of the Portentous height of two thousand yojanas= 18,000 miles, and the Baka of 3090 yojanas. They first assail each other with their wings; then the Baka smites his antagonist in the same manner, while the Ari strikes with his talons. Falling mountains, overturned by the blasts of wind raised by the flapping of their wings, shake the whole earth, the waters of the ocean overflow, the earth itself, thrown off its perpendicular slopes downwards to Patala, the lower regions. Many creatures perished by these various convulsions. Attracted by the dire disorder, Brahma arrives, attended by all the gods, on the spot, and commands the combatants to desist from their fray. They were too fiercely infuriated to regard this injunction; but Brahma put an end to the conflict by restoring them to their natural forms and counselling them to be reconciled."*

The next episode in which they came in as opponents is connected with Ambarisha, king of Ayodhya:

"The story relates that Ambarisha was engaged in performing a sacrifice, when Indra carried away the victim. The priest said that this ill-omened event had occurred owing to the king's bad administration; and would call for a great expiation, unless a human victim could be produced. After a long search the royal-rishi (Ambarisha) came upon the Brahmin rishi, Richika, a descendant of Bhrigu, and asked him to sell one of his sons for a victim, at the price of a hundred thousand cows. Richika answered that he would not sell his eldest son and his wife added that she would not sell the youngest; 'youngest sons' she observed, 'being generally the favourites of their mothers.' The second son, Shunasshepa, then said that in that case he regarded himself as the one who was to be sold, and desired the king to remove him. The hundred thousand cows, with ten millions of gold pieces and heaps of jewels, were paid down and Shunasshepa carried away. As they were passing through Pushkara, Shunasshepa beheld his maternal uncle Vishvamitra who was engaged in austerities there with other rishis, threw himself into his arms, and implored his assistance, urging his orphan, friendless and helpless state, as claims on the sage's benevolence. Vishvamitra soothed him; and pressed his own sons to offer themselves as victims in the room of Shunasshepa. This proposition met with no favour from Madhushyanda and the other sons of the royal hermit, who answered with haughtiness and derision: 'How is it that thou sacrificest thine own sons and seekest to

> *rescue those of others? We look upon this as wrong, and like the eating of one's own flesh. 'The sage was exceedingly wroth at this disregard of his injunction, and doomed his sons to be born in the most degraded classes, like Vashishtha's sons, and to eat dog's flesh, for a thousand years. He then said to Shunasshepa: 'When thou art bound with hallowed cords, decked with a red arland, and anointed with unguents and fastened to the sacrificial post of Vishnu, then address thyself to Agni, and sing these two divine verses (gathas), at the sacrifice of Ambarisha: then shall thou attain the fulfilment (of thy desire)'. Being furnished with the two gathas, Shunasshepa proposed at once to king Ambarisha that they should set out for their destination. When bound at the stake to be immolated, dressed in a red garment, he celebrated the two gods, Indra and his younger brother (Vishnu), with the excellent verses. The thousand-eyed (Indra) was pleased with the secret hymn; and bestowed long life on Shunasshepa."*

The last episode recorded in which the two had ranged themselves on opposite sides is connected with king Kalmashapada. The episode is recorded in the Adi Parvan of the Mahabharata:

> *"Kalmashapada was a king of the race of Ikshvaku. Vishvamitra wished to be employed by him as his officiating priest; but the king preferred Vashishtha. It happened however that the king went out to hunt, and after having killed a large quantity of games, he became very much fatigued, as well as hungry and thirsty. Meeting Shakti, the eldest of Vashishtha's hundred sons, on the road, he ordered him to get out of his way. The priest civilly replied:' The path is mine, O king; this is the immemorial law; in all observations the king must cede the way to the Brahmin.' Neither party would yield, and the dispute waxing warmer, the king struck the muni with his whip. The muni, resorting to the usual expedient of offended sages, by a curse doomed the king to become a man-eater. It happened that at that time enmity existed between Vishvamitra and Vashishtha on account of their respective claims to be priest to*

Kalmashapada. Vishvamitra had followed the king; and approached while he was disputing with Shakti. Perceiving, however, the son of his rival Vashishtha, Vishvamitra made himself invisible, and passed them, catching this opportunity. The king began to implore Shakti's clemency; but Vishvamitra wishing to prevent their reconciliation, commanded a Rakshasa (a man-devouring demon) to enter into the king. Owing to the conjoint influence of the Brahman-rishi's curse, and Vishvamitra's command, the demon obeyed the injunction. Perceiving that his object was gained, Vishvamitra left things to take their course, and absented himself from the country. The king having happened to meet a hungry Brahmin, and sent him, by the hand of his cook (who could procure nothing else), some human flesh to eat, was cursed by him also to the same effect as by Shakti. The curse, being now augmented in force, took effect, and Shakti himself was the first victim, being eaten up by the king. The same fate befell all the other sons of Vashishtha at the instigation of Vishvamitra. Perceiving Shakti to be dead, Vishvamitra again and again incited the Rakshasa against the sons of Vashishtha and accordingly the furious demon devoured those of his sons who were younger than Shakti as a lion eats up the small beasts of the forest. On hearing the destruction of his sons by Vishvamitra, Vashishtha supported his affliction as the great mountain sustains the earth. He meditated his own destruction, but never thought of exterminating the Kaushikas. This divine sage hurled himself from the summit of Meru, but fell upon the rocks as if on a heap of cotton. Escaping alive from his fall, he entered a glowing fire in the forest; but the fire, though fiercely blazing, not only failed to bum him, but seemed perfectly cool. He next threw himself into the sea with a heavy stone attached to his neck; but was cast up by the waves on the dry land. He then went home to his hermitage; but seeing it empty and desolate, he was again overcome by grief and sent out and seeing the river Vipasa which was swollen by the recent rains, and sweeping along many trees torn from its banks, he conceived the design of drowning himself into its waters; he accordingly tied himself firmly with cords, and threw himself in; but the river severing his bonds, deposited him unbound (Vipasa) on dry land; whence the name of the stream, as imposed by the sage. He afterwards saw and threw himself into the dreadful Satadru (Sutlej), which was full of alligators, etc., and derived its name rushing away in a hundred directions on seeing the Brahmin brilliant as fire. In consequence of this, he was once more stranded; and seeing that he could not kill himself, he went back to his hermitage."

There are particular instances in which Vashishtha and Vishvamitra had come into conflict with each other. But there was more than these occasional conflicts between the two. There was general enmity between them. This general enmity was of a mortal kind so much so that Vishvamitra wanted even to murder Vashishtha as will be seen from the Shalyaparvan of the Mahabharata. Says the author of the Mahabharata:

"There existed a great enmity, arising from rivalry in their austerities, between Vishvamitra and the Brahmin rishi Vashishtha. Vashishtha had an extensive hermitage in Sthanutirtha, to the east of which was Vishvamitra's. These two great ascetis were every day exhibiting intense emulation in regard to their respective austerities. But Vishvamitra beholding the might of Vashishtha was the most chagrined; and fell into deep thought. The idea of this sage, constant in duty, was the following: This river Sarasvati will speedily bring to me on her current the austere Vashishtha, the most eminent of all utterers of prayers. When that most excellent Brahmin has come, I shall most assuredly kill him.' Having thus determined, the divine sage Vishvamitra, his eyes reddened by anger, called to mind the chief of rivers. She being thus the subject of his thoughts became very anxious, as she knew him to be very *powerful and very irascible. Then trembling, pallid and with joined hands, the Saraswati stood before the chief of munis like a woman whose husband has been slain; she was greatly distressed, and said to him 'what shall I do?' The incensed muni replied, 'Bring Vashishtha hither speedily, that I may slay him.'*

The lotus-eyed goddess, joining her hands trembled in great fear, like a creeping plant agitated by the wind. Vishvamitra, however, although he saw her condition, repeated his command. The Sarasvati, who knew how sinful was his design, and that the might of Vashishtha was unequalled, went trembling and in great dreed of being cursed by both the sages, to Vashishtha and told him what his rival had said. Vashishtha seeing her emaciated, pale and anxious, spoke thus. Deliver thyself, o chief of rivers; carry me unhesitatingly to Vishvamitra, lest he curse thee.' Hearing these words of the merciful sage, the Sarasvati considered how she could act most wisely. She reflected, 'Vashishtha has always shown me great kindness, I must seek his welfare.' Then observing the Kaushika sage praying and sacrificing on her brink, she regarded that as a good opportunity, and *swept away the bank by the force of her current. In this way the son of Mitra and Varuna (Vashishtha) was carried down; and white he was being borne along, he thus celebrated the river. Thou, o Sarasvati, issuest from the lake of Brahma, and pervadest the whole world with thy excellent streams. Residing in the sky, thou dischargest water into the clouds. Thou alone art all waters. By thee we study.' Thou art nourishment, radiance, fame, perfection, intellect, light. Thou art speech, thou art svaha; this world is subject to thee. Thou, in fourfold form, dwellest in all creatures.' Beholding Vashishtha brought near by the Saratvati, Vishvamitra searched for a weapon with which to make an end of him. Perceiving his anger, and dreading lest Brahmanicide should ensue, the river promptly carried away, Vashishtha in an easterly direction thus fulfilling the commands of both sages, but eluding Vishvamitra. Seeing Vashishtha so carried away. Vishvamitra, impatient and enraged by vexation, said to her, 'Since thou, o chief of rivers, has eluded me, and hast receded, roll in waves of blood acceptable to the chief of demons' (which are fabled to gloat on blood). The Saratvati being thus cursed, flowed for a year in a stream mingled with blood. Rakshasas came to the place of pilgrimages where Vashishtha had been swept away, and revelled in drinking to satiety the bloody stream in security, dancing and laughing, as if they had conquered heaven. Some rishis who arrived at the spot some time after were horrified to see the bloodstained water, and the Rakshasas quaffing it, and made the most strenuous efforts to rescue the Sarasvati."*

The enmity between Vashishtha and Vishvamitra was not an enmity between two priests. It was an enmity between a Brahmin priest and a Kshatriya priest. Vashishtha was a Brahmin. Vishvamitra was a Kshatriya. He was a Kshatriya of royal lingeage. In the Rig Veda (iii.33.11) Vishvamitra is spoken of as the son of Klishika. The Vishnu Purana gives further details about Vishvamitra.

It says that Vishvamitra was the son of Gadhi who was descended from king Pururavas. This is confirmed by the Harivamsha. From the Rig Veda (iii:l: 21) we know that the family of Vishvamitra has been keeping 'fire' kindled in every generation. We also know from the Rig Veda that Vishvamitra was the author of many hymns of that Veda and was admitted to be a Rajarishi. He was the author of the hymn which is held to be the holiest in the whole of the Vedas namely the Gayatri hymn in the Rig Veda (iii.62.10). Another important fact we know about him is that he was a Kshatriya and his family belonged to the clan of the Bharatas.

It seems that about this time a dispute was going on between Brahmins and Kshatriyas on the following points:

(1) The right to receive gifts. Gift means payment made without work. The contention of the Brahmins was that nobody could receive gifts. To receive gifts was the right of the Brahmins *only.*

(2) The right to teach the Vedas. The Brahmins' contention was that the Khastriya had only the right to study the Vedas. He had no right to teach the Vedas. It was the privilege of the Brahmins only.

(3) The right to officiate at a sacrifice. On this point the Brahmins' contention was that Kshatriya had the right to perform sacrifices, but he had no right to officiate as a purohit (priest) at a sacrifice. That was the privilege of the Brahmins.

What is important to note is that even in disputes on these points and particularly on the third point they did not fail to play their part as the opponents of each other. This is confirmed by the story of Trishanku narrated in the Ramayana and which runs as follows:

> *"King Trishanku, one of Ikshvaku's descendants, had conceived the design of celebrating a sacrifice by virtue of which he should ascend bodily to heaven. As Vashishtha on being summoned, declared that the thing was impossible* (asakyam), *Trishanku travelled to the south, where the sage's hundred sons were engaged in austerities, and applied to them to do what their father had declined. Though he addressed them with the greatest reverence and humility, and added that the Ikshvakus regarded their family-priests as their highest resource in difficulties, and that, after their father, he himself looked to them as his tutelary deities,' he received from the haughty priests the following rubuke for his presumption: "Fool, thou hast been refused by the truth-speaking preceptor. How is it that, disregarding his authority thou hast resorted to another school (shakha)? The family-priest is the highest oracle of all the Ikshvakus; and the command of that veracious personage cannot be transgressed. Vashishtha, the divine rishi, has declared that 'the thing cannot be: ' how can we undertake the sacrifice? Thou art foolish, king; return to thy capital. The divine (Vashishtha) is competent to act as priest of the three works; how can we shew him disrespect?"*

Trishanku then gave them to understand, that as his preceptor and "his preceptor's sons had declined compliance with his requests, he should think of some other expedient "In consequence of his venturing to express this presumptous intention, they condemned him by their imprecation to become a Chandala. As this curse soon took effect, and the unhappy king's form was changed into that of a degraded outcast, he resorted to Vishvamitra (who, as we have seen, was also dwelling at this period in the south), enlarging on his own virtues and piety, and bewailing his fate. Vishvamitra commiserated his condition and promised to sacrifice on his behalf, and exalt him to heaven in the same Chandala form to which he had been condemned by his preceptor's curse. "Heaven is now as good as in the possession, since thou hast resorted to the son of Kushika.' "He then directed that preparations should be made for the sacrifice, and that all the rishis, including the family of Vashishtha, should be invited to the ceremony.

The disciples of Vishvamitra who had conveyed his message, reported the result on their return in these words: "Having heard your message, all the Brahmins are assembling in all the countries, and have arrived, excepting Mahodaya (Vashishtha). Hear what dreadful words those hundred Vashishtha, their voices quivering with rage, have uttered: 'How can the gods and rishis consume the oblation at the sacrifice of that man, especially if he be a Chandala, for whom a Kshatriya is officiating priest? How can illustrious Brahmins ascened to heaven, after eating the food of a Chandala, and being entertained by Vishvamitra?" These ruthless words all the Vashishtha, together with Mahodaya, uttered, their eyes inflamed with anger." Vishvamitra who was greatly incensed on receiving this message, by a curse doomed the sons of Vashishtha to be reduced to ashes, and reborn as degraded outcasts *(mritapah),* for seven hundred births, and Mahodaya to become a Nishada.

Knowing that this curse had taken effect Vishvamitra then, after eulogizing Trishanku, proposed to the assembled rishis that the sacrifice should be celebrated. To this they assented, being actuated by fear of the terrible sage's wrath, Vishvamitra himself officiated at the sacrifice as Yajaka; and the other rishis as priests (ritvijah) (with other functions) performed all the ceremonies."

In this dispute between Vashishtha and Vishvamitra, Sudas seems to have played an important part. Vashishtha was the family priest of Sudas. It was Vashishtha who performed his coronation ceremony. It was Vashishtha who helped him to win the battle against the ten kings. Notwithstanding this, Sudas removed Vashishtha from office. In his place he appointed Vishvamitra as his purohita who performed yajna for Sudas. This is the first deed of Sudas which created enmity between Sudas and Vashishtha. There was another deed which Sudas committed which widened and intensified the enmity. He threw into fire Shakti the son of Vashishtha and burned him alive. The story is reported in the Satyayana Brahmana. The Satyayana

Brahmana does not give the reason for such an atrocious act. Some light is thrown on it by Shadgurushishya in his Commentary on Katyayana's Anukramanika to the Rig Veda. According to Shadgurushishya, a sacrifice was performed by Sudas at which there was a sort of public debate between Vishvamitra and Shakti, the son of Vashishtha and in this debate, to use the words of Shadgurushishya:

> *"The power and speech of Vishvamitra were completely vanquished by Shakti, son of Vashishtha; and the son of Gadhi (Vishvamitra) being so overcome, became dejected."*

Here is the reason why Sudas threw Shakti into fire. Obviously, Sudas did it to avenge the dishonour and disgrace caused to Vishvamitra. Nothing could avert a deadly enmity growing up between Sudas and Vashishtha. This enmity does not seem to have ended with Sudas and Vashishtha. It appears to have spread to their sons. This is supported by the Taittiriya Samhita which says:

> *"Vashishtha, when his son had been slain, desired, 'May I obtain offspring; may I overcome the Saudasas.' He beheld this* ekasmannapanchasa, *he took it and sacrificed with it. In consequence he obtained offspring, and overcame the Saudasas."*

This is confirmed by the Kaushitaki Brahmana which says:

> *"Vashishtha, when his son had been slain, desired, 'May I be fruitful in offspring and cattle and overcome the Saudasas. He beheld this form of offering, the Vashishtha-sacrifice; and having performed it, he overcame the Saudasas."*

The conflict between Sudas and Vashishtha is not the only conflict between kings and the Brahmins. The Puranas record other conflicts also between kings and Brahmins. It is desirable to assemble them here. The first relates to king Vena. The story of his conflict with Brahmins has been told by various authorities. The following account is taken from the Harivamsa:

> *"There was formerely a Prajapati (Lord of creatures), a protector of righteousness called Anga, of the race of Atri, and resembling him in power. His son was the Prajapati Vena who was but indifferently skilled in duty,*

and was born of Sunita, the daughter of Mrityu. This son of the daughter of Kala (Death), owing to the taint derived from his maternal grandfather, threw his duties behind his back, and lived in covetousness under the influence of desire. This king established an irreligious system of conduct; transgressing the ordinances of the Veda, he was devoted to lawlessness. In his reign men lived without study of the sacred books and without the Vashatkara, and the gods had no Soma libations to drink at sacrifices. 'No sacrifice or oblation shall be offered'— such was the ruthless determination of that Prajapati, as the time of his destruction approached. I,' he declared, ' am the object, and the performer of sacrifice, and the sacrifice itself; it is to me that sacrifice should be presented, and oblations offered.' This transgressor of the rules of duty, who arrogated to himself what was not his due, was then addressed by all the great rishis headed by Marichi: 'We are about to consecrate ourselves for a ceremony which shall last for many years; practise *not unrighteousness, Vena; this is not the eternal rule of duty. Thou art in very deed a Prajapati of Atri's race, and thou hast engaged to protect thy subjects.' The foolish Vena, ignorant of what was right, laughingly answered those great rishis, who had so addressed him; 'who but myself is the ordainer of duty? Or whom ought I to obey? Who on earth equals me in sacred knowledge, in prowess, in austere fervour, in truth? Ye, who are deluded and senseless, know not that I am the source of all beings and duties. Hesitate not to believe that I, if I willed, could burn up the earth, or deluge it with water, or close up heaven and earth.' When owing to his delusion and arrogance Vena could not be governed, then the mighty rishis becoming incensed, seized the vigorous and struggling king, and rubbed his left thigh. From this thigh, so rubbed, was produced a black man, very short in stature, who, being alarmed, stood with joined hands. Seeing that he was agitated, Atri said to him 'Sit down'* (nishida). *He became the founder of the race of the Nishadas, and also progenitor of the Dhivaras (fisherman), who sprang from the corruption of Vena."*

The next king who came in conflict with the Brahmins was Pururavas. This Pururavas is the son of Ila and grandson of Manu Vaivastava. The details of his conflict with the Brahmins are given in the Adi Parvan of the Mahabharata:

> *"Subsequently, the wise Pururavas was born of Ila, who, as we have heard, was both his father and his mother. Ruling over the thirteen islands of the ocean, and surrounded by beings who were all superhuman, himself a man of great renown, Pururavas, intoxicated by his prowess, engaged in a conflict with the Brahmins, and robbed them of their jewels, although they loudly remonstrated. Sanatkumara came from Brahma's heaven, and addressed to him an admonition, which, however, he did not regard. Being then straightaway cursed by the incensed rishis, he perished, this covetous monarch, who, through pride of power, had lost his understanding."*

The third king in this series is Nahusha. This Nahusha is the grandson of Pururavas, the account of whose conflict with the Brahmins has been recounted above. The story of Nahusha and his conflict with the Brahmins has been told in two places in the Mahabharata, once in the Vanaparvan and again in the Udyogaparvan. The account, which follows, is taken from the Udyogaparvan. It says:

After his slaughter of the demon Vritra, Indra became alarmed at the idea of having taken the life of a Brahmin (for Vritra was regarded as such), and hid himself in the waters. In consequence of the disappearance of the king of the gods, all affairs, celestial as well as terrestrial, fell into confusion. The rishis and gods then applied to Nahusha to be their king. After first excusing himself on the plea of want of power, Nahusha at length, in compliance with their solicitations, accepted the high function. Up to the period of his elevation he had led a virtuous life, but he now became addicted to amusement and sensual pleasure; and even aspired to the possession of Indrani, Indra's wife, whom he had happened to see.

The queen resorted to the Angiras Vrihaspati, the preceptor of the gods who engaged to protect her. Nahusha was greatly incensed on hearing of this interference; but the gods endeavoured to pacify him, and pointed out the immorality of appropriating another person's wife. Nahusha, however, would listen to no remonstrance, and insisted that in his adulterous designs he was no worse than Indra himself. The renowned Ahalya, a rish's wife, was formerly corrupted by Indra in her husband's lifetime. Why was he not prevented by you? And many barbarous acts, and unrighteous deeds, and frauds were perpetrated of old by Indra; why was he not prevented by you?' The gods, urged by Nahusha, went to bring Indram; but Vrihaspati would not give her up. At his recommendation, however, she solicited Nahusha for some delay, till she should ascertain what had become of her husband.

This request was granted. Indrani now went in search of her husband; and by the help of Upashruti (the goddess of night and reveller of secrets) discovered him existing in a very subtle form in the stem of a lotus growing in a lake situated in a continent within an ocean north of the Himalayas. She made known to him the wicked intentions of Nahusha, and entreated him to exert his power, rescue her from danger and resume his dominion. Indra declined any immediate interposition on the plea of Nahusha's superior strength; but suggested to his wife a device by which the usurper might be hurled from his position. She was recommended to say to Nahusha that if he would visit her on a celestial vehicle borne by rishis, she would with pleasure submit herself to him.'

The queen of the gods accordingly made this proposal:' I desire for thee, king of the gods, a vehicle hitherto unknown, such as neither Vishnu nor Rudra, nor the Ashuras, nor the Rakshasas employ. Let the eminent rishis, all united, bear thee, lord, in a car; this idea pleases me'. Nahusha receives favourably this appeal to his vanity, and in the course of his reply thus gives utterance to his self-congratulation; 'He is a personage of no mean prowess who makes the munis his bearers. I am a fervid devotee of great might. Lord of the past, the future, and the present. If I were angry, the world would no longer stand; on me everything depends. Wherefore, goddess, I shall, without doubt, carry out what you propose. The seven rishis and all the Brahmin rishis, shall carry me. Behold, beautiful goddess, my majesty and my prosperity.'

The narrative goes on: Accordingly this wicked being, irreligious, violent, intoxicated by the force of conceit, and arbitrary in his conduct, attached to his car the rishis, who submitted to his commands, and compelled them to bear him. Indrani then again resorts to Vrihaspati who assures her that vengeance will soon overtake Nahusha for his presumption; and promises that he will himself perform a sacrifice with a view to the destruction of the oppressor, and the discovery of Indra's lurking place. Agni is then sent to discover and bring Indra to Vrihaspati and the latter, on Indra's arrival, informs him of all that had occurred during his absence. While Indra, with Kubera, Yama, Soma and Varuna was devising means for the destruction of Nahusha, the sage Agastya came up, congratulated Indra on the fall of his rival, and proceeded to relate how it had occurred.

Wearied with carrying the sinner, Nahusha, the eminent divine-rishis, and the spotless Brahmin-rishis, asked that divine personage, Nahusha (to solve) a difficulty; 'Dost thou, O Vasava, most excellent of conquerors, regard as authoritative or not those Brahmana texts which are recited at the immolation of king?' 'No', replied Nahusha, whose understanding was enveloped in darkness. The rishis rejoined; Engaged in unrighteousness, thou attainest not unto righteousness; these tests, which were formerely uttered by great rishis, are regarded by us as authoritative.'

Then (proceeds Agastya) disputing with the munis, Nahusha impelled by unrighteousness touched me on the head with his foot. In consequence of this, the king's glory was smitten and his prosperity departed. When he had instantly become agitated and oppressed with fear, I said to him, 'Since thou, a fool, condemnest that sacred text, always held in honour, which has been composed by former sages, and employed by Brahmin-rishis and hast touched my head with thy foot, and employest the Brahma-like and irresistible rishis as bearers to carry thee, therefore, shorn of thy lustre and all thy merit exhuasted, sink down, sinner, degraded from heaven to earth. For ten thousand years thou shall crawl in the form of a huge serpent. When that period is completed, thou shalt again ascend to heaven.' So fell that wicked wretch from the sovereignty of the gods. Happily, O Indra, we shall now prosper, for the enemy of the Brahmins has been smitten. Take possession of the three worlds, and protect their inhabitants, O husband of Shachi (Indrani), subduing the senses, overcoming thine enemies, and celebrated by the great rishis."

The fourth king to come into conflict with the Brahmins was Nimi. The details of the story are related in the Vishnu Purana which says:

> *"Nimi had requested the Brahmin-rishi, Vashishtha to officiate at a sacrifice, which was to last a thousand years. Vashishtha in reply pleaded a pre-engagement to Indra for five hundred years, but promised to return at the end of that period. The king made no remark, and Vashishtha went away, supposing that he had assented to his arrangement. On his return, however, the priest discovered that Nimi had retained Gautama (who was, equally with Vashishtha a Brahmin-rishi) and others to perform the sacrifice; and being incensed, he cursed the King, who was then asleep, to lose his corporeal form. When Nimi awoke and learnt that he had been cursed without any previous warning, he retorted by utering a similar curse on Vashishtha, and then died. Nimi's body was embalmed. At the close of the sacrifice which he had begun, the gods were willing, on the intercession of the priests, to restore him to life; but he declined the offer; and was placed by the deities, according to his desire, in the eyes of all living creatures. It is in consequence of this that they are always opening and shutting (Nimisha means 'the twinkling of the eye')."*

These foregoing cases of conflict have been referred to by Manu in his Smriti:

> *"Through a want of modesty many kings have perished, together with their belongings; through modesty even hermits in the forest have gained kingdoms. Through a want of humility Vena perished, likewise king Nahusha, Sudas, the son of Pijavana, Surnukha, and Nimi."*

Unfortunately, the bearing of these cases on the position of the Sudra has not been realised as fully as it should have been. The reason is that nobody has realised that this conflict was a conflict between Brahmins and Sudras. Sudas definitely was a Sudra. The others although they have not been described as Sudras are described as having been descended from Ikshvaku.

Sudas is also described as a descendant of Ikshvaku. There is nothing far-fetched in saying that they were all Sudras. Even Manu had no idea of this. He represents these cases as cases of conflict between Brahmins and Kshatriyas. Dr. Muir has failed to realise that Sudas was a Sudra and has in recounting these stories represented that the parties to these conflicts were Brahmins on the one hand and the Kshatriyas on the other. In a sense, it is true that the conflict was between Brahmins and Kshatriyas because the Sudras were also a branch of the Kshatriyas.

It would, however, have been far more illuminating if they had been described in more precise terms as conflicts between Brahmins and Sudras. The misunderstanding having been caused, it has remained and has continued to conceal the real nature of so important a part of the history of the Indo-Aryan society. It is to clear this misunderstanding that the hearing given to this Chapter is 'Brahmins *versus* Sudras' and not 'Brahmins *versus* Kshatriyas'. Understood as a history of conflict between Brahmins and Sudras, it helps one to understand how the Sudras came to be degraded from the second to the fourth Varna.

The Degradation of the Sudras

What is the technique which the Brahmins employed to bring about the degradation of the Sudras from the rank of the second to the rank of the fourth Varna?

The discussion has so far centred round two questions as to whether or not the Sudras were originally a part of the second or Kshatriya Varna and whether or not the Brahmins had not received sufficient provocation to degrade the Sudras. It is now necessary to deal with the question, which is logically next in order of sequence. What is the technique of degradation employed by the Brahmins?

My answer to the question is that the technique employed by the Brahmins for this purpose was to refuse to perform the Upanayana of the Sudras. I have no doubt that it is by this technique that the Brahmins accomplished their end and thereby wreaked their vengeance upon the Sudras. It is perhaps necessary to explain what Upanayana means and what importance it had in the Indo-Aryan Society. The best way to give an idea of Upanayana is to give a description of the ceremony.

As a rite *Upanayana* was originally a very simple ceremony. The boy came to the teacher with a *samidh* (a grass blade) in his hand and told the teacher that he desired to become a Brahmachari (*i.e.* a student) and begged the teacher to allow him to stay with him for purposes of study. At a later date it became a very elaborate ceremony. How elaborate it had become may be realised from the following description of *Upanayana* in the Ashvalayana Grihya Sutra:

Let him initiate the boy who is decked, whose hair (on the head) is shaved (and arranged), who wears a new garment or an antelope skin if a Brahmana, ruru skin if a Kshatriya, a goat's skin if a Vaishya; if they put on garments they should put on dyed ones, reddish-yellow, red and yellow (for a Brahmana, Kshatriya, Vaishya respectively); they should have girdles and staffs (as described above). While the boy takes hold of (the hand of) his teacher, the latter offers (a homa of clarified butter oblations) in the fire (as described above), and seats himself to the north of the fire with his face turned to the east, while the other one (the boy) stations himself in front (of the teacher) with his face turned to the west The teacher then fills the folded hands of both himself and of the boy with water and with the verse 'we choose that of Savitri' (Rg.V. 82.1) the teacher drops down the water in his own folded hands on to the water in the folded hands of the boy; having thus poured the water, he should seize with his own hand the boy's hand together with the thumb (of the boy) with the formula' by the urge (or order) of the god Savitri, with the arms of the two Ashvins, with the hands of Pushan, I seize thy hand, oh so, and so,' with the words 'Savitri has seized thy hand, oh so and so' a second time (the teacher seizes the boy's hand) with the words 'Agri is thy teacher oh so and so' a third time.

The teacher should cause (the boy, to look at the sun, while the teacher repeats 'God Savitri, this is thy brahmachari protect him, may he not die' and (the teacher should further) say Whose brahmachari art thou? Thou art the brahmachari of Prana. Who does initiate thee and whom (does he initiate)? I give thee to Ka (to Prajapati).' With the half verse (Rg. 111.8.4) 'the young man well attired and dressed, come hither' he (the teacher) should cause him to turn round to the right and with his two hands placed over (the boy's) shoulders he should touch the place of the boy's heart repeating the latter half (of Rg. III. 8.4). Having wiped the ground round the fire, the brahmachari should put (on the fire) a fuel stick silently, since it is known (from sruti) 'what belongs to Prajapati is silently done,' and the brahmachari belongs to Prajapati. Some do this (offering of a fuel stick) with a mantra to Agni: I Have brought a fuel stick, to *the* great Jatavedas; by the fuel stick mayst thou increase. Oh agni and may we (increase) through *Brahman'* (prayer or spiritual lore), svaha.'

Having put the fuel stick (on the fire) and having touched the fire, he (the student) thrice wipes off his face with the words I anoint myself with lustre,' it is known (from sruti) for he does anoint himself with lustre. 'May Agni bestow on me, insight, offspring and lustre: on me may Indra bestow insight, offspring and vigour (Indriya); on me may the sun bestow insight, offspring and radiance; what thy lustre is. Oh Agni, may I thereby become lustrous; what the strength is, Agni, may I thereby become strong; what thy consuming power is, Agni, may I thereby acquire consuming power.'

Having waited upon (worshipped) Agni with these formulae, (the student) should bend his knees, embrace (the teachers feet) and say to him 'recite. Sir, recite. Sir, the Savitri.' Seizing the student's hands with the upper garment (of the student) and his own hands, the teacher recites the Savitri first pada by pada, then hemstitch by hemstitch (and lastly) the whole verse. He (the teacher) should make him (the student) recite (the Savitiri) as much as *he* is able. On the place of the student's heart the teacher lays his hand with the fingers upturned with the formula place thy heart unto duty to me, may thy mind follow my mind; may you attend on my words single-minded; may Vrihaspati appoint thee unto me.' Having tied the girdle round him (the boy) and having given him the staff, the teacher should instruct him in the observances of a brahmachari with the words 'a brahmachari art thou, sip water, do service, *do* not sleep by day, depending (completely) on the teacher learn the Veda.' He (the student) should beg (food) in the evening and the morning; he should put a fuel stick (on fire) in the evening and morning. That (which he has received by begging) he should announce to the teacher; he should not sit down (but should be standing) the rest of the day.

The Upanayana ends with the teaching by the Acharya to the boy of the Vedic Mantra known as the Gayatri Mantra. Why the Gayatri Mantra is regarded as so essential as to require the ceremony of Upanayana before it is taught it is difficult to say.

From this description of the Upanayana ceremony two things are clear. First is that the purpose of Upanayana was to initiate a person in the study of the Vedas which commenced with the teaching of Gayatri Mantra by the Acharya to the Brahmachari. The second thing that is clear is that certain articles were regarded as very essential for the Upanayana ceremony. They are (1) two garments one for the lower part of the body technically called *Vasa* and the other for the upper part of the body called *Uttariya,* (2) Danda or wooden staff, (3) Mekhala or a girdle of grass tied across the waist.

Any one who compares this description of Upanayana as it was performed in ancient times with the details of the ceremony as performed in later days is bound to be surprised at the absence of any mention of thread called *Yajnopavita* to be worn by the Brahmachari as a part of his Upanayana. The centre of the modern ceremony of Upanayana is the wearing of this thread and the whole purpose of the Upanayana has come to be the wearing of this *Yajnopavita.* So important a part this *Yajnopavita* has come to play that most elaborate rules have come to be framed about its manufacture and its use.

The *Yajnopavita* should have three threads, each thread to be of nine strands well twisted. One *tantu* (strand) stands for one devata (deity). The *Yajnopavita* should reach as far as the navel, should not reach beyond the navel, nor should it be above the chest.

A person could wear more than one *Yajnopavita.*

A man must always wear *Yajnopavita.* If he took his meals without wearing the *Yajnopavita,* or answers the call of nature without having the *Yajnopavita* placed on the right ear, he had to undergo prayascitta, *viz.*, to bathe, to mutter prayers and fast. Wearing of another's *Yajnopavita* along with several other things (such as shoes, ornament, garland and kamandalu) is forbidden. Three ways of wearing the *Yajnopavita* are recognised: (1) nivita, (2) pracinavita and (3) upavita. When the cord is carried over the neck, both shoulders and the chest and is held with both the thumbs (of the two hands) lower than the region of the heart and above the navel, it is called *nivita.* Suspending the cord over the left shoulder in such a way that it hangs down on his right side, it becomes *upavita.* Suspending it on his right shoulder in such a way that it hangs down on his left side, it becomes *pracinavita.*

How did this *Yajnopavita* come in? Mr. Tilak offers an explanation which is worth quoting. Mr. Tilak says: "Orion or Mrigashiras is called Prajapati in the Vedic works, otherwise called Yajna. A belt or girdle of cloth round the waist of Orion or Yajna will therefore be naturally named after him as *Yajnopavita,* the *upavita* or the cloth of *yajna*

The term, however, now denotes the sacred thread of the Brahmins, and it may naturally be asked whether it owes its character, if not the origin, to the belt of Orion. I think it does on the following grounds:

The word yajnopavita is derived by all native scholars from *Yajna + Upavita;* but there is a difference of opinion as to whether we should understand the compound to mean an *upavita* for yajna i.e. for sacrificial purposes, or, whether it is the 'upavita of Yajnas.' The former is not incorrect, but authority is in favour of the latter. Thus the Prayoga-writers quote a *smriti* to the effect that 'the High Soul is termed *Yajna* by the hotris, this is his *upavita;* therefore it is *yajna-upavita.* 'A mantra, which is recited on the occasion of wearing the sacred thread means, 1 bind you with the *upavita* of *yajna",* while the first half of the general formula with which a Brahmin always puts on his sacred thread is as follows:

Yagnyopaveetham paramapavithram prajhapatheryathsahajam purasthaath

The Mantra is not to be found in any of the existing Samhitas, but is given in the Brahmopanishad and by Baudhayana. This verse is strikingly similar to the verse quoted above from the Haoma Yesht. It says, 'yajnopavita is high and sacred; it was born with Prajapati, of old.' The word *purastat* corresponds with *paurvanim* in the Avesta verse and thus decides the question raised by Dr. Haug, while *sahaja,* born with the limbs of Prajapati, conveys the same meaning as *mainyutastem.* The coincidence between these verses cannot be accidental, and it appears to me that the sacred thread must be derived from the belt of Orion. Upavita, from *ve* to weave, literally means a piece of cloth and not a thread. It appears, therefore, that a cloth worn round the waist was the primitive form *of yajnopavita,* and that the idea of sacredness was introduced by the theory that it was to be a symbolic representation of Prajapati's waistcloth or belt."

This explanation by Mr. Tilak is no doubt very interesting. But it does not help to explain some of the difficulties. It does not explain the relation of the *Yajnopavita* to the two garments the *Uttariya,* and the *vasa,* which are necessary for a person to wear while undergoing *Upanayana.* Was the *Yajnopavita* in addition to the two garments? If so, how is it that there is no mention of it in the early description of the ceremony of the *Upanayana?* It does not explain another difficulty. If that thread is a substitute for the cloth, how is it that the wearing of the cloth is retained in the *Upanayana?*

There seems to be another explanation. I offer it for what it is worth. According to it, the wearing of the thread had to do with the adoption of the *gotra.* Its object was to tie oneself to a particular *gotra.* It had nothing to do with the *Upanayana* as such, the object of which was to initiate a person in the study of the Vedas. It is not sufficiently realized that under the Ancient Aryan Law, a son did not naturally inherit the *gotra* of his father. The father had to perform a special ceremony to give his *gotra* to his son. It is only when this ceremony was performed that the son became the same *gotra* as the father. In this connection, reference may be made to two rules observed by the Indo-Aryan Society. One is the rule of impurities.

The other is the rule of adoption. With regard to the rule of impurity, brought about by death, the days of impurity vary with the kinship with the dead. If the kinship is very close, the days of impurity are greater than those in the case where the kinship is less close. The impurities attached to the death of a boy who has not been invested with the thread are very meagre, not extending for more than a few days. With regard to the rule of adoption, it lays down that a boy who was invested with the thread was not eligible for adoption. What is the idea behind these rules? The idea seems to be quite clear. The impurities are nominal because there being no thread, the boy had not formally entered into the *gotra* of his father. Adoption means entering into the *gotra* of the adoptive father. Once the thread ceremony had taken place the boy had already and irrevocably entered another *gotra,*.

There was no room for adoption left. Both these rules show that the thread ceremony was connected with *gotra* and not with *Upanayana.* The view that the thread has connection with gotra seems to receive support from Jain literature. Shloka 87 of the fourth Parvan of the Padmapurana by Acharya Ravishena reads as follows: "Bhagwan! you have told us, the origin of Kshatriya, Vaishya and Sudra. I am anxious to know the origin of those who wear the thread in their neck."

The words 'those who wear the thread in the neck' are very important There is no doubt that it is a description of the Brahmins. From this it is clear that there was a time when the Brahmins alone wore the thread and no other class did. Read with the fact that the *gotra* relationship was confined only to the Brahmins, it is clear that the thread ceremony was connected with bringing the boy into— actually tying him up to the *gotra*— of his father, and had nothing to do with *Upanayana* which was connected with the initiation in the teaching of the Vedas.

If this is true, then the thread ceremony and the *Upanayana* ceremony had different purposes to serve. At some later date the two merged into one. The reason for this merger appears to be very natural. The Upanayana without the thread ceremony involved the danger of the Acharya taking the boy in his *gotra.* It was to avoid the danger that the father of the boy performed the thread ceremony before handing him over to the Acharya. This is the probable reason why the two ceremonies came to be performed simultaneously.

Be that as it may, *Upanayana* means the teaching of the Veda by the Vedic Brahmin.

While I am convinced that my thesis is sound, it would be over confident to think that there will not be found persons who will not raise objections to it. I anticipate the following:

(1) Is absence of *Upanayana* the test of Sudradom;

(2) Did the Sudra ever have the right to *Upanayana?*

(3) How can the loss of *Upanayana* result in the general degradation of Sudras?

(4) What power did the Brahmins have to deny *Upanayana* to the Shadras?

Having stated the possible objections to my thesis, I like to give my reply to them.

To begin with the first. The best way to deal with this objection is to refer to the judicial decisions in order to find out what the Courts in India have regarded as the surest criterion for determining who is a Sudra.

The first case to which reference may be made is to be found in 7, M.I.A.18. It was decided by the Privy Council in 1837. The question at issue was whether at the relevant time there were in India any Kshatriyas. The contention of one side was that there were. The contention on the other side was that there were none. The latter contention was based upon the theory propagated by the Brahmins that the Brahmin Parashurama had killed all the Kshatriyas and that if any were left they were all exterminated by the Sudra king Mahapadma Nanda, so that thereafter there were no Kshatriyas left and that there were any Brahmins and Sudras.

The Privy Council did not accept this theory which they regarded as false and concocted by the Brahmins and held that the Kshatriyas still existed in India. The Privy Council did not however lay down any test by which a Kshatriya could be distinguished from a Sudra. In their view, the question must be determined in each case on its own facts.

The second case on the subject is to be found in I.L.R.10 Cal. 688. The question raised in the case was whether the Kayasthas of Bihar were Kshatriyas or Sudras. The High Court decided that they were Sudras. The partisans of the Kayasthas took the position that the Kayasthas of Bihar were different from the Kayasthas of Bengal, the Upper Provinces and Benares and that while those in the Upper Provinces and Benares were Sudras, the Kayasthas of Bihar were Kshatriyas. The court refused to make this distinction and held that the Kayasthas of Bihar were also Sudras.

The validity of this judgement was not accepted by the Allahabad High Court. In I.L.R.12 All. 328. Justice Mahamood at page 334 observed as follows:

> *"I entertain considerable doubts as to the soundness of the view which seems to have been adopted by both the Courts below, that the literary caste of* Kayasthas *in this part of the country, to which the parties belong, falls under the category of* Sudras, *as understood in the division of mankind in (he Institute of Manu or elsewhere in authoritative texts of the Hindu Law. The question is one of considerable difficulty not only ethnologically, but also from a legal point of view, so far as the administration of the Hindu Law to this important section of the population is concerned. I do not take the question to be settled by any adjudication of the Lords of the Privy Council either in* Sri Narayan Mitter *vs.* Sree Mutty Kishen Soondoory Dassee, *or in* Mahashova Shosinath Ghose *vs.* Srimati Krishna Soondari Dasi *in both of which the cases referred to adoption by Kayasthas of Lower Bengal, who may be distinguishable from the twelve castes of Kayasthas in Upper India, such as the North-western Provinces and Oudh. Nor do I think that the unreported decision of the learned Chief Justice and my brother Tyrell in* Chaudhari Hazari Lal *versus* Bishnu Dial *(First Appeal No. 113 of 1886, decided on the 15th June 1887), which was also an adoption case, settles the question. But I need not pursue the subject any further...."*

The third case is reported in (1916) 20 Cal. W.N.901. Here the question raised was whether Kayasthas of Bengal were Kshatriyas or Sudras. The High Court of Calcutta held that they were Sudras. The case was taken to the Privy Council by way of appeal against the decision of the Calcutta High Court. The decision of the Privy Council is reported in (1926) 47 I.A. 140. The question whether the Bengali Kayasthas are Sudras or Kshatriyas was not decided upon by the Privy Council but was left open. In between 1916 and 1926 the Calcutta High Court gave two decisions which held that intermarriages between Kayasthas of Bengal and *Tantis* and *Domes* two of the low castes, were legal on the ground that both of them were sub-castes of Sudras.

These decisions which caused further deterioration in the position of the Kayasthas were followed by another which is reported in I.L.R. 6 Patna 506. In a most elaborate judgement extending over 47 pages Mr. Justice Jwala Prasad went into every Purana and every Smriti in which there was a reference to the Kayasthas. He differed from the Calcutta High Court and held that the Kayasthas of Bihar were Kshatriyas.

Next come cases in which the question at issue was whether the Maharattas are Kshatriyas or Sudras. The first case in which this issue was raised is reported in 48 Mad. 1. This was an interpleader suit filed by the Receiver of the estate of Raja of Tanjore in which all the descendants as well as the distant a gnates and cognates of the Raja were made defendants in the suit. The kingdom of Tanjore was founded by Venkoji, otherwise called Ekoji, who was a Mahratta and the brother of Shivaji the founder of the Mahratta Empire. The judgement in the case covers 229 pages and the question whether the Mahrattas were Kshatriyas was dealt with in a most exhaustive manner. The decision of the Madras High Court was that the Mahrattas were Sudras and not Kshatriyas as was contended by the defendants.

The next case which also relates to the Mahrattas is reported in I.L.R. (1928) 52 Bom.497. The Court decided that: "There are three classes among the Mahratthas in the Bombay Presidency: (1) the five families; (2) the ninety-six families; (3) *the* rest. Of these, the first two classes are legally Kshatriyas."

The last case to which reference may be made is reported in I.L.R. (1927) 52 Mad. 1. The issue was whether the Yadavas of Madura were Kshatriyas. The Yadavas claimed themselves to be Kshatriyas. But the Madras High Court negatived the claim and held that they were Sudras.

Such is the course of judicial pronouncements on the issue as to how to determine who is a Kshatriya and who is a Sudra. It is a most confusing medley of opinion which settles little and unsettles much. The Kayasthas of Bihar, of the Upper Provinces (now U.P) and Benares are Kshatriyas, while the Kayasthas of Bengal are Sudras!! According to the Madras High Court all Mahrattas are Sudras. But according to the Bombay High Court, Mahrattas belonging to five families and 96 families are Kshatriyas and the rest are Sudras!! The Yadava community to which Krishna belonged is popularly believed to be Kshatriyas.

But according to the Madras High Court, the Yadavas are Sudras!!

More important for our purpose are the criteria which the courts have adopted in coming to their decisions than the particular decisions in the cases referred to. Among the criteria which the courts have laid down, the following may be noted:

(1) In I.L.R. 10 Cal. 688, the criteria adopted were *(i)* use of Das as surname, *(ii)* wearing the sacred thread, *(iii)* ability to perform the *homa, (iv)* the period of impurity, *(v)* competence or incompetence of illegitimate sons to succeed.

(2) In I.L.R. 6 Patna 606, the criterion seems to be general repute. If a community is Kshatriya by general repute it is to be treated as a Kshatriya community.

(3) In 48 Madras I, a variety of criteria were adopted. One was the consciousness of the community. The second was undergoing the ceremony of *Upanayana* as distingished from wearing the sacred thread. The third criterion was that all non-Brahmins are Sudras unless they prove that they are Kshatriyas or Vaishyas.

(4) In I.L.R. Bom. 497, the tests adopted were *(i)* the consciousness of the caste *(ii)* its custom, and *(iii)* the acceptance of that consciousness by other castes.

No one who knows anything about the subject can say that the criteria adopted by the various courts are the right ones. A criterion such as the period of impurity is irrelevant and of no value for determining the question. A criterion such as the capacity for performing *homa* is relevant but not valid. It mistakes effect for a cause. The criterion of consciousness is hardly a fair criterion. A community may have lost its consciousness by long disuse of necessary religious observances due to causes over which it has no control. The criterion of *Upanayana* stands on a different footing.

The courts have not put it properly. But there is no doubt that rightly understood and properly put the criterion of *Upanayana* is sound. The Courts have not made any distinction between the *de facto* position of the community and its position *de jure* in regard to *Upanayana,* and have proceeded on the assumption that what is true *de facto* must also be true *de jure.*

It is this fault in the application of the criterion of *Upanayana* which has produced anomalies and absurdities, such as one community having one status in one area and quite a different status in a different area— or allowing any pretender community to wear the thread and by continuing its pretence for a period to acquire a vested right or contrariwise punishing a community by declaring that it had no *de jure* right to wear the thread merely because it has not been wearing it *defacto.* The real criterion is not the wearing of the sacred thread but the right to wear the sacred thread. Understood in its proper sense, it may be said without fear of contradiction that the right to *Upanayana* is the real and the only test of judging the status of a person whether he is a Sudra or a Kshatriya.

The second objection is quite untenable. To assume, as the objection does, that from the very beginning the Aryan Society treated its different classes differently in the matter of *Upanayana* is to my mind a very unnatural supposition. Primitive society does not begin with differentiation. It begins with uniformity and ends in diversity. The natural thing would be to suppose that in the matter of the *Upanayana* the ancient Aryan society treated all its classes on the same footing. It may however be argued, on the other side, that such an original tendency in favour of uniformity need not be accepted as being universal, that it may well be that in the ancient Aryan society the Sudras and the women were excluded from *Upanayana.* Fortunately for me, it is not necessary for me to rely on logic alone though I contend that l*ogic* is on my side. For there is ample evidence both circumstantial as well as direct to show that both Sudras as well as women had at one time the right to wear the sacred thread.

That the ancient Aryan society regarded *Upanayana* as essential for all will be evident if the following facts are borne in mind.

Upanayana was allowed for the deaf, the dumb, the idiot and even the impotent. A special procedure was prescribed for the *Upanayana* of the deaf and dumb and idiots. The principal points in which their *Upanayana* differs from that of others are that the offering of *Samidh,* treading on a stone, putting on a garment, the tying of *mekhala,* the giving of deer skin and staff are done silently, that the boy does not mention his name, it is the *achary a* himself who makes offering of cooked food or of clarified butter, all the *mantras* are muttered softly by the *achary a* himself. The same procedure is followed as to other persons who are impotent, blind, lunatic, suffering from such diseases as epilepsy, white leprosy or black leprosy, etc.

The six *anuloma* castes were also eligible for *Upanayana;* this is clear from the rules for the Upanayana of Kshatriyas, Vaishyas and of mixed castes like Rathakara, Ambashtha, etc.

Upanayana was permitted to *Patitasavitrikas.* The proper age for the *Upanayana* of a Brahman boy was 8th year from birth, of a Kshatriya 11th year and of a Vaishya 12th year. But a certain latitude was allowed so that the time for *Upanayana* was not deemed to have passed upon the 16th, the 22nd and the 24th year in the case of Brahmins, Kshatriyas and Vaishyas respectively. After these years are passed without *Upanayana* taking place, a person was held to have become incompetent thereafter for learning the Savitri (the sacred Gayatri verse). Such persons were then called *Patitasavitrika* or *savitripatita.* According to the strict interpretation of rules, no *Upanayana* is to be thereafter performed for them, they are not to be taught the Veda, nor is anyone to officiate at their sacrifices and there is to be no social intercourse with them (*i.e.*, no marriage takes place with them). But even in their case, there was readiness to relax the rules subject to certain penances.

Upanayana was permitted in the case of Brahmaghnas. A Brahmaghna is a person whose father or grandfather had failed to perform *Upanayana.* The original rule was that if a person's father and grandfather also had not the *Upanayana* performed for them then they (*i.e.*, the three generations) are called slayers of *brahma* (holy prayers or lore); people should have no intercourse with them, should not take their food nor should enter into marriage alliance with them. But even in their case the rule was relaxed and they were allowed *Upanayana* if they desired, provided they performed the prescribed penance.

A further relaxation was made in the case of a person whose generation beginning with the great grandfather had not the Upanayana performed on them. Even they were allowed to have their Upanayana performed if they desired, provided they performed penance which included studenthood for twelve years and bath with the Pavamani, and other verses. On his Upanayana, instruction in the duties of the householder was imparted to him, and though he himself could not be taught the Veda, his son may have the samskara performed as in the case of one who is himself a *patitasavitrika* so that his son will be 'one like other Arya'.

Upanayana was permitted to the Vratyas. It is difficult to state exactly who the Vratyas were, whether they were Aryans who had for more than three generations failed to perform the Upanayana or whether they were non-Aryans who were never within the Aryan fold and whom the Brahmins wanted to convert to the Aryan faith. It is possible that it included both. Be that as it may, there is no doubt that Upanayana was open to the Vratyas provided they performed Vratyastomas. Vratyas were those who lead the Vratya life, were base and were reduced to a baser state since they did not observe studenthood (brahmacharya) nor did they till the soil nor engage in trade.

There were four Vratyastomas, the first of which is meant for all Vratyas, the second is meant for those who are *Abhishasta* who are wicked or guilty of heavy sins and are censured and lead a Vratya life, the third for those who are the youngest and lead a Vratya life and the fourth for those who are very old and yet lead a Vratya life. In each of the four Vratyastomas, Sodasastoma is always performed. It is by the Sodasastoma that they can attain this (superior status). The Sodasastoma was supposed to have the power to remove the guilt of these. By performing the Vratyastoma sacrifice, they should cease to be Vratyas and become eligible for social intercourse with the Orthodox Aryas, to have the sacrament *(samskara* of Upanayana) performed of them and then be eligible to study the Veda.

In the Vratyata-shuddisamgraha provision is made for the purification of Vratyas even after twelve generations subject to appropriate penances.

Upanayana was so highly thought of that Baudhayana (ii.10) allowed Upanayana for the Asvattha tree.

Given these facts, it is difficult to believe that the women and Sudras were excluded from the Upanayana by the Aryan society from the very beginning. In this connection, attendon may be drawn to custom prevalent among the Indo-Iranians who were very closely related to the Indo-Aryans in their culture and religion. Among the Indo-Iranians, not only both men and women but men and women of all classes are invested with the sacred thread. It is for the opponents to prove why the system was different among the Indo-Aryans. It is, however, not quite necessary to depend upon circumstantial evidence. There is enough direct evidence to show that there was a time when both women and Sudras had the right to Upanayana and did have it performed.

As to the Upanayana of women the statements contained in the Hindu religious books are quite explicit. Anyone who examines them will find that Upanayana was open to women. Women not only learned the Vedas but they used to run schools for teaching the Vedas, are even known to have written commentaries on the Women Purva Mimamsa. As to the Sudras, the evidence is equally positive. If Sudas was a king, if Sudas was a Sudra, if his coronation ceremony was performed by Vashishtha and he performed the Rajasuya Yaga, then there can be no doubt that the Sudras did at one time wear the sacred thread. In addition to circumstantial evidence and the evidence of the authors mentioned before, the Sanskara Ganapati cited by Max Muller contains an express provision declaring the Sudra to be eligible for Upanayana.

The only difference between the women and the Sudras is that in the case of women there is some plausible explanation given as to why the Upanayana of women was stopped, while there is no such explanation for stopping the Upanayana of the Sudras. It is argued that the Upanayana of women continued as long as the age of Upanayana and the age of marriage continued to be different. It is said that in ancient times the age of Upanayana was 8 and the age for marriage was considerably later. But at a later stage, the age of marriage was brought down to 8, with the result that the Upanayana as an independent ceremony ceased to exist and became merged in marriage. Whether this explanation is right or wrong is another matter. The point is that in the case of the Sudra, the Upanayana was at one time open to him, that it was closed to him at a later stage and that there is no explanation for this change.

Those who, in spite of the evidence to which I have referred, think that they must insist upon their objection should remember the weakness of their side. Assuming that the Sudras had never had the benefit of Upanayana, the question they have to face is why were the Sudras not allowed the benefit of the Upanayana. The orthodox theory merely states the fact that there is no Upanayana for a Sudra. But it does not say why the Sudra is not to have his Upanayana performed. The explananation that there was no Upanayaa of the Sudra because he was a non-Aryan is a modern invention which has been shown to be completely baseless. Either there was once an Upanayana and it was stopped or the Upanayana was from the very beginning withheld. Either may be true. But before one or the other is accepted to be true, it must be accompanied by reasons. There being no reason why the benefit of the Upanayana was withheld from the Sudra, the presumption must be in favour of my thesis which states that they had the right to Upanayana, that they were deprived of it and gives reasons why they were deprived of its validity.

The third objection is no objection at all. Only a person who does not know fully all the incidents of Upanayana can persist in upholding its validity.

The Aryan society regarded certain ceremonies as Samskaras. The Gautama Dharma Sutra (VIII. 14-24) gives the number of Samskaras as forty. They are: Garbhadhana Pumsavana, Simantonnayana, Jatakarma, namakarana, annaprasana, caula, Upanayana, the four vratas of the Veda, Snana (or Samavartana), vivaha, five daily mahayajnas (for deva, pitri, manushya, bhuta, and Brahma); seven pakayajnas (*viz.*, astaka, parvanasthalipaka, sraddha sravani, agrahayani, caitri, asvayuji); seven haviryajnas (in which there is burnt offering but no Soma, *viz.*, Agnyadheya, Agnihotra, Darsapuramasa, Agrayana, Caturmasyas, Nirudhapasubandha and Sautramani); seven soma sacrifices (Agnistoma, Atyagnistoma, Ukthya, Sodasin, Vajapeya, Atiratra, Aptoryama).

At a late stage a distinction appears to have been drawn between Samskaras in the narrower sense and Samskaras in the wider sense. Samskaras in the wider sense were really sacrifices and were therefore not included in the Samskaras in the proper sense, which were reduced to sixteen.

At a late stage a distinction appears to have been drawn between Samskaras in the narrower sense and Samskaras in the wider sense. Samskaras in the wider sense were really sacrifices and were therefore not included in the Samskaras in the proper sense, which were reduced to sixteen.

There is nothing strange about the Samskaras. Every society recognises them. For instance, the Christians regard Baptism, Cofirmation, Matrimony, Extreme Unction, Eucharist, the Lord's Supper and the Holy Communion as sacraments. There however seems to be a difference between the notions of the Indo-Aryans and say the Christians about the Samskaras. According to Christian notions, the Samskara or Sacrament is a purely spiritual matter—drawing in of God's grace by particular rites. It had no social significance. Among the Indo-Aryans the Samskaras had originally a purely spiritual significance. This is clear from what Jaimini the author of the *Purva Mimamsa* has to say about the Samskaras. According to Jaimini the general theory is that Samskaras impart fitness. They act in two ways. They remove taints and they generate fresh qualities. Without such Samskaras, a person may not get the reward of his sacrifice on the ground that he is not fit to perform it. Upanayana was one of the Samskaras and like other Samskaras, its significance was just spiritual. The denial of the Upanayana to the Sudras necessarily brought about a change in its significance. In addition to its spiritual significance it acquired a social significance which it did not have before.

When Upanayana was open to everyone, Aryan or non-Aryan, it was not a matter of social significance. It was a common right of all. It was not a privilege of the few. Once it was denied to the Sudras, its possession became a matter of honour and its denial a badge of servility. The denial of Upanayana to the Sudras introduced a new factor in the Indo-Aryan society. It made the Sudras look up to the higher classes as their superiors and enabled the three higher classes to look down upon the Sudras as their inferiors. This is one way in which the loss of Upanayana brought about the degradation of the Sudras.

There are other incidents of Upanayana. Since idea of these can be had if one refers to the rules laid down in the *Purva Mimamsa* One of these rules is that all property is meant primarily for the purpose of providing a person with the means of performing a sacrifice. The right to property is dependent upon capacity to sacrifice In other words, anyone who suffers from an incapacity to perform a sacrifice has no right to property. Capacity to sacrifice depends upon Upanayana. This means that only those who are entitled to Upanayana have a right to own property.

The second rule of the *Purva Mimamsa* is that a sacrifice must be accompanied by Veda mantras. This means that the sacrificer must have undergone a course in the study of the Veda. Aperson who has not studied the Vedas is not competent to perform the sacrifices. The study of the Veda is open only to those persons who have undergone the Upanayana ceremony. In other words, capacity to acquire knowledge and learning—which is what the study of Veda means-is dependant upon Upanayana. If there is no Upanayana the road to knowledge is closed. Upanayana is no empty ceremony. Right to property and right to knowledge are the two most important incidents of Upanayana.

Those who cannot realise how loss of Upanayana can bring about the degradation of the Sudras should have no difficulty in understanding the matter if they will bear in mind the rules of the Purva Mimamsa referred to above. Once the relation of Upanayana to education and property is grasped, all difficulty in accepting the thesis that the degradation of the Sudra was entirely due to loss of Upanayana must vanish.

It will be seen, from what has been said above, how the sacrament of Upanayana was in the ancient Aryan society fundamental and how the social status and personal rights of persons depended upon it. Without Upanayana, a person was doomed to social degradation, to ignorance and to poverty. The stoppage of Upanayana was a most deadly weapon-discovered by the Brahmins to avenge themselves against the Sudras. It had the effect of an atomic bomb. It did make the Sudra, to use the language of the Brahmins, a graveyard.

That the Brahmins possessed the power to deny Upanayana is beyond question. The doubt probably arises from the fact that there is nowhere an express statement showing the conferment of such a power upon the Brahmins. All the same, whatever doubt there may be lurking in the minds of persons who are not aware of the operative parts of the religious system of the

Indo-Aryans must vanish if account is taken of two things: (1) the exclusive right of the Brahmin to officiate at the Upanayana and (2) the penalities imposed upon the Brahmin for performing unauthorised Upanayana.

It is probable that in most ancient times it was the father who taught his son the *Gayatri,* with which the study of the Veda begins and for which the ceremony of Upanayana was devised at a later stage. But it is beyond question that from a very early time the function of performing Upanayana had been assigned to a guru or a teacher called the Acharya and the boy went and stayed in the Acharya's house. The questions as to who should be the Acharya and what should be his qualification have been the subject of discussions from very ancient times.

The Acharya must be a man learned in the Vedas. A Brahmana text says, "he, whom a teacher devoid of learning initiates, enters from darkness into darkness and he also (*i.e.* an acharya) who is himself unlearned (enters into darkness)."

The Ap. Dh. S. (1.1.1.12—13), lays down that an Acharya selected for performing one's Upanayana should be endowed with learning and should be one whose family is hereditarily learned and who is serene in mind; and that one should study Vedic lore under him up to the end (of brahmacharya) as long as the teacher does not fall off from the path of Dharma.

But the first and foremost qualification of an Acharya is that he must be a Brahmana: It was only in times of difficulty (*i.e.*, when a Brahmana is not available) that a person was allowed to have a Kshatriya or a Vaishya teacher. This exception was permitted only during the period when the distinction between the right to learn the Vedas and the right to teach the Vedas had not been made.

But when that distinction came to be made—and it was made in very early times— in fact the conflict between Vashishtha and Vishvamitra was just on this very point—the Brahmin alone came to possess the right to be an Acharya fit to officiate at an Upanayana. One thing therefore must be taken as well-established, namely that none but a Brahmin could perform the Upanayana ceremony. Upanayana performed by anybody else is not a valid Upanayana.

The other operative part of the Indo-Aryan religious system is the obligation imposed upon the Brahmin not to do any unauthorised act of a religious character. A Brahmin guilty of any such conduct was liable to punishment or penance. Many such penalties are to be found in the ancient Law Books. I refer to Manu and Parashara.

Manu (III.150ff.), lays down what class of Brahmins are to be deemed unworthy (to partake) of oblations to the gods and manes. In this list he includes:

III. 156.— "He who teaches for a stipulated fee and he who is taught on that condition, he who instructs Sudra pupils and he whose teacher is a Sudra, he who speaks rudely, the son of an adulteress, and the son of a widow."

Parashara says: "That Brahmana, who for the sake of dakshina (gift of money or fee) offers oblation into fire on behalf of a Sudra, would become a Sudra, while the Sudra (for whom he offers) would become a Brahman;" that, according to Madhava, propounds that the merit of the rite "goes to the Sudra and the Brahmana incurs sin."

Those who may ask what powers the Brahmins had to deprive the Sudra of his right to Upanayana may consider the combined effect of these two facts: (1) the Brahmin's exclusive right to officiate at an Upanayana, and (2) the penalties to which he is made liable for performing an unauthorized Upanayana. If they do, they will have no doubt that the combined effect of these two factors was to vest in the Brahmin the power of performing as well as of denying Upanayana. It is true that such a power has not been expressly vested in the Brahmin. That was because it was unnecessary to do by express terms what was in fact done by indirect but more effectual means. That the Brahmins are conscious of the possession of this power to deny Upanayana? is also beyond doubt.

So far as the records go, there are 16 reported cases in which they have threatened various communities by putting it into operation against them. In nine cases, they challenged the Kayasthas, in four they challenged the Panchalas, in one they challenged the Palshes. What is important is that they challenged even two Maratha Kings. These instances have occurred between 556 to 1904 AD. It is true that they do not belong to ancient times. It must however be remembered that these instances are mere evidences of the exercise by the Brahmins of their power to deny Upanayana. The power itself must have been acquired in much more ancient times. That they have acquired it earlier is not an empty assertion without support. Satyakama Jabali's instance which is very ancient is cited generally to prove that the Varna of a man was determined by his *guna* (mental and moral qualities) and not by his birth. While this is true, it is equally true that Jabali's case proves that even in ancient times the Brahmins had acquired the right to refuse to perform Upanayana.

The enumeration of these cases has very little value for the purpose in hand unless we know the deductions that could be drawn from the decisions arrived at in them. To be able to do this, we must know the details of each case. Unfortunately, in most of them beyond the decision other details are not sufficiently full for the purpose. There is only one case that of the Brahmins *versus* Shivaji in respect of which the details are full and well-known. The case is sufficiently important and it is therefore well worth detailed examination. The deductions deducible from it are not only interesting and instructive but they throw a flood of light on the point under discussion.

As is well known, Shivaji after having established a Hindu independent kingdom in the western part of Maharashtra thought of proclaiming himself a king by having his coronation performed. It was felt by Shivaji and his friends that the coronation ceremony if it was at all to be of any value must be performed according to Vedic rites. But in carrying out his wishes Shivaji found himself faced with many difficulties. He found that whether his coronation could be performed with Vedic rites dependent entirely upon the Brahmins. Nobody was from religious point of view qualified to perform the ceremony except a Brahmin. Secondly, he found that no such ceremony could be performed unless it was proved that he was a Kshatriya. There was a third difficulty, namely, that even if he was found to be a Kshatriya, he was past the age of Upanayana and without Upanayana there could be no coronation.

The third difficulty was a minor one for it could be got over by the performance of the Vratya Stoma ceremony. The first difficulty was the greatest stumbling block. It related to Shivaji's status. The question was, was he a Kshatriya? If that could be got over, the rest was easy. Shivaji's claim that he was Kshatriya was opposed by many. His principal opponents were Brahmins who were led by his own Prime Minister Moro Pant Pingle. Unfortunately for Shivaji even his Maratha Sardars had refused to give him social precedence and had ranged themselves against him.

In their view, he was a Sudra. Shivaji's claim was also in direct conflict with the well established thesis long insisted upon by the Brahmins that there were no Kshatriyas in the Kali age. Shivaji was living in the Kali age. Obviously he could not be a Kshatriya. This objection to his claim for the status of Kshatriya was further strengthened by the non-performance of the ceremony of Upanayana or the investiture of the sacred thread at the proper time, which was fixed by the Sastras to be the eleventh year in the case of the Kshatriyas. This was taken to be evidence of his being a Sudra. He was however fortunate in securing the services of one Gagabhat, a renowned Brahmin, resident of Benares, learned both in the Vedas and Sastras. Gagabhat solved all difficulties and performed Shivaji's coronation# on 6th June 1674 at Raigad first after performing the Vratya Stoma and then the Upanayana.

It seems that some Brahmins were prepared to perform Shivaji's coronation but with non-Vedic, *i.e.*, with Pauranic rites as is done in the case of Sudras. They predicted all sorts of evils to happen if Shivaji had his coronation performed with Vedic rites. Unfortunately these evils did take place and Shivaji who undoubtedly was superstitious had another coronation performed according to non-Vedic rites. The following account of this second coronation taken from Mr. C. V. Vaidya makes interesting reading: Obstructive and dissatisfied Brahmins there were even then as always. They did not deem the ceremony satisfactory, though it was acclaimed by the whole of Maharashtra. A poem named *Rajyabhisheka Kalpataru,* a copy of which is in the Library of the Bengal Royal Asiatic Society and which has been published from it *by* Itihas S. Mandal of Poona (Quarterly, Vol. X-I), embodies some objections raised against the coronation ceremony gone through.

This poem is not quite contemporary, as it mentions the later idea that Shivaji was an incarnation of Shiva (not of

Vishnu as represented by the earlier Shivabharata) though it is of the time of Rajaram. It gives an imaginary conversation between Nischalpuri, a learned Brahmin ascetic of Benares who was an opponent of Gagabhat, and Govindbhat Barve as taking place in Konkan. It recounts the ill omens which preceded and followed the coronation, such as the death of Prataprao Gujar, the death of Kashibai, wife of Shivaji, etc., and the wound caused to Gagabhat himself on the nose by the falling of a rafter. The poem expressly says that Gagabhat engaged for the ceremony those Brahmins only who were his followers and refused to employ those recommended by Nis'chalpuri. Many defects in the ceremony itself, are next mentioned.

Thus when Shivaji was getting into the chariot after the ceremony of ascending the throne Gagabhat himself first sat in the chariot and then Shivaji. After seeing the whole ceremony through Nis'chalpuri left the fort but told Shivaji that bad events would happen on the 13th, 22nd and 55th days. On the 13th day accordingly, Shivaji's mother died. Next a horse-shed was burnt at Pratapgad with good many horses in it and an elephant died on Sinhgad. These incidents induced Shivaji to call Nis'chalpuri back and through him and his Brahmins Shivaji performed afresh the ceremony of ascending the throne, not with Vedic rites, but Tantrik or magical. This ceremony is also described in detail. There are mentioned some Vedic mantras from Sama Veda as recited; but the ceremony was not Vedic. It was performed on Ashvin Suddha 5 (Lalita Panchami day S. 1596), as'is stated at the end of the peorn. This ceremony is also mentioned by J and Nis'chapuri is also spoken of in a Mohammedan record.'

Shivaji's case is important for several reasons. It is important because it proves that nobody except a Brahmin has the right to perform the Upanayana and that nobody can compel a Brahmin to perform it if he is not prepared to do so. Shivaji was the ruler of an independent kingdom and had already started styling himself Maharaja and Chhatrapati. There were many Brahmins who were his subjects. Yet, Shivaji could not compel anyone of them to perform his coronation.

It is important because it proves that the ceremony to be valid must be performed by a Brahmin. A ceremony performed by a non-Brahmin would be infructuous. It was open to Shivaji to have his coronation performed by a non-Brahmin. But he did not dare to do it. For he knew it would be without any social or spiritual efficacy.

In the third place, it is important because it proves that the power of determining the status of a Hindu depends entirely upon the will of the Brahmins. The decision in favour of Shivaji is sought to be justified by the genealogy which was brought from Mewar by Shivaji's friend, Balaji Avaji, and which connected Shivaji with the Sisodyas of Mewar who were reckoned as Kshatriyas. It has been alleged that the genealogy was a fabrication got up for the occasion.

Assuming it was not a fabrication, how can it justify the recognition of Shivaji's claim to be a Kshatriya? Far from establishing that Shivaji was a Kshatriya, the genealogy could do no more than raise another question, namely, whether the Sisodiyas were Kshatriyas. The Sisodiyas were Rajputs. There is considerable doubt as to whether the Rajputs are the descendants of the original Kshatriyas who formed the second Varna of the ancient Indo-Aryan community. One view is that they are foreigners, remnants of the Huns who invaded India and established themselves in Rajputana and whom the Brahmins raised to the status of Kshatriyas with the object of using them as means to suppress Buddhism in Central India by a special ceremony before the sacred fire and who were therefore known as the Agnikul Kshatriyas. This view has the support of many erudite scholars who are entitled to speak on the subject. Vincent Smith says:

In this place I want to draw attention to the fact, long suspected and now established by good evidence that the foreign immigrants into Rajputana and the upper Gangetic valley were not utterly destroyed in the course of their wars with the native princes. Many of course perished but many survived and were mixed in the general population of which no inconsiderable part is formed by their descendants. These foreigners like their forerunners the Sakas and the Yue-chi universally yielded to the wonderful assimilative power of Hinduism and rapidly became Hinduised. Clans or families which succeeded in winning chieftainships were admitted readily into the frame of Hindu polity as Kshatriyas or Rajputs and there is no doubt that the Parihars and many other famous Rajput clans of the north were developed out of the barbarian hordes which poured into India during the fifth and sixth centuries. The rank and file of the strangers became Gujars and the castes ranking lower than Rajputs in their precedence. Further to the south, various indigenous or aboriginal tribes and clans underwent the same process of Hinduised social promotion in venue of which Gonds, Bhars, Kharwas and so forth emerged as Chandels, Rathors, Gaharwars and other well-known Rajput clans duly equipped with pedigree reaching back to the sun AND the moon.

William Crooke says: Recent research has thrown much light on the origin of Rajputs. A wide gulf lies between the Vedic Kshatriyas and the Rajputs of mediaeval times which it is now impossible to bridge. It is now certain that the origin of many clans dates from the Saka or Kushan invasions of more certainly from that of the White Huns who destroyed the Gupta empire about 480 A.D. The Gujar tribe connected with the latter people adopted Hinduism and their leaders formed the main stock from which the higher Rajput families sprang. When these new claimants to princely honour accepted the faith and the institution of Brahmanism the attempt would naturally be made to connect them with the heroes of the Mahabharata and the Ramayana.

Hence arose the body of legend recorded in these annals by which a fabulous origin from the sun and the moon was ascribed to these Rajput families... The group denoted by the name Kshatriya or Rajput depended on status rather than on descent and it was therefore possible for foreigners to be introduced into these tribes without any violation of the prejudices of caste, which was then only partially developed. But it was necessary to disguise this admission of foreigners under a convenient fiction. Hence arose the legend how by a solemn act of purification or initiation under the superintendence of the ancient Vedic Rishis, *fire—born* septs were created to help the Brahmins in repressing Buddhism and other heresies. This privilege was confined to four septs known as Agnikula or fire-born-*viz.*, the Parmar, Parihar, Chalukya and Chauhan.

Dr. D. R. Bhandarkar also holds the same view. According to him, the Rjaputs are the descendents of Gujars, the Gujars were foreigners and that the Rajputs are therefore the descendants of foreigners.

The Brahmins engaged for the coronation could not have been ignorant of the origin of the Rajputs, and their claim to be descended from the Kshatriyas. But assuming that they did not know this fact they knew that there was already a previous decision of the Brahmins, namely, that there were no Kshatriyas in the Kali age. This was an old, long-standing decision. And if the Brahmins had respect for precedent, they were bound to throw out the claim of Sisodiyas as well as of Shivaji. Nobody would have blamed them, if they had done so. But the Brahmins had never accepted the law of precedent as binding upon them. With them there was no such thing as *stare* decisis.

Fourthly, it is important because it shows that the decisions of the Brahmins on matters of status were open to sale like the indulgences of the Catholic clergy. That the decision of Gagabhat was not an honest decision is obvious from the amount of money which Gagabhat and other Brahmins received as officiating priests. The amount of money spent on the coronation by Shivaji and how much of it went to Gagabhat and the Brahmins will be seen from the following details collected by Mr. Vaidya.:

> *"These ministers were presented each with* one *lakh of hon, one elephant, one horse, garments and ornaments. Gagabhat was given one lakh of rupees for seeing the whole ceremony through. The Dakshinas granted by Shivaji on the several occasions of the coronation ceremony were very large, as was suited to the occasion. Sabhasad reports that the whole expenditure amounted to one crore and forty-two lakhs of hons or 426 lakhs of rupees.*
>
> *Sabhasad relates that 50,000 Vaidika Brahmins had collected on the occasion of Shivaji's coronation. Besides these there were Jogis, Sanyasis, etc., by thousands. These were fed* or *given com below the fort It is related in contemporary papers that Shivaji, before coronation, was weighed against gold and almost every other metal as well as auspicious thing. Dutch record describing the ceremony in detail* on *3rd October PS. 1684 states that Shivaji weighed 17,000 hons or 160 Ibs. and he was also weighed against silver, copper, iron, etc., and against camphor, salt, sugar, butter, various kinds of fruit,*

betel-nuts, etc., and the value of the whole was distributed amongst Brahmins. On the 7th June, the day after the coronation, Dakshina was given in general and every Brahmin got three to five rupees and everyone else, whether woman or child two rupees and one rupee. In all, the Dakshina amounted to one and a half lakhs of hon in value.

Oxenden also states in his diary from 18th May *to 13th June that Shivaji was weighed against gold and the weight 16,000 hons, together with one lakh of hons in addition were distributed as Dakshinas among Brahmins.*

The above noted Dutch record further states that for the Vratya ceremony 7,000 hons were given to Gagabhat and 17,000 to other Brahmins. On the 5th of June Shivaji bathed in holy Ganges water and every Brahmin present was given 100 hons."

Can the amount paid to Gagabhat be taken as representing nothing more than a *fee* properly payable to a priest? There is one circumstance which may be depended upon to show that Gagabhat was not even paid enough. It is that what Gagabhat got was comparatively much less than what the Ministers of Shivaji got. Two facts must however be noted as telling on the other side before any conclusion is drawn from this fact. They completely nullify the argument. The first is that the ministers themselves had made large *presents* to Shivaji on his coronation. Moropant Pingle the Peshwa or Prime Minister of Shivaji, the Mujamdar had paid 7,000 hons and the other two ministers 5,000 hons each. Deducting these, the presents given to them by Shivaji must be said to be much smaller than they appear to be.

The second fact is that these ministers of Shivaji were the greatest opponents of Shivaji in this project of coronation. They were staunch in their view that he was a Sudra and that he was not entitled to have his coronation performed as it was a right which belonged to the Kshatriya only. It is therefore, no surprise if Shivaji gave them large presents with a view to silence them and win them over permanently to his side. The amount of money paid to the ministers by Shivaji is therefore no criterion to determine whether the amount paid to Gagabhat was no more than a fair fee for officiation. Indeed there are so many twists and turns taken by Gagabhat that one is forced to the conclusion that it was more than fair fee and that it included some part as illegal gratification to keep him straight.

In this business of coronation the man who took the most leading part in bringing it about was a Kayastha from Maharashtra by name Balaji Avaji who was the Personal Secretary to Shivaji. The first step Balaji took was to send three Brahmins as messengers from Shivaji to fetch Gagabhat from Benares with full information as to the status and purpose of Shivaji. What did Gagabhat do? He sent back the three messengers with a letter refusing to accept the invitation on the ground that in his view Shivaji was a Sudra and was therefore not fit for coronation.

The next step Balaji took was to collect evidence in support of Shivaji's claim to the status of a Kshatriya. He succeeded in obtaining a genealogy which showed that Shivaji was a Kshatriya descended from the Sisodyas who were Rajputs and rulers of Mewad. This evidence he sent with another messenger, to Gagabhat. Gagabhat seemed to have been impressed by the evidence for he agreed to come to Raigad to perform the coronation ceremony. What did Gagabhat do on his arrival? He said that he had re-examined the evidence and had come to the conclusion that Shivaji was a Sudra and was therefore unfit for coronation.

This is not the only somersault which Gagabhat took in this business. He took another and a very queer turn and declared that he was prepared to perform the coronation of Balaji Avaji for he was a Kayastha and therefore a Kshatriya but not of Shivaji who was Sudra. Gagabhat did not stop there. He again turned round and gave his opinion that Shivaji was a Kshatriya and that he was prepared to perform his coronation and even went so far as to write a treatise known as Gagabhatti in which he sought to prove that the Kayasthas were bastards. What do these twists and turns show? Do they not show he was a most unwilling priest and that his willingness has had to be bought by cash? If this argument is sound then there is no doubt that his decision that Shivaji was Kshatriya was sold by him for illegal gratification.

Lastly Shivaji's case is important because it shows that the Brahmins in the matter of status did not recognise as being bound by the principle of *res judicata.* They regard themselves as free to reopen a case already decided by them. For how long did the Brahmins respect their decision that Shivaji was a Kshatriya?

Shivaji started a new era from the day of his coronation, namely, 6th June 1674 which he called the Rajyabhisheka Era. How long did it remain in vogue? Only so long as Shivaji and his descendants remained as active rulers on the throne. The moment effective sovereignty passed into the hands of the Brahmin Peshwas, they issued an order to discontinue it. Not only did they stop the use of the Era, they began using the style of the Muslim Emperors, namely, the Fasli year. The Brahmins did not stop there. They went further and began to question the very status of Shivaji's descendants as Kshatriyas. They could do nothing to the two sons of Shivaji, Sambhaji and Rajaram. Shivaji had their Upanayana performed in his life-time by Brahmins with Vedic rites. They could do nothing to his grandson, Shahu because the Brahmins had no ruling power in their hands.

The moment Shahu transferred his sovereign powers to his Brahmin Peshwa their road to repudiation became clear. There is no evidence whether Ramjee Raje the successor and adopted son of Shahu, who was minor and whose guardians were the Peshwas, had his Upanayana performed and if so, whether it was performed with Vedic rites. But there is definite evidence that the Upanayana ceremony of his successors, Shahu II, who was adopted in 1777 had been performed with *Pauranic* rites and by the direction of the Peshwas

The performance of Upanayana of Shahu II with *Pauranic* rites was tantamount to his being regarded by the Peshwas as a Sudra. For it is only in the case of a Sudra that the ceremonies are performed with *Pauranic* rites. What happened to Maharaja Pratapsing who succeeded Shahu II in 1808 whether or not his Upanayana was performed and if performed whether it was performed with Vedic rites or *Pauranic* rites it is not possible to be definite. One thing, however, is definitely known that in about 1827 the Shankarcharya of Karvir in his judgement about the status of the Kayasthas of Sangli stated *"that there were no Kshatriyas in the Kali age and that documents showing that neither Shivaji, nor Sambhaji nor Shahu were Kshatriyas exist in his Daftar*". It is alleged that this statement is not to be found in the original judgement but was interpolated by the Brahmin Raja of Sangli. Be that as it may, it was a direct challenge to the status of Pratapsinha as a descent of Shivaji. Pratapsinha had to put the issue to a conference of Brahmins which was held in Satara in 1830. The majority gave a decision in favour and saved Pratapsinha from being degraded to the status of a Sudra.

Foiled in their attempt to level down one line of Shivaji to the status of a Sudra, the Brahmins began their attack on the status of the second line of Shivaji which had established itself at Kolhapur. In the reign of one of the rulers of Kolhapur by name Babasaheb Maharaj, the Palace Priest by name Raghunath Sastri Parvate took into his head to perform all ceremonies in the Palace with *Pauranic* rites. It is said that he was stopped from continuing the practice. Babasaheb died in 1886. From 1886 to 1894, all rulers were minors and the administration was in the hands of the British. There is no direct evidence as to the exact manner and mode of ceremonial performances adopted by the Palace priest.

In 1902, the late Shahu Maharaj issued order to the Palace priest to perform all ceremonies in the Vedic manner. The priest refused and insisted on performing it in the *Pauranic* manner suggesting thereby that the rulers of Kolhapur were Sudras and not Kshatriyas. The part played by Sankaracharya of Karvir Math in this affair is very noteworthy. At the time of the controversy the head of the Math called Guru, had adopted a disciple (Sishya) by name Brahmanalkar and had given him all the rights of the head of the Math. At first both the Guru and the Sishya were on the side of the Palace Priest and against the Maharaja. Later on, the disciple took the side of the Maharaja and accepted his status as a Kshatriya. The Guru who remained on the side of the Priest excommunicated the Sishya. The Maharaja later on tried to create his own Sankaracharya but he too proved false to the Maharaja.

Shivaji was recognised as a Kshatriya. Obviously, that status was not a personal honour conferred on him. It was a status in tail and belonged to his family as well as to his descendants. Nobody could question it. It could be lost by a particular descendant by doing some act which was inconsistent with it.

It could not be lost generally. No act inconsistent with the Kshatriya status was attributed to any of the descendants of Shivaji. Yet the Brahmins came forward to repudiate the decision on their status.

This could happen only because the Brahmins claimed the power to do and undo the status of any Hindu at any time. They can raise a Sudra to the status of a Kshatriya. They can degrade the Kshatriya to the status of a Sudra. Shivaji's case proves that their sovereignty in this matter is without limit and without challenge.

These instances are no doubt drawn from the Bombay Presidency only. But the principles from them are clear and general in their application. They are:

(1) That the Brahmins have the exclusive right to perform the Upanayana. Neither Shivaji, nor Pratap Sinha nor the Kayasthas, Panchals or Palashes wanted the Upanayana to be performed by a non-Brahmin. It is only once that the Kayasthas resolved to have their ceremonies performed by Kayasthas. But it was only a paper resolution.

(2) The Brahmin has the right to say whose Upanayana he will perform and whose he will not perform. In other words, the Brahmin is the sole judge of deciding whether a given community is entitled to Upanayana.

(3) The support of the Brahmins for the performance of Upanayana need not be based on honest grounds. It could be purchased by money. Shivaji got the support of the Brahmin Gagabhat on payment of money.

(4) The denial of Upanayana by the Brahmins need not be on legal or religious ground. It is possible for the denial to be based on purely political grounds. The refusal by the Brahmins of Upanayana to Kayasthas was entirely due to political rivalry between the two.

(5) The right of appeal against the denial of an Upanayana by a Brahmin is only to a Vidvat-Parishad and the Vidvat-Parishad is an assembly for which a Brahmin alone is eligible to be a member.

From the foregoing discussion. It must be clear to all that the Brahmins did possess the power to deny Upanayana. Given the powers and the motive, there is nothing strange if they used it against the Sudras.

The Story of Reconciliation

So far I have attempted to establish the following propositions:

(1) That it is the Brahmins who brought about the fall of the Sudras from the second to the fourth Varna in the Indo-Aryan Society;

(2) That the technique adopted by the Brahmins to degrade the Sudras was to deny them the benefit of the Upanayana;

(3) That this act of degradation was born out of the spirit of revenge on the part of the Brahmins who were groaning under the tyrannies and oppressions and indignities to which they were subjected by the Sudra kings.

While all this is crystal clear, there may be some who may yet have some such questions to ask, namely:

(i) Why should a quarrel with a few kings make the Brahmins the enemies of the whole Sudra community?

(ii) Was the provocation so great as to create a feeling of hatred and desire to seek vengeance?

(iii) Were not the parties reconciled? If they were, then their was no occasion for the Brahmins to degrade the Sudras.

(iv) How did the Sudras suffer this degradation?

These questions I admit have in them enough force and substance to call for serious consideration. It is only proper that they should be answered. The question why the Brahmins, because of their quarrels with a few kings, should proceed to degrade the whole community of Sudras is not only relevant but is also very pertinent. There would, however, be no difficulty to answer this question if two things are borne in mind.

In the first place, the conflicts described between the Brahmins and the Sudra kings were not individual conflicts though they appear to be so. On the side of the Brahmins there is no doubt that the whole class was involved. Barring the episode relating to Vashishtha, all other episodes relate to

Brahmins in general. On the side of the kings, it is true that the episodes mention individual kings as being involved in this conflict with the Brahmins. But it must not be forgotten that they all belonged to the same line to which Sudas belonged.

In so far as Sudas is concerned, the conflict was between the Brahmins and the Sudra clan of Kshatriyas. Of this, there can be no doubt. We have no direct evidence to say that the other offending kings also belonged to the Sudra clan of Kshatriyas. But we have other evidence which leads to the conclusion that they belonged to the same line of descent as Sudas. Attention is invited to the following genealogical tree appearing overleaf which is taken from the Adi Parvan of the Mahabharata.

The interrelationship of the Kshatriya kings who came in conflict with the Brahmins throws some interesting light On the subject, *Pururavas* is the son of Ila and the grandson of Manu Vaivasvata. *Nahusha* is the grandson of Pururavas. *Nimi* is one of the sons of Ikshvaku, who is the son of Manu Vivasvat. *Trishanku* is 28th in descent from Ikshvaku. *Sudas* is descended from Ikshvaku and is 50th in descent from him. *Vena* is the son of Manu Vaivasvata. All of them claimed descent from Manu, some from him and some from Ikshvaku. Being descendants of Manu and Ikshvaku, it is possible to argue that they were all kindred of Sudas. Given the fact that Sudas is a Sudra, it follows logically that all these kings belonged to the Sudra group.

We have no direct evidence, but there would be nothing unnatural in supposing that in these conflicts with the Brahmins, the whole Sudra community, not merely a few Sudra kings, was involved. This conflict, it must be remembered, has taken place in the ancient past when life was tribal in thought and in action, and when the rule was that what was done by one individual belonging to the tribe was deemed to be done by the whole tribe.

In all ancient societies the unit was the tribe or the community and not the individual, with the result that the guilt of the individual was the guilt of the community and the guilt of the community was the guilt of every individual belonging to it. If this fact is borne in mind, then it would be quite natural to say that the Brahmins did not confine their hatred to the offending kings, but extended it to the whole of the Sudra community and applied the ban against Upanayana to all the Sudras.

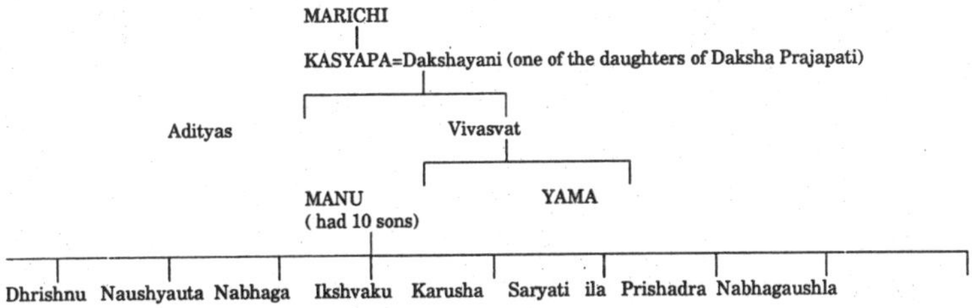

As to whether there was enough provocation, the matter is hardly open to question. Tempers must have risen high on both sides. There was enough combustible material on both sides for an explosion to take place.

On the side of the Brahmins, it is evident that their pretensions to social superiority and their claim for special privileges had become outrageous in character and unbearable in extent. The following is a catalogue of the pretensions put fourth by the Brahmins:

(i) The Brahmin must be acknowledged to be the guru to all Vamas by the mere fact of his birth;

(ii) The Brahmana has the sole right of deciding upon the duties of all other classes, what conduct was proper to them and what should be their means of livelihood; and the other classes were to abide by his directions and the king was to rule in accordance with such directions;

(iii) The Brahmana is not subject to the authority of the king. The king was the ruler of all except the Brahmana;

(iv) The Brahmana is exempt from (1) whipping; (2) fetters being put on him; (3) the imposition of fines; (4) exile; (5) censure and (6) abandonment.

(v) A Shrotriya (a Brahmana learned in Vedas) is free from taxes.

(vi) A Brahmana is entitled to claim the whole of the treasure trove if he found it If the king found it he must give half to the Brahmana.

(vii) The property of a Brahmana dying without an heir shall not go to the king, but shall be distributed among Shrotriyas or Brahmanas.

(viii) The king meeting a Shrotriya or a Brahmana on the road must give way to the Brahmana.

(ix) The Brahmana must be saluted first

(x) The person of a Brahmana is sacred. No death sentence could be passed against a Brahmana even if he is guilty of murder.

(xi) Threatening a Brahmana with assault, or striking him or drawing blood from his body is an offence.

(xii) For certain offences the Brahmana must receive a lesser punishment than members of other classes.

(xiii) The king should not summon a Brahmana as a witness where the litigant is not a Brahmana.

(xiv) Even when a woman has had ten former husbands who are not Brahmanas, if a Brahmana marries such a woman, it is he alone who is her husband and not a Rajanya or a Vaishya to whom she may have been married.

After discussing these pretensions and privileges claimed by the Brahmanas, Mr. Kane says : "Further privileges assigned to Brahmanas are: free access to the houses of other people for the purpose of begging alms; the right to collect fuel, flowers, water and the like without its being regarded as a theft, and to converse with other men's wives without being restrained (in such conversation) by others; and the right to cross rivers without paying any fare for the ferry-boat and to be conveyed (to the other bank) before other people. When engaged in trading and using a ferry boat, they shall have to pay no toll. A Brahmana who is engaged in travelling, who is tired and has nothing to eat, commits no wrong by taking two canes of sugar or two esculent roots."

These privileges have no doubt grown in course of time and it is difficult to say which of them had become vested rights when these conflicts were raging. But there is no doubt that some of the most annoying ones such as (i), (ii), (iii), (viii) and (xiv) had then come into existence. These were enough to infuriate any decent and self-respecting body of men.

On the side of the Kshatriya kings they could not be supposed to be willing to take things lying low. How could they? It must not be forgotten that most of the Kshatriya kings who came into conflict with the Brahmins, belonged to the solar line. They differed from the Kshatriyas of the lunar line in learning, in pride and in martial spirit The Kshatriyas who belonged to the solar line were a virile people, while those who belonged to the lunar line were an imbecile lot without any self-respect. The former challenged *the* Brahmins. The latter succumbed to them and became their slaves. This was as it should be. For while the Kshatriyas of the lunar line were devoid of any learning, those belonging to the solar line were not merely the equals of Brahmins in the matter of learning, they were their superiors. Several of them were the authors of the Vedic hymns and were known as Rajarishis. This was particularly true of those who came into conflict with the Brahmins.

According to the Anukramanika to the Rig Veda as well as according to tradition the following hymns are said to have been composed by the under mentioned kings: "vi.15: Vitahavya (or Bharadvaja); x.9: Sindhuvipa, son of Ambarisha (or Trisiras, son of Tvashtri); x.75: Sindhukshit, son of Priyamedha; x. 133, *Sudas* son of Pijavana; x. 134, Mandhatri, son of Yuvanasva; x. 179, Sibi, son of Usinara, Pratardana, son of Divodasa and king of Kasi, and Vasumanas, son of Rohidasva; and x. 148 is declared to have had *Prithi Vainya."*

The Matsya Purana also gives the lists of those who composed the hymns of the Rig Veda in a passage which says: "Bhrigu, Kashya, Prachetas, Dadhicha, Atmavat, Aurva, Jamadagni, Kripa, Sharadvata, Arshtishena, Yudhajit, Vitahavya, Suvarchas, *Vaina, Prithu, Divodasa,* Brahmasva, Gritsa, Saunaka—these are the nineteen Bhrigus, composers of hymns. Angiras, Vedhasa, Bharadvaja, Bhalandana, Ritabadha, Garga, Siti, Sankriti, Gurudhira, Mandhatri, Ambarisha, Yuvanasva, Purukutsa, Pradyumna, Shravanasya, Ajamidha, Haryashva, Takshapa, Kavi, Prishadashva, Virupa, Kanva, Mudgala, Utathya, Sharadvat, Vajasravas, Apasya, Suvitta, Vamadeva, Ajita, Brihaduktha, Dirghatamas, Kakshivat, are recorded as thirty-three eminent Angirases.

These were all composers of hymns. Now learn the Kasyapas... *Vishvamitra,* son of Gadhi, Devaraja, Bala the wise Madhuchhandas, Rishabha, Aghamarshana, Ashtaka, Lohita, Bhritakila, Vedasravas, Devarata, Puranashva, Dhananjaya, the glorious Mithila, Salankayana,—these are to be known as the thirteen devout and eminent Kusikas. Manu Vaivasvata, Ida, king *Pururavas,* these are to be known as the eminent utterers of hymns among the Kshatriyas. Bhalanda, Vandya, and Sanskirti these are always to be known as the three eminent persons among the Vaishyas who were composers of hymns. Thus ninety-one persons have been declared by whom hymns have been given birth to, Brahmanas, Kshatriyas and Vaishyas.

In the list of the authors of the Vedic hymns there are not only names of many Kshatriyas, there are names of many of the Kshatriyas who had come into conflict with the Brahmins. The Kshatriyas were the leaders among the Vedic hymn makers. The most famous Vedic hymn namely the Gayatri mantra is the production of Vishvamitra who was a Kshatriya. It was impossible for the Kshatriyas of this calibre not to take up this challenge of the Brahmins.

Their pride which was born out of their prowess and their learning must have been so greatly wounded by the pretensions of the Brahmins that when they did take up the challenge of the Brahmins they did it in a ruthless spirit.

They hit the Brahmins hip and thigh. Vena forced them to worship him and no other god; Pururavas looted their wealth. Nahusha yoked them to his chariot and made them drag it through the city. Nimi flouted the exclusive and hereditary right of a family priest to perform all the ceremonies in the family and Sudas went to the length of burning alive the son of Vashishtha who was once his family priest. Surely, there cannot be greater cause to provoke the Brahmins to seek their vengeance upon the Sudras.

On the point of possible reconciliation between the Brahmins and the Sudras, there is no doubt some evidence on which some people might rely. Before stating my views upon the worth of this evidence, it is desirable to draw attention to it. The evidence consists of stories of reconciliation which are scattered throughout the Mahabharata and the Puranas. The first story of reconciliation concerns the two tribes, the Bharatas to whom Vishvamitra belonged and the Tertius to whom Vashishtha belonged. That the Bharatas were enemies of Vashishtha or Tertius is clear from the Rig Veda itself which says:

III. 53.24.—"These sons of Bharata, O Indra, desire to avoid (the Vashishtha), not to approach them."

The story of their reconciliation is told in the Adi Parvan of the Mahabharata and runs as follows: "And the hosts of their enemies also smote the Bharatas. Shaking the earth with an army of four kinds of forces, the Panchalya chief assailed him having rapidly conquered the earth and vanquished him with ten complete hosts. Then the king Samvarana with his wives, ministers, sons and friends fled from that great cause of alarm and dwelt in the thickets of the great river Sindhu (Indus) in the country bordering on the stream, and near a mountain. There the Bharatas abode for a long time, taking refuge in a fortress. As they were dwelling there, for a thousand years, the venerable rishi Vashishtha came to them. Going out to meet him on his arrival, and making obeisance, the Bharatas all presented him with the *arghya,* offering, showing every honour to the glorious rishi. When he was seated, the king himself solicited him: 'Be thou our priest; let us strive to regain my kingdom.' Vashishtha consented to attach himself to the Bharatas, and as we have heard, invested the descendant of Puru with the sovereignty of the entire Kshatriya race, to be a horn (to have a mastery) over the whole earth. He occupied the splendid city formerly inhabited' by Bharata, and made all kings again tributary to himself."

The second story relates to the conflict between the Bhrigus and the Kshatriya king Kritavirya and their subsequent reconciliation. It occurs in the Adi Parvan of the Mahabharata: "There was a king named Kritavirya, by whose liberality the Bhrigus, learned in the Vedas, who officiated as his priests, had been greatly enriched with cows and money. After he had gone to heaven, his descendants were in want of money, and came to beg for a supply from the Bhrigus, of whose wealth they were aware. Some of the latter hid their money underground, others bestowed it on Brahmins, being afraid of the Kshatriyas, while others again gave these last what they wanted. It happened, however, that a Kshatriya while digging the ground, discovered some money buried in the house of a Bhrigu.

The Kshatriyas then assembled and saw this treasure, and, being incensed, slew in consequence all the Bhrigus, whom they regarded with contempt, down to the children in the womb. The widows, however, fled to the Himalaya mountains. One of them concealed her unborn child in her thigh. The Kshatriyas, hearing of its existence from a Brahmani informant sought to kill it, but it issued forth from his mother's thigh with lustre, and blinded the persecutors. After wandering about bewildered among the mountains for a time, they humbly supplicated the mother of the child for the restoration of their sight; but she referred them to her wonderful infant Aurva, into whom the whole Veda, with its six Vedangas, had entered, as the person who (in retaliation of the slaughter of his relatives) had robbed them of their eye-sight, and who alone could restore it They accordingly had recourse to him, and their eye-sight was restored. Aurva, however, mediated the destruction of all living creatures, in revenge for the slaughter of the Bhrigus, and entered on a course of austerities which alarmed both gods, ashuras and men; but his progenitors (Pitris), themselves appeared, and sought to turn him from his purpose by saying that they had no desire to be revenged on the Kshatriyas.

It was *not* from weakness that the devout Bhrigus overlooked the massacre perpetrated by the murderous Kshatriyas. 'When we became distressed by old age, we ourselves desired to be slaughtered by them. The money which was buried by some one in a Bhrigu's house was placed there for the purpose of exciting hatred, by those who wished to provoke the Kshatriyas. For what had we who were desiring heaven, to do with money?' They added that they hit upon this device because they did not wish to be guilty of suicide, and concluded by calling upon Aurva to restrain his wrath, and abstain from the sin he was meditating: 'Destroy not the Kshatriyas, o son, nor the seven worlds. Suppress thy kindled anger which nullifies the power of austere fervour.' Aurva, however, replies that he cannot allow his threat to remain unexecuted. His anger, unless wreaked upon some other object, will, he says, consume himself, and he argues, on grounds of justice, expediency and duty, against the clemency which his progenitors recommended.

He is, however, persuaded by the Pitris to throw the fire of his anger into the sea, where they say it will find exercise in assailing the watery element, and in this way his threat will be fulfilled. It accordingly became the great Hayasiras, known to those who are acquainted with the Veda, which vomits forth that fire and drinks up the waters." The third story concerns the conflict between Aijuna, son of Kritavirya, the king of the Haihayas and Parashurama and the subsequent reconciliation between them. It occurs in the Vanaparvan of the Mahabharata and runs as follows: "Arjuna, son of Kritavirya and king of the Haihayas, had, we are told, a thousand arms. He obtained from Dattatreya an aerial car of gold, the march of which was irresistible. He thus trod down gods, Yakshas, rishis, and oppressed all creatures.

The gods and rishis applied to Vishnu and he along with Indra, who had been insulted by Arjuna, devised the means of destroying the latter. At this time, the story goes on, there lived a king of Kanyakubja, called Gadhi, who had a daughter named Satyavati. The marriage of this princess to the rishi Richika and the birth of Jamadagni, are then told in nearly the same way as above narrated. Jamadagni and Satyavati had five sons, the youngest of whom was the redoubtable Parashurama. By his father's command he kills his mother (who, by the indulgene of impure desire, had fallen from her previous sanctity), after the four elder sons had refused this matricidal office, and had in consequence been deprived of reason by their father's curse. At Parashurama's desire, however, his mother is restored by his father to life, and his brothers to reason; and he himself is absolved from all the guilt of murder; and obtains the boon of invincibility and long life from his father. His history now begins to be connected with that of king Arjuna (or Kritavirya).

The latter had come to Jamadagni's hermitage, and had been respectfully received by his wife; but he had requited this honour by carrying away by force the calf of the sage's sacrificial cow, and breaking down his lofty trees. On being informed of this violence, Parashurama was filled with indignation, attached Arjuna, cut off his thousand arms, and slew him. Arjuna's son, in return slew the peaceful sage Jamadagni, in the absence of Parashurama. Parashurama incensed at the slaughter of his father, having vowed in consequence to sweep away all Kshatriyas from the earth, seized his weapons and slaying all the sons and grandsons of Arjuna, with thousands of the Haihayas, he turned the earth into a mass of ensanguined mud. Having thus cleared the earth of Kshatriyas he became penetrated by deep compassion and retired to the forest.

After some thousands of years had elapsed, the hero, naturally irascible, was taunted by Paravasu, the son of Raibhaya and grartdson of Vishvamitra, in a public assembly in these words: 'Are not these virtuous men, Pratardana and the others, who are assembled at the sacrifice in the city of Yayati—are they not Kshatriyas? Thou hast failed to execute thy threat, and vainly boastest in the assembly. Thou hast withdrawn to the mountain from the fear of those valiant Kshatriyas, while the earth has again become overturn by hundreds of their race,' Hearing these words, Rama seized the weapons.

The hundreds of Kshatriyas who had before been spared had now grown powerful kings. Those, however, Parashurama, now slew with their children, and all the numerous infants then unborn as they came into the world. Some, however, were preserved by their mothers. Having twenty-one times cleared the earth of the Kshatriyas, Rama gave her as a sacrificial fee to Kasyapa at the conclusion of an Ashvamedha."

After telling the story of the conflict the author of the Mahabharata proceeds to narrate the story of reconciliation in the following terms: "Having one and twenty times swept away all the Kshatriyas from the earth, the son of Jamadagni engaged in austerities on Mahendra, the most excellent of mountains. After he had cleared the world of Kshatriyas, their widows came to the Brahmins, praying for offspring. The religious Brahmins, free from any impulse of lust, cohabited at the proper seasons with these women, who in consequence became pregnant, and brought forth valiant Kshatriya boys and girls, to continue the Kshatriya stock. Thus was the Kshatriya race virtuously begotten by Brahmins on Kshatriya women and became multiplied and long-lived. Thence there arose four castes inferior to the Brahmins."

The above instances of conflicts and conciliations between Brahmins and Kshatriyas do not relate to those Kshatriya kings who have figured in history as having declared war on the Brahmins. To turn to instances of their stories of reconciliation with the Brahmins the first is that of Kalmashapada. He is said to be the son of Sudas. The story is given in the Adiparvan of the Mahabharata. That part of the story which narrates the enmity between Kalmashapada and Vashishtha has already been recounted. The part of the story which deals with reconciliation runs as follows: "After roaming about over many mountains and countries, he (Vashishtha) was followed home by his daughter-in-law Adrisyanti, Shaktri's widow, from whose womb he heard a sound of the recitation of the Vedas, as she was pregnant with a child, which, when born, received the name of Parasara. Learning from her that there was thus a hope of his line being continued, he abstained from further attempts on his own life.

King Kalmashapada, however, whom they encountered in the forest, was about to devour them both when Vashishtha stopped him by a blast from his mouth, and sprinkling him with water consecrated by a holy text, he delivered him from the curse by which he had been affected for twelve years. The king then addressed Vashishtha thus: 'Most excellent sage, I am Saudasa, whose priest thou art, what can I do that would be pleasing to thee?' Vashishtha answered: 'This which has happened has been owing to the force of destiny; go, and rule thy kingdom; but, o monarch, never condemn the Brahmins.' The king replied, 'Never shall I despise the most excellent Brahmins; but submitting to thy commands I shall pay thee all honour. And I must obtain from thee the means of discharging my debt to the Ikshvakus. Thou must give me the offspring which I desire.' Vashishtha promised to comply with his request. They then returned to Ayodhya. And Vashishtha having been solicited by the king to beget an heir to the throne, the queen became pregnant by him, and brought forth a son at the end of twelve years."

The second instance occurs in the Anushasanaparvan of the Mahabharata: "At the time the eloquent king Saudasa sprung from the race of Ikshvaku proceeded, after salutation, to make an enquiry of his family priest Vashishtha, the eternal saint, the most excellent of rishis, who was able to traverse all the world, and was a treasure of sacred knowledge: 'What, o, venerable and sinless man, is declared to be the purest thing in the three worlds, by constantly celebrating which one may acquire the highest merit?' Vashishtha in reply expatiates at great length on the merit resulting from bestowing cows, and ascribes to these animals some wonderful properties so that they are the 'support of all beings,' the present and the future, and describes the cow as 'pervading the universe, mother of the past and the future'. The great self-subduing king, considering that these words of the rishi were most excellent, lavished on the Brahmins very great wealth in the shape of cows and obtained the worlds. So here we find the son of Saudasa extolled as a saint."

The third instance relates to the reconciliation in which there is reference to Sudasa's descendants. It occurs in the Shanti Parvan of the Mahabharata: "Having received the dominion over the earth, Kasyapa made it an abode of Brahmins, and himself withdrew to the forest.

Sudras and Vaishyas then began to act lawlessly towards the wives of the Brahmins, and in consequence of there being no government, the weak were oppressed by the strong, and no one was master of any property.

The earth being distressed by the wicked, in consequence of that disorder, and unprotected according to rule by the Kshatriyas, the guardians of justice, descended to the lower regions. Perceiving her moving from place to palce in terror, Kasyapa upheld her with his thigh *(uru)*. From this circumstance she derives her name of *urvi*. The goddess Earth then propitiated Kasyapa and supplicated him for protection, and for a king. 1 have,' she said, 'preserved among females many Kshatriyas who have been born in the race of Haihayas; let them be my protectors.

There is the heir of Pauravas, the son of Viduratha, who has been brought up by bears on the mountain Rikshavat; let him protect me. So, too, the heir of Saudasa, has been preserved by the tender-hearted and glorious priest.

Parasara who had performed, though a Brahmin, all menial offices for him like a Sudra whence the prince's name Sarvakarman. 'After enumerating other kings who had been rescued, the Earth proceeds: 'All these Kshatriya descendants have been preserved in different places, abiding continually among the classes of dyokaras and goldsmiths. If they protect me, I shall continue unshaken. Their fathers and grandfathers were slain on my account by Rama, energetic in action. It is incumbent on me to avenge their cause.

For I do not desire to be always protected by an extraordinary person (such as Kasyapa); but I will be content with an ordinary ruler. Let this be speedily fulfilled.' Kasyapa then sent for these Kshatriyas who had been pointed out by the Earth, and installed them in the kingly office."

Such is the evidence. Can anybody accept it as reliable? In my opinion, far from accepting it, one should beware of such evidence. In the first place, all these stories of reconciliation end, for the Kshatriyas, in peace without honour. In every case, the Kshatriyas are shown to have undergone an abject surrender. The Bharatas are the enemies of Vashishtha. Suddenly there is a famine in their country. They leave the country and lose their kingdom. They implore Vashishtha their age-old enemy and pray that he become their priest and save them from the calamity.

In the story of the Bhrigus and the Kshatriyas, the credit is given to the Brahmins as being too proud to fight. In the story of the Haihaya Kshatriyas and the Saudasa such as Kalmashpada, the surrender of the Kshatriyas was so to say purchased by them by offering their women to the victorious Brahmins. The stories are all doctored with a view to glorify the Brahmins and humiliate the Kshatriyas. Who can take such dirty, filthy, abominable and vainglorious stories of reconciliation as true historical facts? Only a supporter of Brahminsm can do so.

Such is the general character of the evidence on the question of reconciliation. Coming to the particular case of reconciliation between the Brahmins and the Sudras, the descendants of Sudas, there is ample evidence to show that no such reconciliation had taken place. In the first place, it cannot be gainsaid that Parasara, the son of Shakti or Shaktri, the son of Vashishtha, when he heard of the way in which his father had met his death—namely, that he was burnt alive by Sudas, the Sudra king,—determined to execute a general slaughter of all creatures.

The general slaughters is, of course, a figurative term. What is meant is that Vashishtha took a vow of general vengeance against the descendants of Sudas, namely, the Sudras. It is no doubt said in the Mahabharata that Vashishtha restrained Parasara and persuaded him not to carry out his threat of vengeance by telling him how the Bhrigus and the Kshatriyas had come into conflict and how the former won against the latter by adopting non-violence. But this story cannot be true; for, like other stories it is doctored with a view to bring glory to the Brahmins.

In the second place, the strongest proof in support of the contention that there was no reconciliation between the Brahmins and the Sudras comes from the legislaıion enacted by the Brahmins against the Sudras.

The laws against the Sudras have already been referred to. Their growth and their extraordinary character have been pointed out. All that remains to do is to say that against this background of black laws any suggestion regarding reconciliation must appear to be wholly untenable.

The Brahmins not only did not forgive the Sudras, they pursued even the progeny of the Sudras-with the same spirit of relentless revenge. As many people do not seem to have any idea of this, it may be desirable to state a few facts regarding the Chandala and the Nishada.

The Chandala and Nishada are the issues of mixed marriages. Nishada is an anuloma while the Chandala is a Pratiloma. The anulomas are held to be eligible for Upanayana. But curiously enough an exception is made to this rule. Nishada who is the son of Brahman from a Sudra woman, though an anuloma, is held not to be eligible for Upanayana. It is interesting to know why this exception was made. The only answer seems to be that this arbitrary act is an act of revenge against the children of one's enemy.

There are six anulomas as shown in the following table:

Father	*Mother*	*Name of the Progeny*
Brahmin	Kshatriya	Murdhavasikta
Brahmin	Vaishya	Ambashtha
Brahmin	Sudra	Nishada
Kshatriya	Vaishya	Mahishya
Kshatriya	Sudra	Urga
Vaishya	Sudra	Karana

Turning to the Pratilomas, Manu no doubt calls, all of them as the best of men.

Father	*Mother*	*Name of the Caste*
Sudra	Brahmin	Chandala
Sudra	Kshatriya	Kshattar
Sudra	Vaishya	Ayogava
Vaishya	Brahmin	Suta
Vaishya	Kshatriya	Vaidehaka
Kshatriya	Brahmin	Magadha

At the same time, the stigma on the Pratilomas is not evenly distributed among all of them. In the matter of rights and privileges, the Ayogava and the Kshattar are treated with incredible consideration, while the Chandala is subjected to unspeakable condemnation. As an illustration of this discrimination one can cite the following provisions in the Manusmriti:

As to the Ayogava, the *Manusmriti* merely says:

Carpenting (shall be the occupation) of an Ayogava.—x.46. As to the Kshattar the *Manusmriti* says:

Catching and killing animals that live in holes (is the occupation) of Kshattar.—x.49.

They are only assigned low occupations.

Compare with this what the Manusmriti has to say about the Chandala: "A Chandala and a boar, a cock and also a dog, and a woman in her courses and an eunuch, may not see the Brahmins eating."— iii. 239.

One may not abide with outcasts, nor Chandalas, nor Pukkasas, nor idiots, nor proud (people), nor with the low-born (people) nor with Antyavasayins.—iv.79.

One becomes pure by bathing if one has touched a Chandala, or a woman in her courses, an outcaste, also a woman lying-in, a corpse or one who has touched it.—v.85.

Manu declared the flesh of (a beast) killed by dogs (to be pure); also the flesh of an animal killed by other carnivorous (animals) (or) by Chandala (and) other Dasyus.— v.131.

Two-fold should be the fine of a criminal sentenced within a year, and just as much if one cohabit with a-Vratya woman or a Chandala woman.— viii.373.

The man, however, who foolishly allows this to be done by any other (wife) than the one of his own caste when the latter is at hand, has been, of old, looked upon as (no whit better than) a Chandala.—ix.87.

The dwelling of Chandalas and Svapacas (should be) outside the village; they should be deprived of dishes (apapatra); their property (consists of) dogs and asses.—x.51.

Moreover, Vishvamitra, well knowing right and wrong, being oppressed by hunger proceeded to eat the ramp of a dog, having it from the hand of a Chandala.—x. 108.

At no time should a Brahmin beg property from a Sudra for the sake of sacrifice, for on offering sacrifice after begging (from a Sudra) he is born after death as a Chandala.—vi.24.

On having (carnal) intercourse with Chandala women (or low born woman), on eating their food or receiving (presents) from them, a Brahmin (if he has done so) unwittingly, falls; but (if he has done so) wittingly, he comes to an equality (with them).— xi.175.

The slayer of a Brahmin enters the womb of dogs, boars, asses, camels, cows, goats, sheep, (forest) animals, birds, Chandalas and Pukkasas—xi.55.

How different is the treatment accorded to the Chandala as compared to the treatment accorded to the Ayogava and the Kshattar when all of them are Pratilomas? Why should the Chandala be singled out as the most infamous of the Pratilomas? Only because he is the progeny of the hated Sudra. It is just an act of revenge against the children of one's enemy.

All this leaves no doubt that there was no reconciliation between the Brahmins and the Sudras.

Coming to the last objection, it appears that behind it there is a feeling that the Sudras must have been a very large part of the Indo-Aryan society. With such a feeling it does appear rather strange that the Sudras should have suffered silently the perpetration of such an act as the denial of the Upanayana. Because the Sudras in the Hindu Society form such a vast proportion of the population, so the Sudras of the Indo-Aryan Society must also have formed a very large proportion of the population, can be the only basis for such a feeling. Such an inference is without any foundation, for the Sudras of the Indo-Aryan Society are absolutely different in race from the Sudras of the Hindu Society. The Sudras of the Hindu Society are not the racial descendants of the Sudras of the Indo-Aryan Society.

This confusion has arisen because of the failure to realise that the meaning of the word 'Sudras' in the Indo-Aryan society is quite different from the meaning it has in the Hindu society. In the Indo-Aryans the word Sudra was proper name of one single people. It was the name of a people who belonged to a particular race. The word Sudra, as used in the Hindu society, is not a proper name at all. It is an epithet for a low uncultured class of people.

It is a general cognomen of a miscellaneous and heterogeneous collection of tribes and groups, who have nothing in common except that they happen to be on a lower plane of culture. It is wrong to call them by the name Sudras. They have very little to do with their namesakes of the Aryan society, who had offended the Brahmins. It is a pity that these innocent and backward people of later days have been rolled up with the original Sudras and subjected to the same penalties for which they had given no cause.

That the Sudras of the Indo-Aryan and the Sudras of the Hindu Society are different and distinct is a fact which was present at one time to the minds of the Dharma Sutrakaras is quite clear. This is evident from the distinction they made between *Sacchudra* and *Asac-ckudra* and between *Aniravasita* Sudras and *Niravasita* Sudras. *Sachudra* means a cultured Sudra and asac-*chudra* means an uncultured Sudra. Nirvasita Sudra means a Sudra living in the village community. Anirvasita Sudra means a Sudra living outside the village community.

It is quite wrong to say as some do that this division indicates that the condition of Sudras in the eyes of the lawgivers was improving, in that some were admitted to social intercourse when formerly none was. The correct interpretation is the Sacchudra and Nirvasita Sudra refer to the Sudras of the Aryan society and the *osac-chudra* and the *Anirvasita* Sudra refer to the Sudras by epithet who had begun to form part of the Hindu society. We are concerned with the Sudra of the Aryan society. They have no connection with the later-day Sudras of the Hindu society. That being so, the fact that the Sudras of the Hindu society form such a large number cannot be made the basis for an argument that the Sudras of the Indo-Aryans must have also been a very large body of people.

We do not know exactly whether the Sudras were a tribe, a clan or a moiety or a group of families. But even if they were as big as a tribe, they could not have been larger than a few thousand. The Bharatas are being expressly spoken of in the Rig Veda, vii.33.6, as being small in number. The Satapatha Brahmana referring to a horse sacrifice performed by the Panchala king Son Satrasaha says: "When Satrasaha makes the Ashvamedha offering the Taurvasas arise, six thousand and six and thirty, clad in mail."

If it is any indication that the tribe of Taurvasas numbered six thousand, the Sudras could not be very many.

Apart from the question of numbers, what could the Sudras have done to prevent the calamity? If some Brahmins whom they had offended refused to perform their Upanayana, could they have got the services of other Brahmins whom they had not offended? Such a possibility would of course depend upon various circumstances. In the first place, we do not know whether all the Brahmins had formed a common front and whether it was possible to break up that front. We do not know that at the time when the issue was a burning issue the Brahmins had become a caste. But it is clear that even in the times of the Rig Veda, Brahmins were a class by themselves, had developed class consciousness and were keen on maintaining class interests. In that event it would have been difficult for the Sudras to break up the conspiracy of the Brahmins. Secondly, it might also be that the performance of Upanayana had become the exclusive right of the family priest. The story of king Nimi shows that the performance of sacrifices had become the exclusive right of the family priest. If there is substance in these suggestions, then obviously the Sudras could not have done much to prevent the common front of the Brahmins operating against them.

Another possibility was the forging of a common front among all the Kshatriyas which might have had the effect of weighing down the opposition of the Brahmins. Whether such a thing was possible can only be a matter of speculation. In the first place, did the Sudras realise what the effect of the loss of Upanayana was going to be on their future status? I am sure they did not. Secondly, were the Kshatriyas a united body of people? I doubt if they were. Thirdly, had the other Kshatriya kings any symapathy for the Sudras? If the story of the Dasharajna Yuddha told in the Rig Veda is true, it is quite obvious that there was not much love lost between the Sudras and the other non-Sudra Kshatriyas.

Taking all these circumstances into consideration, there is nothing strange if the Sudras suffered the denial of the Upanayana by the Brahmins to be a fact.

The Theory in the Crucible

The object of this essay was to trace the origin of the Sudras and discover the causes of their degradation. After an examination of historical material and of theories suggested by various writers— orthodox as well as modern—1 have put forth a new thesis. In the preceding chapters, it has been presented in parts for the facility of laying the foundation of each part separately. It is time these parts were assembled together for a full and complete understanding of what the thesis is. It may be summarized as follows:

(1) The Sudras were one of the Aryan communities of the Solar race.

(2) The Sudras ranked as the Kshatriya Varna in the Indo-Aryan Society.

(3) There was a time when the Aryan Society recognized only three Vamas, namely. Brahmins, Kshatriyas and Vaishyas. The Sudras were not a separate Varna but a part of the Kshatriya Varna.

(4) There was a continuous feud between the Sudra kings and the Brahmins, in which the Brahmins were subjected to many tyrannies and indignities.

(5) As a result of the hatred towards the Sudras due to their tyrannies and oppressions, the Brahmins refused to invest the Sudras with the sacred thread.

(6) Owing to the loss of the sacred thread the Sudras became socially degraded, fell below the rank of the Vaishyas and came to form the fourth Varna.

It now remains to assess the validity of this thesis. It is usual for the author to leave this to others to do it. I propose to make a departure and myself enter upon the task of putting my thesis to test. I do so because it gives me an opportunity of vindicating my thesis.

I can well imagine my critics to allege that my thesis rests upon a single statement from the Mahabharata in which Paijavana is described as a Sudra; that identification of Paijavana with Sudas is not proved beyond the shadow of doubt; that the description of Paijavana as a Sudra does not occur in any other place except in a single place in the Mahabharata. How can a theory built on such weak foundations be acceptable? They are bound to invoke the usual agreement that a chain is not stronger than its weakest link. I am sure that my thesis cannot be discredited and demolished in such an easy manner.

In the first place, I do not admit that a thesis cannot be built up on a single piece of evidence. It is a well-known principle of the law of evidence that witness must be weighed and not numbered. The number of witnesses is a less important consideration than the weight to be attached to the individual testimony of each or to the sum of the testimonies of all taken together. There is no reason to doubt the truth of the statement that Paijavana was a Sudra. The author of the Mahabharata has no reason to give a false description. Writing after such a long time, no motive, no partiality could be attributed to him. The only conclusion one can draw is that the author was recording a true tradition.

The fact that Paijavana is not described as a Sudra in the Rig Veda does not militate against the truth of the statement which occurs in the Mahabharata. Many explanations can be given for the absence of the word Sudra from the description of Paijavana in the Rig Veda. The first explanation is that it is wrong to expect such a description in the Rig Veda. The Rig Veda is a book of religion. A description such as Sudra could not be expected in a book of religion. It would be irrelevant. But such a description may well be expected to occur in a book of history such as the Mahabharata wherein as a matter of fact it does.

The other explanation for the infrequent mention of the word Sudra in connection with Sudas which I can think of is that it was unnecessary. Descriptions in terms of kula, gotra, tribe, etc., are really speaking marks of identification. Marks of identification are necessary in the case of lesser people. They are unnecessary in the case of famous men. There is no doubt that Sudas was the most famous man of his time. It was unnecessary to describe him as Sudra for the purpose of identifying him to the people. This is not altogether a mere matter of speculation. One can cite historical instances. Take the case of Bimbisara and Pasenadi, two kings who lived in the time of Buddha. All other kings who were their contemporaries are described in the literature of the time by their *gotra* name. But these two are just spoken of by their personal names. Prof. Oldenberg who noticed this fact explains this on the ground that they were well-known and did not stand in need for being described by their *gotra* names.

But it is really wrong to suppose that my theory is based on the solitary passage in the Mahabharata or on the identification of Paijavana with Sudas. Nothing of the kind. The thesis is not supported by a single chain and therefore the argument that a chain is not stronger than its weakest link does not apply to it. The case is supported by several parallel chains. The weakness of a link in one of them cannot be said to weaken the support. The weakness of one link in one chain throws the whole weight on other chains. Consequently, before concluding that the theory has broken down, it is necessary to prove that the other chains are not able to sustain the weight.

The description of Paijavana as Sudra and the identification of Paijavana with Sudas of the Rig Veda is not the only chain which supports the thesis. There are other chains. One of these is the admission in the Satapatha and Taittiriya Brahmanas that there were only three Vamas and the Sudras did not form a separate Varna. The second consists of evidence that Sudras were kings and ministers of State. The third consists of evidence that the Sudras were at one time entitled to Upanayana. All these are strong chains quite capable of taking all extra weight arising out of a possible breakdown of the first chain.

As far as evidence is concerned, absolute certainty amounting to demonstration is seldom to be had and I do not claim absolute certainty for my thesis. But I do claim that the evidence in support of the theory is both direct as well as circumstantial, and where it is conflicting it is supported by strong probabilities in favour of it.

I have shown what strength there is in the thesis I have presented. I will now proceed to show that the thesis is a valid one. There is one test which I think is generally accepted as the right one by which to appraise the validity of a thesis. It is that a thesis which demands acceptance must not only suggest a solution, but must also show that the solution it proposes answers the riddles which surround the problem which it claims to have solved. It is this test that I propose to apply to my thesis.

Let me begin by listing in one place the riddles of the Sudra. The following include the most important of them:

(1) The Sudras are alleged to be non-Aryans, hostile to the Aryans, whom the Aryans are said to have conquered and made slaves. How is it then that the rishis of the Yajur Veda and the Atharva Veda should wish glory to the Sudras and express a desire to be in favour of the Sudras?

(2) The Sudras are said not to have the right to study the Vedas. How is it then that Sudas, a Sudra, was the composer of the hymns of the Rig Veda?

(3) The Sudras are said to have no right to perform sacrifices. How is it that Sudas performed the Ashva-Medha sacrifice? Why does the Satapatha Brahmana treat the Sudra as a sacrificer and give the formula of addressing him?

(4) The Sudras are said not to have the right to Upanayana. If this was so from the very beginning, why should there be a controversy about it? Why should Badari and the Samskara Ganpati say that he has a right to Upanayana?

(5) The Sudra is not permitted to accumulate property. How is it that the Maitrayani and Kathaka Samhitas speak of the Sudras being rich and wealthy?

(6) The Sudra is said to be unfit to become an officer of the State. How is it then that the Mahabharata speaks of Sudras being ministers to kings?

(7) It is said that the duty of the Sudra is to serve, in the capacity of a menial, the three Vamas. How is it then that there were kings among the Sudras as testified by

the case of Sudas and other cases mentioned by Say ana?

(8) If the Sudra had no right to study the Vedas, if he had no right to Upanayana, if he had no right to sacrifice, why was he not given the right to have his Upanayana, to read the Vedas and to perform sacrifice?

(9) The performance of Upanayana of the Sudra, his learning to read the Vedas, his performing the sacrifices, whether they were of any value to the Sudra or not, were certainly occasions of benefit to the Brahmins in as much as it is the Brahmins, who had the monopoly of officiating at ceremonies and of teaching the Vedas. It is the Brahmins who stood to earn large fees by allowing the Sudra the right to Upanayana, the performance of sacrifices and the reading of the Vedas. Why were the Brahmins so determined to deny these concessions to the Sudras, when granting them would have done no harm and would have increased their own earnings?

(10) Even if the Sudra had no right to Upanayana, sacrifices and Vedas, it was open to the Brahmins to concede him these rights. Why were these questions not left to the free will of the individual Brahmins? Why were penalties imposed upon a Brahmin if he did any of these prohibited acts?

How can these riddles be explained? Neither the orthodox Hindu nor the modem scholar has attempted to explain them. Indeed they do not seem to be aware of the fact that such riddles exist. The orthodox Hindu does not bother about them. He is content with the divine explanation contained in the *Purusha Sukta* that the Sudra was born from the feet of the Purusha.

The modern scholar is content with the assumption that the Sudra in his origin is a non-Aryan aboriginal, for whom the Aryan quite naturally prescribed a different code of laws. It is a pity that none of these classes of people have cared to acquaint themselves with the riddles which surround the problem of the Sudra, much less have they thought of suggesting a theory of the origin of the position of the Sudra capable of solving them.

With regard to my thesis it will be seen that it can explain everyone of these riddles. Postulates (1) to (4) explain how the

Sudras could be kings and ministers and why the rishis should praise them and desire to be in their good books. Postulates (5) and (6) explain why there was a controversy over the Upanayana of the Sudra, also why the law not only denied the right to the Sudra but imposed penalties upon a Brahmin, helping to make it effective.

Indeed there is no riddle which the thesis does not solve. The thesis, if I may say so, is a close and a perfect fit. Few theses can therefore have a better title deed than this.

A Comparative Survey

Untouchability among Non-Hindus: Who are the Untouchables and what is the origin of Untouchability? These are the main topics which it is sought to investigate and the results of which are contained in the following pages. Before launching upon the investigation it is necessary to deal with certain preliminary questions. The first such question is: Are the Hindus the only people in the world who observe Untouchability? The second is: If Untouchability is observed by Non-Hindus also how does Untouchability among Hindus compare with Untouchability among non-Hindus? Unfortunately no such comparative study has so far been attempted. The result is that though most people are aware of the existence of Untouchability among the Hindus they do not know what are its unique features. A definite idea of its unique and distinguishing features is however essential not merely for a real understanding of the position of the Untouchables but also as the best means of emphasising the need of investigating into their origin.

It is well to begin by examining how the matter stood in Primitive and Ancient Societies. Did they recognise Untouchability? At the outset it is necessary to have a clear idea as to what is meant by Untouchability. On this point, there can be no difference of opinion. It will be agreed on all hands that what underlies Untouchability is the notion of defilement, pollution, contamination and the ways and means of getting rid of that defilement.

Examining the social life of Primitive Society in order to find out whether or not it recognised Untouchability in the sense mentioned above there can be no doubt that Primitive Society not only did believe in the notion of defilement but the belief had given rise to a live system of well-defined body of rites and rituals.

Primitive Man believed that defilement was caused by:

(1) the occurrences of certain events;

(2) contact with certain things; and

(3) contact with certain persons.

Primitive Man also believed in the transmission of evil from one person to another. To him the danger of such transmission was peculiarly acute at particular times such as the performance of natural functions, eating, drinking, etc. Among the events the occurrence of which was held by Primitive Man as certain to cause defilement included the following:

(1) Birth

(2) Initiation

(3) Puberty

(4) Marriage

(5) Cohabitation

(6) Death

Expectant mothers were regarded as impure and a source of defilement to others. The impurity of the mother extended to the child also.

Initiation and puberty are stages which mark the introduction of the male and the female to full sexual and social life. They were required to observe seclusion, a special diet, frequent ablutions, use of pigment for the body and bodily mutilation such as circumcision. Among the American Tribes not only did the initiates observe a special dietary but also took an emetic at regular intervals.

The ceremonies which accompanied marriage show that marriage was regarded by the Primitive Man as impure. In some cases the bride was required to undergo intercourse by men of the tribe as in Australia or by the chief or the medicine man of the tribe as in America or by the friends of the grooms as among the East African Tribes. In some cases there takes place the tapping of the bride by a sword by the bridegroom. In some cases, as among the Mundas, there takes place marriage to a tree before marriage with the bridegroom. All these marriage observances are intended to neutralise and prepare the individual against the impurity of marriage.

To the Primitive Man the worst form of pollution was death. Not only the corpse, but the possession of the belongings of the deceased were regarded as infected with pollution. The widespread custom of placing implements, weapons, etc., in the grave along with the corpse indicates that their use by others was regarded as dangerous and unlucky.

Turning to pollution arising out of contact with objects. Primitive Man had learned to regard certain objects as sacred and certain others as profane. For a person to touch the sacred was to contaminate the sacred and to cause pollution to it. A most striking example of the separation of the sacred and the profane in Primitive Society is to be found among the Todas, the whole of whose elaborate ritual and (it would not be too much to say) the whole basis of whose social organisation is directed towards securing the ceremonial purity of the sacred herds, the sacred dairy, the vessels, and the milk, and of those whose duty it is to perform connected rites and rituals. In the dairy, the sacred vessels are always kept in a separate room and the milk reaches them only by transfer to and fro of an intermediate vessel kept in another room. The dairyman, who is also the priest, is admitted to office only after an elaborate ordination, which in effect is a purification. He is thereby removed from the rank of ordinary men to a state of fitness for sacred office. His conduct is governed by regulations such as those which permit him to sleep in the village and only at certain times, or that which entails that a dairyman who attends a funeral should cease from that time to perform his sacred function. It has, therefore, been conjectured that the aim of much of the ritual is to avert the dangers of profanation and prepare or neutralise the sacred substance for consumption by those who are themselves unclean.

The notion of the sacred was not necessarily confined to objects. There were certain classes of men who were sacred. For a person to touch them was to cause pollution. Among the Polynesians, the tabu character of a Chief is violated by the touch of an inferior, although in this case the danger falls upon the inferior. On the other hand, in Efate, the 'sacred man' who comes into contact with Namin (ceremonial uncleanliness) destroys his sacredness. In Uganda, before building a temple, the men were given four days in which to purify themselves. On the other hand, the Chief and his belongings are very often regarded as sacred and, therefore, as dangerous to others of an inferior rank. In the Tonga island, anyone who touches a Chief contacted tabu; it was removed by touching the sole of the foot of a superior chief. The sacred quality of the chief in Malaya Peninsula also resided in the Royal Regalia and anyone touching it was invited with serious illness or death.

Contact with strange people was also regarded as a source of Untouchability by the Primitive Man. Among the Bathonga, a tribe in South Africa, it is believed that those who travel outside their own country are peculiarly open to danger from the influence of foreign spirits and in particular from demoniac possession. Strangers are tabu because, worshipping strange gods, they bring strange influence with them. They are, therefore, fumigated or purified in some other way. In the Dieri and neighbouring tribes even a member of the tribe returning home after a journey was treated as a stranger and no notice was taken of him until he sat down.

The danger of entering a new country is as great as that which attaches to those who come from thence. In Australia, when one tribe approaches another, the members carry lighted sticks to purify the air, just as the Spartan kings in making war had sacred fires from the alter "arried before them to the frontier.

In the same manner, those entering a house from the outside world were required to perform some ceremony, even if it were only to remove their shoes, which would purify the incomer from the evil with which otherwise he might contaminate those within, while the threshold, door-posts and lintel—important as points of contact with outer world— are smeared with blood or sprinkled with water when any member of household or of the community has become a source of pollution, or a horseshoe is suspended over the door to keep out evil and bring goodluck.

Of course, the rites and ceremonies connected with birth, death, marriage, etc., do not positively and unequivocally suggest that they were regarded as sources of pollution. ' But that pollution is one element among many others is indicated by the fact that in every case there is segregation. There is segregation and isolation in birth, initiation, marriage, death and in dealing with the sacred and the strange.

In birth the mother is segregated. At puberty and initiation there is segfegadon and seclusion for a period. In marriage, from the time of betrothal until the actual ceremony bride and bridegroom do not meet. In menstruation a woman is subjected to segregation. Segregation is most noticeable in the case of death. There is not only isolation of the dead-body but there is isolation of all the relatives of the dead from the rest of the community. This segregation is evidenced by the growth of hair and nail and wearing of old clothes by the relatives of the dead which show that they are not served by the rest of the society such as the barber, washerman, etc. The period of segregation and the range of segregation differ in the case of death but the fact of segregation is beyond dispute. In the case of defilement of the sacred by the profane or of defilement of the kindred or by intercourse with the non-kindred there is also the element of segregation. The profane must keep away from the sacred. So the kindred must keep away from the non-kindred. It is thus clear that in Primitive Society pollution involved segregation of the polluting agent.

Along with the development of the notion of defilement. Primitive Society had developed certain purificatory media and purificatory ceremonies for dispelling impurity.

Among the agents used for dispelling impurity are water and blood. The sprinkling of water and the sprinkling of blood by the person defiled were enough to make him pure. Among purificatory rites were included changing of clothes, cutting hair, nail, etc., sweat-bath, fire, fumigation, burning of incense and fanning with the bough of a tree.

These were the means of removing impurity. But Primitive Society had another method of getting rid of impurity. This was to transfer it to another person. It was transferred to some one who was already tabu.

In New Zealand, if anyone touched the head of another, the head being a peculiarly 'sacred' part of the body, he became tabu. He purified himself by rubbing his hands on femroot, which was then eaten by the head of the family in female line. In Tonga, if a man ate tabued food he saved himself from the evil consequences by having the foot of a chief placed on his stomach.

The idea of transmission also appears in the custom of the scapegoat. In Fiji, a tabued person wiped his hands on a pig, which became sacred to the chief, while in Uganda, at the end of the period of mourning for a king a 'scapegoat' along with a cow, a goat, a dog, a fowl and the dust and fire from the king's house was conveyed to the Bunyoro frontier, and there the animals were maimed and left to die. This practice was held to remove all uncleanliness from the king and queen. Such are the facts relating to the notion of pollution as it prevailed in Primitive Society.

Turning to Ancient Society the notion of pollution prevalent therein was not materially different from what was prevalent in Primitive Society. There is difference as to the sources of pollution. There is difference regarding purificatory ceremonies. But barring these differences the pattern of pollution and purification in Primitive and Ancient Society is the same.

Comparing the Egyptian system of pollution with the Primitive system there is no difference except that in Egypt it was practised on an elaborate scale.

Among the Greeks the causes of impurity were bloodshed, the presence of ghost and contact with death, sexual intercourse, childbirth, the evacuation of the body, the eating of certain food such as pea-soup, cheese and garlic, the intrusion of unauthorised persons into holy places, and, in certain circumstances, foul speech and quarrelling. The purificatory means, usually called *kaopoia* by Greeks, were lustral water, sulphur, onions, fumigation and fire, incense, certain boughs and other vegetative growths, pitch, wool, certain stones and amulets, bright things like sunlight and gold, sacrificed animals, especially the pig and of these specially the blood and the skin; finally, certain festivals and festival rites particularly the ritual of cursing and the scapegoat. One unusual method was the cutting of the hair of the polluted person or sacrificial communion with the deity.

A striking feature of the Roman notion of pollution and purification is to be found in the belief of territorial and communal pollution and purification. Parallel to the *lustratio* of the house is the periodical purificatory ritual applied to a country district (Pagi). The *lustractio pagi* consisted in a religious procession right round its boundaries, with sacrifice. There seems to have been in ancient days a similar procession round the walls of the city, called *amburbium.* In historical times special purification of the City was carried out when a calamity called for it, *e.g.* after the early disasters in the Second Punic War. The object of all such expiations was to seek reconciliation with the gods. Lustral ceremony accompanied the foundation of a colony.

The *Therminalia* protective of boundaries, and the *Compitalia* of streets in the City were also probably lustral in their origin. Down to the late period, priests called *Luperci* perambulated in the boundaries of the earliest Rome, the settlement on the Palatinate.

Earlier there was an annual solemn progress round the limits of the most ancient territory of the Primitive City. It was led by the Archaic priesthood called the *Arval* brotherhood. The ceremony was called *ambravalia* and it was distinctly piacular. When Roman territory was expanded no corresponding extension of the lustral rite seems ever to have been made. These round-about piacular surveys were common elsewhere, inside as well as outside Italy and particularly in Greece.

The solemn words and prayers of the traditional chant, duly gone through without slip of tongue, seem to have had a sort of magical effect. Any error in the pronouncement of these forms would involve a need of reparation, just as in the earliest Roman legal system, the mispronunciation of the established verbal forms would bring loss of the lawsuit.

Other forms of quaint ancient ritual were connected with the piacular conception. The *Salii,* ancient priests of Mars, made a journey at certain times round a number of stations in the City. They also had a 'cleaning of the weapons' and a 'cleaning of the trumpets' which testify to a primitive notion that the efficiency of the army's weapons required purification. The 'washing' (lustrum) with which the census ended was in essence military; for it was connected with the *Comitia Centuriata,* which is merely the army in civil garb. *Lustratio exercitus* was often performed when the army was in the field, to remove superstitious dread which sometimes attacked it at other times, it was merely prophylactic. There was also a illustration of the fleet.

Like all Primitive people the Hebrews also entertained the notion of defilement. The special feature of their notion of defilement was the belief that defilement was also caused by contact with the carcass of unclean animals, by eating a carcass or by contact with creeping things, or by eating creeping things and by contact with animals which are always unclean such as "every beast which divided the hoof, and is not cloven footed, nor chewed the cud...whatsoever goes upon his paws, among all manner of beasts that go on all four". Contact with any unclean person was also defilement to the Hebrews. Two other special features of the Hebrew notion of defilement may be mentioned. The Hebrews believed that defilement might be caused to persons by idolatrous practices or to a land by the sexual impurities of the people.

On the basis of this survey, we can safely conclude that there are no people Primitive or Ancient who did not entertain the notion of pollution.

Untouchability among Hindus

In the matter of pollution there is nothing to distinguish the Hindus from the Primitive or Ancient peoples. That they recognised pollution is abundantly clear from the Manusmriti. Manu recognises physical defilement and also notional defilement.

Manu treated birth, death and menstruation as sources of impurity. With regard to death, defilement was very extensive in its range. It followed the rule of consanguinity. Death caused defilement to members of the family of the dead person technically called *Sapindas* and *Samanodakas* It not only included maternal relatives such as maternal uncle but also remote relatives It extended even to nonrelatives such as (1) teacher, (2) teacher's son, (3) teacher's wife, (4) pupi (5) fellow student, (6) Shrotriya, (7) king, (8) friend, (9) members of the household, (10) those who carried the corpse and (11) those who touched the corpse. Anyone within the range of defilement could not escape it. There were only certain persons who were exempt. In the following verses Manu names them and specifies the reasons why he exempts them:

"V.93. The taint of impurity does not fall on kings and those engaged in the performance of a vow, or of a Sattra; for the first are seated on the throne of India, and the (last two are) ever pure like Brahman.

94. For a king, on the throne of magnanimity, immediate purification is prescribed, and the reason for that is that he is seated (there) for the protection of (his) subjects.

95. (The same rule applies to the kinsmen) of those who have fallen in a riot or a battle, (of those who have been killed) by lightning or by the king, and for cows and Brahmins, and to those whom the king wishes to be pure (in spite of impurity).

96. A king is an incarnation of the eight guardian deities of the world, the Moon, the Fire, the Sun, the Wind, Indra, the Lords of wealth and water (Kubera and Varuna) and Yama.

Because the king is pervaded by those lords of the world, no impurity is ordained for him for purity and impurity of mortals is caused and removed by those lords of the world."

From this it is clear that the king, the kinsmen of those who have fallen in a noble cause as defined by Manu and those whom the king chose to exempt were not affected by the normal rules of defilement. Manu's statement that the Brahmin was 'ever pure' must be understood in its usual sense of exalting the Brahmin above everything. It must not be understood to mean that the Brahmin was free from defilement. For he was not. Indeed besides being defiled by births and deaths the Brahmin also suffered defilement on grounds which did not affect the Non-Brahmins. The Manusmriti is full of tabus and don'ts which affect only the Brahmins and which he must observe and failure to observe which makes him impure.

The idea of defilement in Manu is real and not merely notional. For he makes the food offered by the polluted person unacceptable.

Manu also prescribes the period of defilement. It varies. For the death of a Sapinda it is ten days. For children three days. For fellow students one day. Defilement does not vanish by the mere lapse of the prescribed period. At the end of the period there must be performed a purificatory ceremony appropriate to the occasion.

For the purposes of purification Manu treats the subject of defilement from three aspects:(1) Physical defilement, (2) notional or psychological defilement, and (3) ethical defilement The rule for the purification of ethical defilement which occurs when a person entertains evil thoughts are more admonitions and exhortations. But the rites for the removal of notional and physical defilement are the same. They include the use of water earth cows urine, the kusa grass and ashes Earth, cow's urine, Kusa grass and ashes are prescribed as purificatory agents for removing physical impurities caused by the touch of inanimate objects. Water is the chief agent for the removal of notional defilement. It is used in three ways (1) sipping, (2) bath, and (3) abludon Later on *panchagavya* became the most important agency for removing notional defilement. It consists of a mixture of the five products of the cow, namely, milk, urine, dung, curds and butter.

In Manu there is also provision for getting rid of defilement by transmission through a scapegoat namely by touching the cow or looking at the sun after sipping water.

Besides the individual pollution the Hindus believe also in territorial and communal pollution and purification very much like the system that prevailed among the early Romans. Every village has an annual *jatra.* An animal, generally a he buffalo, is purchased on behalf of the village. The animal is taken round the village and is sacrificed, the blood is sprinkled round the village and towards the end toe meat is distributed among the villagers. Every Hindu, every Brahmin even though he may not be a beef eater is bound to accept his share of the meat. This is not mentioned in any of the Smritis but it has the sanction of custom which among the Hindus is so strong that it always overrides law.

If one could stop here, one could well say that the notion of defilement prevalent among the Hindus is not different from that which obtained in Primitive and in Ancient Societies. But one cannot stop here. For there is another form of Untouchability observed by the Hindus which has not yet been set out. It is the hereditary Untouchability of certain communities. So vast is the list of such communities that it would be difficult for an individual with his unaided effort to compile an exhaustive list. Fortunately such a list was prepared by the Government of India in 1935 and is attached to the Orders-in-Council issued under the Government of India Act of 1935. To this Order-in-Council there is attached a Schedule.

The Schedule is divided into nine parts. One part refers to one province and enumerates the castes, races or tribes or parts of or groups within steps which are deemed to be Untouchables in that province either in the whole of that province or part thereof. The list may be taken to be both exhaustive and authentic. To give an idea of the vast number of communities which are regarded as hereditary Untouchables by the Hindus. I reproduce below the list given in the Order-in-Council.

Schedule

Madras

(1) Scheduled Castes throughout the Province: Adi-Andhra, Adi-Dravida, Adi-Karnataka, Ajila, Arunthuthiyar, Baira, Bakuda, Bandi, Bariki, Battada, Bavuri Bellara, Bygari Chachati, Chakkiliyan, Chalvadi, Chamar, Chandala, Cheruman, Dandasi, Devendrakulathan, Ghasi, Godagali, Godari, Godda, Gosangi, Haddi, Hasla, Holeya, Jaggali, Jambuvulu, Kalladi, Kanakkan, Kodalo, Koosa, Koraga, Kudumban, Kuravan, Madari, Madiga, Maila, Mala, Mala Dasu, Matangi, Moger, Muchi, Mundala, Natekeyava, Nayadi, Paga dai, Paidi, Painda, Paky, Pallan, Pambada, Pamidi, Panchama, Paniyan, Panniandi, Paraiyan, Parvan, Pulayan, Puthirai Vanaa, Raneyar, Relli Samagara, Samban, Separi, Semman, Thoti, Tiruvalhivr, Valluvan, Valmiki and Vettuvan.

(2) Scheduled Castes throughout the Provinces except in any special constituency constituted under the Government of India Act, 1935, for the election of a representative of backward areas and backward tribes to the Legislative Assembly of the Province: Arnadan, Kattunayakan, Kuruman, Dombo, Kudiya, Malasar, Kadan, Kudubi, Mavilan, Karimpalan, Kurichchan and Pano.

Bombay

Scheduled Castes:

(1) Throughout the Province: Asodi, Dhor, Mang Garudi, Bakad, Garode, Maghval, or Menghwar, Bhambi, Halleer, Mini Madig, Bhangi, Halsar, or Haslar, Mukri, Chakrawadya-Dasar, Hulsavar, Nadia, Chalvadi, Holaya, Shenva, or Shindhava, Chambhar or Mochigar or Khalpa, Shinghdav, or Shingadya, Samagar, Kolcha, or Kolgha, Sochi, Chena-Dasaru, Koli-Dhor, Timali, Chuhar, *or* Chuhra, Lingader, Turi, Dakaleru, Madig, *or* Mang, Vankar, Dhed, Mahar, Vitholia and Dhegu-Megu.

(2) Throughout the Province except in the Ahmedabad, Kaira, Broach and Panch Mahals and Surat Districts—Mochi.

(3) In the Kanara district—Kotegar.

Bengal

Scheduled castes throughout the Province:

Agarua, Bagdi, Bahelia, Baiti, Bauri, Bediya, Beddar, Berua, Bhatiya, Bhiumali, Bhuiya, Kandh, Kandra, Kaora, Kapuria, Karenga, Kastha, Kaur, Khaira, Khatik, Koch, Konai, Konwar, Kora, Kotal, Lalbegi,Bhumij, Bind, Bmjhia, Chamar, Dhenuar, Dhoba, Doai, Dom, Dosadh Garo, Ghasi, Lodha, Lahor, Mahli, Mal, Mahar, Mallah, Mech, Mehtor, Muchi, Munda, Musahar, Nagesia, Namasudm, Natnuniya, Gonrili, Hadi, Hajang, Halalkor, Hari, Ho, Jalia Kaibartta, Jhalo Malo, or Malo, Kadar, Kalpahariya, Kan, Oraon, Paliya, Pan, Pasi, Patni Pod, Rabha, Rajbanshi, Rajwar, Santal, Sunn, Tiyar and Tun.

United Provinces

Scheduled Castes:

(1) *Throughout the Province:* Agaria, Aheriya, Badi, Badhik, Baheliya, Bajaniya, Bajgi, Balahar, Balmiki, Banmaus, Bansphor, Barwar, Basor, Bawariya, Beldar, Bengali, Berya, Bhantu, Bhuiya, Bhuiyar, Boriya, Chamar, Chero, Dabagar, Dhangar, Dhanuk (Bhangi), Dharikar, Dhobi, Dom, Domar, Ghaiami, Ghasiya, Gual, Habura, Hari, Hela, Khairaha, Kalabaz, Kanjar, Kapariya, Karwal,

Kharot, Kharwar (except Benbansi) Khatik, Kol, Korwa, Lalbegi, Majhawar, Nat Pankha, Parahiya, Pasi, Patari, Rawat, Saharya, Sanaurhiya, Sansiya, Shilpkar, Tharu and Turaiha.

(2) Throughout the Province except in the Agra, Meerut and Rohilkhand-divisions—Kori.

Punjab

Scheduled Castes throughout the Province: Ad Dharmis, Marija, or Marecha, Khatik, Bawaria, Bengali, Kori, Chamar, Baiar, Nat, Chuhra, or Balmiki, Bazigar, Pasi, Dagi and Koli, Bhanjra, Pema, Dhumna, Chanal, Sepela, Od, Dhanak, Siridband, Sansi, Gagra, Meghi, Sarera, Gandhila and Ramdasis.

Bihar

Scheduled Castes:

Throughtout the Province: Chamar, Halalkhor, Mochi, Chaupal, Hari, Musahar, Dhobi, Kanjar, Nat, Dusadh, Kurariar, Pasi, Dom and Lalbegi.

In the Patna and Tirhut divisions and the Bhagalpur, Monghyr, Palamau and Pumea Districts: Bauri, Bhumij, Rajwar, Bhogta, Ghasi, Tun, Bhaiiya, Pan.

In the Dhanbad Sub-division of the Manbhum District and the Central Manbhum General Rural Constituency, and the Purulia and Raghunathpur Municipalities: Bauri, Ghasi, Rajwar, Bhogta, Pan, Turi and Bhuiya.

Central Provinces and Berar

Scheduled Castes	*Localities*
Basor, or Burud, Chamar, Dom, Ganda, Mang, Mehtar or Bhangi, Mochi, Satnami	Throughout the Province.
Audhelia	In the Bilaspur distict.
Bahna	In the Arnraoti district

Balahi, or Balai	In the Berar division and the Balaghat, Bhandara Betul, Chanda, Chhindwara, Hoshangabad, Jabbulpore, Mandia, Nagpur, Nimar, Saugor and Wardha districts.
Bedar	In the Akola, Arnraoti and Buldana districts.
Chadar	In the Bhandara and Saugor districts.
Chauhan	In the Durg district.
Dahayat	In the Damoh sub-division of the Saugor district.
Dewar	In the Bilaspur, Durg and Raipur districts.
Dhanuk	In the Saugor district, except in the Damoh sub-division thereof.
Dhimar	In the Bhandara district.
Dhobi	In the Bhandara, Bilaspur, Raipur and Saugor districts and the Hoshangabad and Seoni-Malwa tahsils of the Hoshangabad district.
Dohar	In the Berar division and the Balghat, Bhandara, Chanda, Nagpur and Wardha districts.
Holiya	In the Balaghat and Bhandara districts.
Jangam	In the Bhandara district.
Kaikari	In the Berar division, and in Bhandara, Chanda, Nagpur and Wardha districts.
Ghasia	In the Berar division and in the Balaghat, Bhandara, Bilsaspur, Chanda, Durg, Nagpur, Raipur and Wardha districts.
Katia	In the Berar division, in the Balghat, Betui, Bhandara, Bilaspur, Chanda, Durg, Nagpur, Nimar, Raipur and Wardha districts, in the Hoshangabad and Seoni-Malwa tahsils of the Hoshangabad district, in the Chhindwara district, except in the Seoni sub-division thereof, and in the Saugor district, except in the Damoh sub-division thereof.

Khangar	In the Bhadara, Buldhana and Saugor districts and the Hoshangabad and Sconi Malwa tahsils of the Hoshangabad district.
Khatik	In the Berar division, in' the Balaghat, Bhandara, Chanda, Nagpur and Wardha districts, in the Hoshangabad tahsil of the Hoshangabad district, in the Chhindwara district, except in the Seoni sub-division thereof, and in the Saugor district, except in the Damoh sub-division thereof.
Koli	In the Bhandara and Chanda districts.
Kori'	In the Arnraoti, Balaghat, Betui, Bhandara, Buldana, Chhindwara, Jubbulpore, Mandia, Nimar, Raipur'and Saugor districts, and in the Hoshangabad district, except in the Harda and Sohagpur tahsils thereof.
Kumhar	In the Bhandara and Saugor districts and the Hoshangabad and Seoni-Malwa ṭahsils of the Hoshangabad district.
Madgi	In the Berar division and in the Balaghat, Bhandara, Chanda, Nagpur and Wardha districts.
Mala	In the Balaghat, Betui, Chhindwara, Hoshangabad, Jubbuipwe Mandla, Nimar and Saugor districts.
Mehra or Mahar	Throughout the Province, except in the Harda and Sohagpur tahsils of the Hoshangabad district
Nagarchi	In the Balaghat, Bhandaia, Chhindwara, Mandla, Nagpur and Raipur districts.
Ojha	In the Balaghat, Bhandara and Mandia districts and the Hoshangabad tahsil of the Hoshangabad district
Panka	In the Berar division, in the Balaghat, Bhandara, Bilaspur, Chanda, Durg, Nagpur, Raipur, Saugor and Wardha districts and in the Chhindwara district, except in the Seoni subdivison thereof.

Pardhi	In the Narsinghpura sub-division of the Hoshangabad district.
Pradhan	In the Berar division, in the Bhandara, Chanda, Nagpur, Nimar, Raipur and Wardha districts and in the Chhaindwara district, except in the Seoni sub-division thereof.
Rajjhar	In the Sohagpur tahsil of the Hoshangabad district.

Assam

Scheduled Castes:

In the Assam Valley: Namasudra, Hira, Mehtar, or Bhangi, Kaibartta, Lalbegi, Bansphor, Bania, or Brittial-Bania.

In the Surma Valley : Mali, or Bhuimali, Sutradhar, Kaibartta, or Jaliya, Dhupi, or Dhobi, Muchi, Lalbegi, Dugla, or Dholi, Patni, Mehtar, or Bhangi, Jhalo and Malo, Namasudra, Bansphor and Mahara.

Orissa

Scheduled Castes:

(1) Throughout the Province: Adi-Andhra, Audhelia, Bariki, Bansor, or Burud, Bavuri, Chachati, Chamar, Chandala, Dandasi, Dewar, Dhoba or Dhobi, Ganda, Ghusuria, Godagali, Godari, Godra, Gokha, Haddi, or Hari, Irika, Jaggali, Kandra, Katia, Kela, Kodalo, Madari, Madiga, Mahuria, Mala, Mang, Mangan, Mehra, or Mahar, Mehtar, *or* Bhangi, Mochi or Muchi, Paidi, Painda, Pamidi, Panchama, Panka, Relli, Sapari, Satnami, Siyal and Valmiki.

(2) Throughout the Province except in the Khondmals district, the district of Sambalpur and the areas transferred to Orissa under the provisions of the Government of India (Constitution of Orissa) Order, 1936, from the Vizagapatam and Ganjam Agencies in the Presidency of Madras: Pan, or Pano.

(3) Throughout the Province except in the Khondmals district and the areas so transferred to Orissa from the said Agencies: Dom, or Dambo.

(4) Throughout the Province except in the district of Sambalpur: Bauro, Bhumij, Turi, Bhuiya, Ghasi, or Ghasia.

(5) In the Nawapara sub-division of the district of Sambalpur: Kori, Nagarchi, Pradhan.

This is a very terrifying list. It includes 429 communities. Reduced to numbers it means that today there exist in India 50-60 millions of people whose mere touch causes pollution to the Hindus. Surely, the phenomenon of Untouchability among primitive and ancient society pales into insignificance before this phenomenon of hereditary Untouchability for so many millions of people, which we find in India. This type of Untouchability among Hindus stands in a class by itself. It has no parallel in the history of the world. It is unparalleled not merely by reason of the colossal numbers involved which exceed the number of great many nations in Asia and in Europe but also on other grounds.

There are some striking features of the Hindu system of Untouchability affecting the 429 Untouchable communities which are not to be found in the custom of Untouchability as observed by Non-Hindu communities, primitive or ancient. The isolation prescribed by Non-Hindu societies as a safeguard against defilement, if it is not rational, is at least understandable. It is for specified reasons such as birth, marriage, death, etc.. But the isolation prescribed by Hindu society is apparently for no cause.

Defilement as observed by the Primitive Society was of a temporary duration which arose during particular times such as the performance of natural functions, eating, drinking, etc. or a natural crisis in the life of the individual such as birth, death, menstruation, etc. After the period of defilement was over and after the purificatory ceremonies were performed the defilement vanished and the individual became pure and associable. But the impurity of the 50-60 millions of the Untouchables of India, quite unlike the impurity arising from birth, death, etc., is permanent. The Hindus who touch them and become polluted thereby can become pure by undergoing purificatory ceremonies. But there is nothing which can make the Untouchables pure. They are born impure, they are impure while they live, they die the death of the impure, and they give birth to children who are born with the stigma of Untouchability affixed to them. It is a case of permanent, hereditary stain which nothing can cleanse.

In the third place, Non-Hindu societies which believed in defilement isolated the individuals affected or at the most those closely connected with them. But the Untouchability among the Hindus involves the isolation of a class-a class which today numbers about 50 to 60 million people.

In the fourth place, Non-Hindu societies only *isolated* the affected individuals. They did not *segregate* them in separate quarters. The Hindu society insists on segregation of the Untouchables. The Hindu will not live in the quarters of the Untouchables and will not allow the Untouchables to live inside Hindu quarters. This is a fundamental feature of Untouchability as it is practised by the Hindus. It is not a case of social separation, a mere stoppage of social intercourse for a temporary period. It is a case of territorial segregation and of a *cordon sanitaire* putting the impure people inside a barbed wire into a sort of a cage. Every Hindu village has a ghettto. The Hindus live in the village and the Untouchables in the ghetto.

Such is the Hindu system of Untouchability. Who can deny that it is not altogether different from what is found to exist among Non-Hindu societies? That Untouchability among Hindus is a unique phenomenon is beyond question. Persons were treated by non-Hindu communities as impure but as individuals. Never a whole class was treated as impure. But their impurity was of a temporary duration and was curable by the performance of some purifactory rites. There has never been a case of permanent impurity based on the rule 'once impure always impure'. Persons were treated as impure by Non-Hindu Communities and they were even cut off from social intercourse. But there has never been a case of persons having been put into permanent segregation camps. A whole body of people have been treated as impure by Non-Hindu communities. But they were strangers outside the fold of the kindred. There has never been a case of a people treating a section of their own people as permanently and hereditarily impure.

Untouchability among Hindus is thus a unique phenomenon, unknown to humanity in other parts of the world. Nothing like it is to be found in any other society-primitive, ancient or modern. The many problems that arise out of a study of Untouchability and which call for investigation may be reduced to two:

(1) Why do the Untouchables live outside the village?

(2) What made their impurity permanent, and ineradicable?

The following pages are devoted to finding answers to these two questions.

Problem of Habitat

Why do the Untouchables Live Outside the Village?: That the Untouchables live outside the village is so notorious a fact that it must be taken to be within the cognisance even of those whose knowledge about them is not very profound. Yet, nobody has thought that this was a serious question calling for satisfactory answer. How did the Untouchables come to live outside the village? Were they declared to be Untouchables first and then deported out of the village and made to live outside? Or were they from the very beginning living outside the village and were subsequently declared to be Untouchables? If the answer is that they were living outside the village from the very beginning, there arises a further question, namely, what can be the reason for it?

As the question of the separate settlement of the Untouchables has never been raised before, naturally there exists no theory as to how the Untouchables came to live outside the village. There is, of course, the view of the Hindu Shastras and if one wants to dignify it by calling it a theory one may do so. The Shastras of course say that the *Antyajas* should live and have their abode outside the village. For instance,' Manu says:

"*X. 51.* But the dwellings of the *Chandalas* and the *Shvapakas* shall be outside the village, they must be made *Apapatras* and their wealth (shall be) dogs and donkeys.

X. 52. Their dress (shall be) the garments of the dead, (they shall eat) their food from broken dishes, black iron (shall be) their ornaments and they must always wander from place to place.

X. 53. A man who fulfils a religious duty, shall not seek intercourse with them; their transactions (shall be) among themselves and their marriages with their equals.

X. 54. Their food shall be given to them by others (than an Aryan giver) in a broken dish; at night they shall not walk about in village and in towns.

X. 55. By day they may go about for the purpose of their work, distinguished by marks at king's command, and they shall carry out the corpses (of persons) who have no relatives; that is a settled rule.

X. 56. By the King's order they shall always execute the criminals, in accordance with the law, and they shall take for themselves the clothes, the beds, and the ornaments of (such) criminals."

But what conclusion can one draw from these statements of the Shastras? They are capable of double interpretation. When the Shastras say that the Untouchables should stay outside the village, they may be purporting to say no more than that the Untouchables should stay where they have been staying, *i.e.* outside the village. This is one interpretation. The second interpretation is that those who are declared Untouchables should not be allowed to stay inside the village but should be required to go out of the village and live outside. Following up the alternate interpretations of the Shastras there are two different possibilities which call for consideration.

One is that the Untouchability has nothing to do with the Untouchables living outside the village. From the very beginning they lived outside the village. Thereafter when the stigma of Untouchability fell on them they were prohibited from coming to live inside the village. The other possibility is that Untouchability has everything to do with the Untouchables, living outside the village. In other words, the Untouchables originally lived inside the village and that thereafter when the stigma of untouchability fell on them they were forced to vacate and live outside the village.

Which of the two Possibilities is more Acceptable?: The second possibility is on the face of it absurd and fantastic. One argument is quite enough to expose its absurdity. The phenomenon we are discussing is not confined to a single village or single area. It exists all over India. The transplantation of the Untouchables from within the village to outside the village is a vast operation. How and who could have carried on an operation of such colossal dimensions? It could not have been carried out except by the command of an Emperor having his sway ever the whole of India. Even to him such a transplantation would have been impossible.

But possible and impossible it can only be the work of an Emperor. Who is the Emperor to whom the credit or discredit of this task can be assigned? Obviously, India had no Emperor to perform this task If there was no Emperor to do the transplantation, then the second possibility must be abandoned.

That those who are called Untouchables lived outside the village from the very beginning even before they became Untouchables and that they continued to live outside the village because,of the supervention of untouchability at a later stage is the only possibility worth consideration.

But this raises a very difficult question: Why did they live outside the village? What made them or forced them to do so? The answer is that having regard to the factors which are known to students of Sociology to have influenced the transformation of Primitive Society into Modern Society all over the world it is only natural to suppose that the Untouchables should have from the beginning lived outside the village.

Not many will realise why this is natural without some explanation of the factors which have affected the condition of Primitive Society into Modern Society.

For a clear understanding of the matter it is necessary to bear in mind that Modern Society differs from Primitive Society in two respects. Primitive Society consisted of nomadic communities while Modern Society consists of settled communities. Secondly, Primitive Society consisted of tribal communities based on blood relationship.

Modem Society consists of local communities based on territorial affiliation. In other words there are two lines of evolution along which Primitive Society has proceeded before it became transformed into Modem Society. One line of evolution has led the Primitive Society to become a territorial community from being a tribal community.

There can be no doubt that such a change has taken place. Clear traces of the change are to be seen in the official style of kings. Take the style of the English kings. King John was the first to call himself the king of England. His predecessors commonly called themselves kings of the English. The former represent a territorial community. The latter represent a tribal community. England was once the country which Englishmen inhabited. Englishmen are now the people who inhabit England. The same transformation can be seen to have taken place in the style of the French kings who were once called kings of the Franks and later as kings of France. The second line of evolution had led-Primitive Society to become a settled community instead of the Nomadic community which it was. Here again, the change is so definite and so impressive that no illustration is required to convince anybody of its reality.

For the purpose in hand all we need is to confine ourselves to a consideration of the second line of evolution. How did Primitive Society become a settled community? The story of how Primitive Society became a settled community is too long to be detailed in a chapter-much too long to be compressed in a section thereof. It is enough to note two things. The first thing to understand is what made Primitive Society give up its nomadic life and secondly what happened in the transition from nomadic to settled life.

Primitive Society was no doubt nomadic. But it was nomadic not because of any migratory instinct. Nor was it due to any mental trait peculiar to it. It was the result of the fact that the earliest form of the wealth held by Primitive Society was cattle. Primitive Society was migratory because its wealth, namely the cattle, was migratory. Cattle went after new pastures. Primitive Society by reason of it's love for cattle, therefore, went wherever its cattle carried it. Primitive Society became fixed in its abode, in other words became a settled-community, when a new species of wealth was discovered. This new species of wealth was land. This happened when Primitive Society learned the art of farming and of cultivating land. Wealth became fixed at one place when it changed its form from cattle to land. With this change Primitive Society also became settled at the same place.

This explains why Primitive Society was at one time nomadic and what led it take to settled life.

The next thing is to note the events that have happened when Primitive Society was on the road to becoming a Settled Society. The problems which faced Primitive Society in its transition from Nomadic life to Settled life were mainly two. One confronted the Settled Community. The other confronted the Broken men.

The problem that confronted the Settled community was that of its defence against the Nomadic tribes. The problem which confronted the Broken men was that of the protection and shelter. It may be desirable to elucidate how and why these problems arose.

For an understanding of the problem which confronted the Settled tribes, it is necessary to bear in mind the following facts. All tribes did not take to settled life at one and the same time. Some became settled and some remained nomadic. The second thing to remember is that the tribes were never at peace with one another. They were always at war. When all tribes were in a Nomadic state the chief causes for intra-tribal warfare were (1) stealing cattle, (2) stealing women, and (3) stealthily grazing of cattle in the pastures belonging to other tribes. When some tribes became settled, the tribes that remained nomadic found it more advantageous to concentrate their fight against the settled tribes. It was more paying than a war against other Nomadic tribes.

The Nomadic tribes had come to realise that the Settled tribes were doubly wealthy. Like the Nomadic tribes, they had cattle. But in addition to cattle, they had corn which the Nomadic tribes had not and which they greatly coveted. The Nomadic tribes systematically organized raids on the Settled tribes with the object of stealing the wealth belonging to the Settled tribes. The third fact is that the Settled tribes were greatly handicapped in defending themselves against these raiders. Being engaged in more gainful occupation, the Settled tribes could not always convert their ploughs into swords. Nor could they leave their homes and go in pursuit of the raiding tribes. There is nothing strange in this. History shows that peoples with civilization but no means of defence are not able to withstand the attacks of the barbarians. This explains how and why during the transition period the Settled tribes were faced with the problem of their defence.

How the problem of the Broken men arose is not difficult to understand. It is the result of the continuous tribal warfare which was the normal life of the tribes in their primitive condition. In a tribal war it often happened that a tribe instead of being completely annihilated was defeated and routed. In many cases a defeated tribe became broken into bits. As a consequence of this there always existed in Primitive times a floating population consisting of groups of Broken tribesmen roaming in all directions. To understand what gave rise to the problem of the Broken men it is necessary to realise that Primitive Society was fundamentally tribal in its origanisation. That Primitive Society was fundamentally tribal meant two things. Firstly, every individual in Primitive Society belonged to a tribe. Nay, he must belong to the tribe.

Outside the tribe no individual had any existence. He could have none. Secondly tribal organisation being based on common blood and common kinship an individual born in one tribe could not join another tribe and become a member of it. The Broken Men had, therefore, to live as stray individuals. In Primitive Society where tribe was fighting against tribe a stray collection of Broken Men was always in danger of being attacked. They did not know where to go for shelter. They did not know who would attack them and to whom they could go for protection. That is why shelter and protection became the problem of the Broken Men.

The foregoing summary of the evolution of Primitive Society shows that there was a time in the life of Primitive Society when there existed two groups-one group consisting of Settled tribes faced with the problem of finding a body of men who would do the work of watch and ward against the raiders belonging to Nomadic tribes and the other group consisting of Broken Men from defeated tribes with the problem of finding patrons who would give them food and shelter.

The next question is: How did these two groups solve their problems? Although we have no written text of a contract coming down to us from antiquity we can say that the two struck a bargain whereby the Broken Men agreed to do the work of watch and ward for the Settled tribes and the Settled tribes agreed to give them food and shelter. Indeed, it would have been unnatural if such an arrangement had not been made between the two especially when the interest of the one required the cooperation of the other.

One difficulty, however, must have arisen in the completion of the bargain, that of shelter. Where were the Broken Men to live? In the midst of the settled community or outside the Settled community? In deciding this question two considerations must have played a decisive part. One consideration is that of blood relationship. The second consideration is that of strategy. According to Primitive notions only persons of the same tribe, *i.e.*. of the same blood, could live together. An alien could not be admitted inside the area occupied by the homesteads belonging to the tribe. The Broken men were aliens. They belonged to a tribe which was different from the Settled tribe. That being so, they could not be permitted to live in the midst of the Settled tribe. From the strategic point of view also it was desirable that these Broken men should live on the border of the village so as to meet the raids of the hostile tribes. Both these considerations were decisive in favour of placing their quarters outside the village.

We can now return to the main question, namely, why do the Untouchables live outside the village? The answer to the question can be sought along the lines indicated above. The same processes must have taken place in India when the Hindu Society was passing from Nomadic life to the life of a settled village community. There must have been in Primitive Hindu society, Settled tribes and Broken Men. The Settled tribes founded the village and formed the village community and the Broken Men lived in separate quarters outside the village for the reason that they belonged to a different tribe and, therefore, to different blood. To put it definitely, the Untouchables were originally only Broken Men. It is because they were Broken Men that they lived outside the village. This explains why it is natural to suppose that the Untouchables from the very beginning lived outside and that Untouchability has nothing to do with their living outside the village.

The theory is so novel that critics may not feel satisfied without further questioning. They will ask:

(1) Is there any factual evidence to suggest that the Untouchables are Broken Men?

(2) Is there evidence that the process of settlement suggested above has actually taken place in any country?

(3) If Broken Men living outside the village is a universal feature of all societies, how is it that the separate quarters of the Broken Men have disappeared outside India but not in India?

Are the Untouchables Broken Men?

To the question: Are the Untouchables in their origin only Broken Men, my answer is in the affirmative. An affirmative answer is bound to be followed by a call for evidence. Direct evidence on this issue could be had if the totems of the Touchables and the Untouchables in the Hindu villages had been studied. Unfortunately the study of the totemic organisation of the Hindus and the Untouchables has not yet been undertaken by students of anthropology. When such data is collected it would enable us to give a decisive opinion on the question raised in this Chapter. For the present, I am satisfied from such inquiries as I have made that the totems of the Untouchables of a particular village differ from the totems of the Hindus of the village.

Difference in totems between Hindus and Untouchables would be the best evidence in support of the thesis that the Untouchables are Broken Men belonging to a tribe different from the tribe comprising the village community. It may, however, be admitted that such direct evidence as has a bearing on the question remains to be collected. But facts have survived which serve as pointers and from which it can be said-that the Untouchables were Broken men. There are two sets of such evidentiary facts.

One set of facts comprise the names *Antya, Antyaja* and *Antyavasin* given, to certain communities by the Hindu Shastras. They have come down from very ancient past. Why were these names used to indicate a certain class of people? There seem to be some meaning behind these terms. The words are undoubtedly derivative. They arc derived from the root *Anta.* What does the word *Anta* mean? Hindus learned in the Shastras argue that it means one who is born last and as the Untouchable according to the Hindu order of Divine creation is held to be born last, the word *Antya* means an Untouchable. The argument is absurd and does not accord with the Hindu theory of the order of creation. According to it, it is the Sudra who is born last.

The Untouchable is outside the scheme of creation. The Sudra is *Savarna.* As against him the Untouchable is *Avarna, i.e.* outside the *Varna* system. The Hindu theory of priority in creation does not and cannot apply to the Untouchable. In my view, the word *Antya* means not end of creation but end of the village. It is a name given to those people who lived on the outskirts of the village. The word *Antya* has, therefore, a survival value. It tells us that there was a time when some people lived inside the village and some lived outside the village and that those who lived outside the village, *i.e.* on the *Antya* of the village, were called *Antyaja.*

Why did some people live on the border of the village? Can there be any other reason than that they were Broken Men who were aliens and who belonged to tribes different from those who lived inside the village? I cannot see any. That this is the real reason is to be found in the use of these particular words to designate them. The use of the words *Antya, Antyaja* and *Antyavasin* has thus double significance. In the first place, it shows that living in separate quarters was such a peculiar phenomenon that a new terminology had to be invented to give expression to it. Secondly, the words chosen express in exact terms the conditions of the people to whom it applied namely that they were aliens.

The second set of facts which shows that the Untouchables were Broken men relates to the position of a community called the Mahars. The Mahar community is a principle Untouchable community in Maharashtra. It is the single largest Untouchable community found in Maharashtra. The following facts showing the relations between the Mahars and the Touchable Hindus are worthy of note: (1) The Mahars are to be found in every village; (2) Every village in Maharashtra has a wall and the Mahars have their quarters outside the wall; (3) The Mahars by turn do the duty of watch and ward on behalf of the village; and (4) The Mahars claim 52 rights against the Hindu villagers. Among these 52 rights the most important are:

(i) The right to collect food from the villagers;

(ii) The right to collect corn from each villager at the harvest season; and

(iii) The right to appropriate the dead animal belonging to the villagers.

The evidence arising from the position of the Mahars is of course confined to Maharashtra. Whether similar cases are to be found in other parts of India has yet to be investigated. But, if the Mahars case can be taken as typical of the Untouchables throughout India it will be accepted that there was a stage in the history of India when Broken Men belonging to other tribes came to the Settled tribes and made a bargain whereby the Broken men were allowed to settle on the border of the village, were required to do certain duties and in return were given certain rights. The Mahars have a tradition that the 52 rights claimed by them against the villagers were given to them by the Muslim kings of Bedar. This can only mean that these rights were very ancient and that the kings of Bedar only confirmed them.

These facts although meagre do furnish some evidence in support of the theory that the Untouchables lived outside the village from the very beginning. They were not deported and made to live outside the village *because* they were declared Untouchables. They lived outside the village from the beginning *because* they were Broken Men who belonged to a tribe different from the one to which the Settled tribe belonged.

The difficulty in accepting this explanation arises largely from the notion that the Untouchables were always Untouchables. This difficulty will vanish if it is borne in mind that there was a time when the ancestors of the present day Untouchables were not Untouchables *vis-a-vis* the villagers but were merely Broken Men, no more and no less, and the only difference between them and the villagers was that they belonged to different tribes.

Are there Parallel Cases?

Are there any cases known to history of Broken Men living outside the village? To this question it is possible to give an affirmative answer. Fortunately for us we have two reported cases which show that what is said to have occurred in India particularly has also actually occurred elsewhere. The countries wherein such a development has actually been reported to have taken place are Ireland and Wales.

The organisation of the Irish village in primitive times can be seen from the Brehon Laws of Ireland. Some idea of it as revealed in these Laws may be obtained from the following summary given by Sir Henry Maine. Says Sir Henry Maine :

"The Brehon Law discloses a stage when the tribe has long been settled, in all probability upon the tribal territory. It is of sufficient size and importance to constitute a political unit, and possibly at its apex is one of the numerous chieftain whom the Irish records call kings. The primary assumption is that the whole of the tribal territory belongs to the whole of the tribe, but in fact large portions of it have been permanently appropriated to minor bodies of tribesmen. A part is allotted in special way to the chief as appurtenant to his office, and descends from chief to chief according to a special rule of succession. Other portions are occupied by fragments of the tribe, some of which are under minor chiefs while others, though not strictly ruled by a chief, have somebody of noble class to act as their representative.

All the unappropriated tribelands are in a more special way the property of the tribe as a whole, and no portion can theoretically be subjected to more than a temporary occupation. Such occupations are, however, frequent and among the holders of tribeland, on these terms, are groups of men calling themselves tribesmen, but being in reality associations formed by contract, chiefly for the purpose of pasturing cattle. Much of the common tribeland is not occupied at all, but constitutes, to use the English expression, the 'waste' of the tribe. Still this waste is constantly brought under tillage or permanent pasture by settlements of tribesmen, and upon it *cultivators and servile states are permitted to squat, particularly towards the border.* It is part of the territory over which the authority of the chief tends steadily to increase, and here it is that he settles his 'fuidhir' or stranger-tenants *a very important class-the outlaws and 'broken men' from other tribes who come to him for protection, and who are only connected with their new tribe by their dependence on its chief, and through the responsibility which he incurs for them".*

Who were the Fuidhirs? According to Sir Henry Maine the Fuidhirs were: "Strangers or fugitives from other territories, men in fact, who had broken the original tribal bond which gave them a place in the community, and who had to obtain and then as best they might in a new tribe and new place. Society was violently disordered. The result was probably to fill the country with 'Broken Men' and such men could only find a home and protection by becoming Fuidhir tenants. "The Fuidhir was not a tribesman but an alien. In all societies cemented together by kinship the position of the person who has lost or broken the bond of union is always extraordinarily miserable. He has not only lost his natural place in them but they have no room for him anywhere else".

Now as to Wales. The organisation of the Welsh village in primitive times is described by Mr. Seebhom. According to Mr. Seebhom a village in Wales was a collection of homesteads. The homesteads were separated into two groups, the homesteads of the Free-tenants and the homesteads of the Unfree-tenants. Mr. Seebhom says that this separation in habitation was a common feature of the primitive village in Wales. Why were these Unfree-tenants made to live in a separate and detached place? The reason for this separation is explained by Mr. Seebhom in the following terms:

> *"At first sight there is a great confusion in the class of men mentioned in the ancient Welsh Laws— of tribesmen, Uchelore bryre and innate boneddings: of non-tribesmen, talogo Aillte, Alltude, etc. The confusion vanishes only when the principle underlying the constitution of tribal society is grasped. And this principle would apparently be a very simple one if could be freed from the complications of conquest and permanent settlement of land from the inroads of foreign law, custom, and nomenclature. To begin with there can be little doubt that the ruling principle underlying the structure of tribal society was that of blood relationship among the free tribesmen. No one who did not belong to a kindred could be a member of the tribe, which was in fact, a bundle of Welsh kindred. Broadly then under the Welsh tribal system there were two classes, those of Cymric blood— and those who were stranger in blood. There*

was a deep, if not unpassable, gulf between these two classes quite apart from any question of land or of conquest. It was a division in blood and it soon becomes apparent that the tenacity with which the distinction was maintained was at once one of the strong distinctive marks of the tribal system and one of the main secrets of its strength."

This description of the organisation of the Irish and the Welsh villages in the primitive times leave no doubt that the case of the Untouchables of India is not the only case of a people living outside the village. It proves that in it was exhibited a universal phenomenon, and was marked by the following features:

1. That in primitive times the Village Settlement consisted of two parts. One part occupied by the community belonging to one tribe and another part occupied by the Broken Men of different tribes.
2. The part of the settlement occupied by the tribal community was regarded as the village proper. The Broken Men lived in the outskirts of the village.
3. The reason why the Broken Men lived outside the village was because they were aliens and did not belong to the tribal community.

The analogy between the Untouchables of India and the Fuidhirs of Ireland and the Alltudes of Wales is complete. The Untouchables lived outside the village for the same reason for which the Fuidhirs and Alltudes had to live outside the village in Ireland and Wales. It is, therefore, clear that what is said about the Untouchables on the issue of their living outside the village is not without a parallel elsewhere.

How did Separate Settlements for Broken men Disappear Elsewhere?

That the Fuidhirs of Ireland and the Alltudes of Wales were Broken Men is true. That they lived in separate quarters is also a fact. But it is also true that the separate quarters of those Broken Men disappeared and they became part of the Settled tribe and were absorbed in it. This is somewhat strange. The Broken Men according to the theory set out before were given quarters outside the village because they belonged to a different tribe and, therefore, to different blood. How is it then that they were absorbed by the tribe later on? Why such a thing did not happen in India? These are questions which are natural and which call for an answer.

The question is integrally connected with the process of evolution through which Primitive Society came to be transferred into Modern Society. As has already been said this evolution has proceeded along two different lines. One marked the transformation of Primitive Society from Nomadic into a settled community. The other marked the transformation of Primitive Society from tribal into a territorial community. The question with which we are immediately concerned relates to the second line of evolution. For it is the substitution of common territory for common blood as the bond of union that is responsible for the disappearance of the separate quarters of the Broken Men. Why did Primitive Society substitute common territory for common blood as the bond of union? This is a question for which there is no adequate explanation. The origin of the change is very-obscure. How the change was brought about is however quite clear. At some stage there came into being in Primitive Society a rule whereby a non-tribesman could become a member of the tribe and become absorbed in it as a kindred. It was known as a rule of ennoblement. This rule was that if a non-tribesman lived next to the tribe or married within a tribe for a given number of generations he became their kindred Mr. Seebhom gives the following rules for a non-tribesman becoming a tribesman as it was found in the Welsh village system.

(1) Residence in Cymru (Wales) according to the tradition of South Wales made the descendant of a stranger at last, a Cymru, but not until continued to the ninth generation.

(2) Intermarriage with innate Cymraeses generation after generation made the descendent of a stranger an innate Cymru in the *fourth* generation. In other-words, the original stranger's great grandson, whose blood was at least seven-eighths Cymric was allowed to attain the right to claim the privileges of a tribesman.

Should not such a thing have happened in India? It could have-indeed it should have. For a rule similar to that which existed in Ireland and Wales also existed in India. It is referred to by Manu. In Chapter X, verses 64-67, he says that a Sudra can be a Brahmin for seven generations (if he marries) within the Brahmin Community. The ordinary rule of *Chaturvarna* was that a Sudra could never become a Brahmin. A Sudra was born a Sudra and could not be made a Brahmin. But this rule of antiquity was so strong that Manti had to apply rule of Untouchability to the Sudra. It is obvious that if this rule had continued to operate in India, the Broken Men of India would have been absorbed in the village community and their separate quarters would have ceased to exist.

Why did this not happen? The answer is that the notion of Untouchability supervened and perpetuated difference between kindred and non-kindred, tribesmen and non-tribesmen in another form; namely; between Touchables and Untouchables. It is this new factor which prevented the amalgamation taking place in the way in which it took place in Ireland and Wales, with the result that the system of separate quarters has become a perpetual and a permanent feature of the Indian village.

2

Need for Political Power for Depressed Classes

Dr. Ambedkar's Lecture at the Round Table Conferences

Mr. Chairman, my purpose in rising to address this conference is principally to place before it the point of view of the depressed classes, whom I and my colleague, Rao Bahadur Srinivasan, have the honour to represent, regarding the question of constitutional reform. It is a point of view of 43,000,000 people, or one-fifth of the total population of British India.

The depressed classes form a group by themselves, which is distinct and separate from the Mohammedans, and, although they are included among the Hindus, they in no sense form an integral part of that community. Not only have they a separate existence, but they have also assigned to them a statute which is invidiously distinct from the status occupied by any other community in India. There are communities in India, which occupy a lower and subordinate position; but the position assigned to the depressed classes is totally different.

It is one which is midway between that of the serf and the slave, and which may, for convenience, be called servile with this difference, that the serf and the slave were permitted to have physical contact, from which the Depressed Classes are debarred. What is worse that this enforced servility and bar to human intercourse, due to their untouchability, involves, not merely the possibility of discrimination in public life, but actually works out as a positive denial of all equality of opportunity and the denial of those most elementary of civic rights on which all human existence depends. I am sure that the point of view of such a community, as large as the population of England or of France, and so heavily handicapped in the struggle for existence, cannot but have some bearing on the right sort of solution of the political problem, and I am anxious that this Conference should be placed in possession of that point of view at the very start.

The point of view I will try to put as briefly as I can. It is this that the bureaucratic form of Government in India should be replaced by a Government, which will be a Government of the people, by the people, and for the people. This statement of the view of the depressed classes I am sure will be received with some surprise in certain quarters. The tie that bounds the Depressed Classes to the British has been of a unique character. The Depressed Classes welcomed the British as their deliverers from age long tyranny and oppression by the orthodox Hindus. They fought their battles against the Hindus, the Mussalmans and the Sikhs and won for them this great Empire of India.

The British, on their side, assumed the role of trustees for the depressed classes. In view of such an intimate relationship between the parties, this change in the attitude of the depressed classes towards British Rule in India is undoubtedly a most momentous phenomenon. But the reasons for this change of attitude are not far to seek. We have not taken this decision simply because we wish to throw in our lot with the majority. Indeed, as you know, there is not much love lost between the majority and the particular minority I represent. Ours is an independent decision. We have judged of the existing administration solely in the light of our own circumstances and we have found it wanting in some of the most essential elements of a good Government.

When we compare our present position with the one, which it was our lot to bear in Indian society of the pre-British days, we find that, instead of marching on, we are only marking time. Before the British, we were in the loathsome condition due to our untouchability. Has the British Government done anything to remove it? Before the British, we could not enter the temple. Can we enter now? Before the British, we were denied entry into the Police Force. Does the British Government admit us in the Force? Before the British, we were not allowed to serve in the Military. Is that career now open to us? To none of these questions can we give an affirmative answer.

That the British, who have held so large a sway over us for such a long time, have done some good we cheerfully acknowledge. But there is certainly no fundamental change in our position. Indeed, so far as we were concerned, the British Government has accepted the social arrangements as it found them, and has preserved them faithfully in the manner of the Chinese tailor who, when given an old coat as a pattern, produced with pride an exact replica, rents, patches and all. Our wrongs have remained as open sores and they have not been righted, although 150 years of British rule have rolled away.

We do not accuse the British of indifference or want of sympathy. What we do find is that they are quite incompetent to tackle our problems. If the case was one of indifference only it would have been a matter of small moment, and it would not have made such a profound change in our attitude. But·what we have come to realise on a deeper analysis of the situation is that it is not merely a case of indifference, rather it is a case of sheer incompetence to undertake the task. The depressed classes find that the British Government in India suffers from two very serious limitations.

There is first of all an internal limitation, which arises from the character, motives, and interests of those who are in power. It is not because they cannot help us in these things but because it is against their character, motives and interests to do so. The second consideration that limits its authority is the mortal fear it has of external resistance. The Government of India does realise the necessity of removing the social evils which are eating into the vitals of Indian society and which have blighted the lives of the downtrodden classes for so many years.

The Government of India does realise that the landlords are squeezing the masses dry, and the capitalists are not giving the labourers a living wage and decent conditions of work. Yet it is most painful thing that it has not dared to touch any of these evils. Why? Is it because it has no legal powers to remove them? No. The reason why it does not intervene is because it is afraid that its intervention to amend the existing code of social and economic life will give rise to resistance. Of what good is such a Government to anybody? Under a Government, paralysed between two such limitations, much that goes to make life good must remain held up. We must have a Government in which the men in power will give their undivided allegiance to the best interest of the country. We must have a Government in which men in power, knowing where obedience will end and resistance will begin, will not be afraid to amend the social and economic code of life which the dictates of justice and expediency so urgently call for. This role the British Government will never be able to play, It is only a Government which is of the people, for the people and by the people that will make this possible.

These are some of the questions raised by the Depressed Classes and the answers which in their view these questions seem to carry. This is therefore the inevitable conclusion which the Depressed Classes have come to: namely, that the bureaucratic Government of India, with the best of motives, will remain powerless to effect any change so far as our particular grievances are concerned. We feel that nobody can remove our grievances as well as we can, and we cannot remove them unless we get political power in our own hands. No share of this political power can evidently come to us so long as the British Government remains as it is. It is only in a Swaraj constitution that we stand any chance of getting the political power into our own hands, without which we cannot bring salvation to our people.

There is one thing, Sir, to which I wish to draw your particular attention. It is this, I have not used the expression Dominion Status in placing before you the point of view of the Depressed Classes. I have avoided using it, not because I do not understand its implications nor does the omission mean that the depressed classes object to India's attaining Dominion Status. My chief ground for not using it is that it does not convey the full content of what the Depressed Classes stand for. The Depressed Classes, while they stand for Dominion Status with safeguards, wish to lay all the emphasis they can on one question and one question alone. And that question is, how will Dominion India function? Where will the centre of political power be? Who will have it? Will the Depressed Classes be heirs to it?

These are the questions that form their chief concern. The Depressed Classes feel that they will get no shred of the political power unless the political machinery for the new constitution is of a special make. In the construction of that machine certain hard facts of Indian social life must not be lost sight of. It must be recognised that Indian Society is a gradation of Castes forming an ascending scale of reverence and a descending scale of contempt—a system which gives no scope for the growth of that sentiment of equality and fraternity so essential for a democratic form of Government.

It must also be recognised that while the intelligentsia is a very important part of Indian society, it is drawn from its upper strata and although it speaks in the name of the country and leads the political movement, it has not shed the narrow particularism of the class from which it is drawn. In other words what the Depressed Classes wish to urge is that the political mechanism must take account of and must have a definite relation to the psychology of the society for which it is devised. Otherwise you are likely to produce a constitution which, however symmetrical, will be truncated one and a total misfit to the society for which it is designed.

There is one point with which I should like to deal before I close this matter. We are often reminded that the problem of the Depressed Classes is a social problem and that its solution lies elsewhere than in politics. We take strong exception to this view. We hold that the problem of the Depressed Classes will never be solved unless they get political power in their own hands. If this is true, and I do not think that the contrary can be maintained, then problem of Depressed Classes is I submit eminently a political problem and must be treated as such. We know that political power is passing from the British into the hands of those who wield such tremendous economic, social and religious sway over our existence.

We are willing that it may happen, though the idea of Swaraj recalls to the mind of many of us the tyrannies, oppressions and injustices practised upon us in the past and fear of their recurrence under Swaraj. We are prepared to take the inevitable risk of the situation in the hope that we shall be installed, in adequate proportion, as the political sovereigns of the country along with our fellow countrymen. But we will consent to that on one condition and that is that the settlement of our problems is not left to time. I am afraid the Depressed Classes have waited too long for time to work its miracle. At every successive step taken by the British Government to widen the scope of representative Government the Depressed Classes have been systematically left out. No thought has been given to their claim for political power. I protest with all the emphasis I can that we will not stand this any longer. The settlement of our problem must be a part of the general political settlement and must not be left over to the shifting sands of the sympathy and goodwill of the rulers of the future. The reasons why the Depressed Classes insist upon it are obvious. Every one of us knows that the man in possession is more powerful than the man who is out of possession.

Everyone of us also knows that those in possession of power seldom abdicate in favour of those who are out of it. We cannot therefore hope for the effectuation of the settlement of our social problem. If we allow power to slip into the hands of those who stand to lose by settlement unless we are to have another revolution to dethrone those, whom we today help to ascend the throne of power and prestige. We prefer being despised for too anxious apprehensions, than ruined by too confident a security, and I think it would be just and proper for us to insist that the best guarantee for the settlement of our problem is the adjustment of the political machine itself so as to give us a hold on it, and not the will of those who are contriving to be left in unfettered control of that machine.

What adjustments of the political machine the Depressed Classes want for their safety and protection I will place before the Conference at the proper time. All I will say at the present moment is that, although we want responsible Government, we do not want a Government that will only mean a change of masters. Let the Legislature be fully and really representative if your Executive is going to be fully responsible.

I am sorry Mr. President. I had to speak in such plain words. But I saw no help. The Depressed Classes have had no friend. The Government has all along used them only as an excuse for its continued existence. The Hindus claim them only to deny them or, better still, to appropriate rights. The Mohammedans refuse to recognise their separate existence, because they fear that their privileges may be curtailed by the admission of a rival. Depressed by the Government, suppressed by the Hindu and disregarded by the Muslim, we are left in a most intolerable position of utter helplessness to which I am sure there is no parallel and to which I was bound to call attention.

Regarding the other question, which is set down for discussion, I am sorry it was decided to tag it on to a general debate. Its importance deserved a session for itself. No justice can be done to it in a passing reference. The subject is one in which the Depressed Classes are deeply concerned and they regard it as a very vital question. As members of a minority, we look to the Central Government to act as a powerful curb on the provincial majority to save the minorities from the misrule of the majority. As an Indian, interested in the growth of Indian nationalism, I must make it plain that I am a strong believer in the Unitary form of Government and the thought of disturbing it I must confess does not please me very much. This Unitary Government has been the most potent influence in the building up of the Indian nation. That process of unification, which has been the result of a unified system of Government, has not been completed and I should be loathed to withdraw this most powerful stimulus in the formative period and before it has worked out its end.

However, the question in the form in which it is placed is only an academic question and I shall be prepared to consider a federal form, if it can be shown that in it local autonomy is not inconsistent with central unity. Sir, all that I, as a representative of the depressed classes, need say on their behalf I have said. May I crave your indulgence to permit me as an Indian to say a word or two generally on the situation, which we have to meet. So much has been said regarding its gravity that I shall not venture to add a word more to it, although I am no silent spectator of the movement.

What I am anxious about is to feel whether we are proceeding on right lines in evolving our solution. What that solution should be rests entirely upon the view that British delegates choose to take. Addressing myself to them I will say, whether you will meet the situation by conciliation or by applying the iron heel must be a matter for your judgement for the responsibility is entirely yours. To such of you as are particular to the use of force and believe that a regime of Letters de Cachet and the Bastille will ease the situation, let me recall the memorable words of the greatest teacher of political philosophy, Edmund Burke. This is what he said to the British nation when it was faced with the problem of dealing with the American colonies:

> *"The use of force alone is but temporary. It may endure for a moment, but it does not remove the necessity of subduing again; a nation is not governed which is perpetually to be conquered. The next objection to force is its uncertainty. Terror is not always the effect of force, and an armament is not a victory. If you do not succeed, you are without resource; for conciliation failing, force remains, but force failing, no further hope of reconciliation is left. Power and authority are sometimes bought by kindness, but they can never be begged as alms by an impoverished and defeated violence. A further objection to force is that you impair the object by your very endeavours to preserve it. The thing you fought for (to wit the loyalty of the people) is not the thing you recover but depreciated, sunk, wasted and consumed in the contest."*

The worth and efficacy of this advice you all knew. You did not listen to it and you lost the great continent of America. You followed it to the lasting good of yourself and the rest of the Dominions that are with you. To such of you as are willing to adopt a policy of conciliation I should like to say one thing. There seems to be prevalent an impression that the Delegates are called here to argue for and against a case for Dominion Status and that the grant of Dominion Status will be dependent upon which side is the victor in this battle of wits. With due deference to all who are sharpening their wits, I submit that there can be no greater mistake than to make the formula of logic govern so live an issue. I have no quarrel with logic and logicians. But I warn them against the disaster that is bound to follow if they are not careful in the selection of the premises they choose to adopt for their deductions.

It is all a matter of temper whether you will abide by the fall of your logic, or whether you will refute it, as Dr. Johnson did the paradoxes of Berkeley by trampling them under his feet. I am afraid it is not sufficiently realised that in the present temper of the country, no constitution will be workable which is not acceptable to the majority of the people.

The time when you were to choose and India was to accept is gone, never to return. Let the consent of the people and not the accident of logic be the touchstone of your new constitution, if you desire that it should be worked.

Committee of the Whole Conference

Comments on the Interim Report of Sub-Committee No. I (Federal Structure)—16th December 1930.

Dr. Ambedkar: I should like to raise the point, which my friend Mr. Joshi made before we adjourned. The Lord Chancellor, as the Chairman of this Sub-Committee, invited some of the delegates to submit any views they might have on these particular matters, and a few delegates including myself submitted a letter to the Chairman of the Sub-Committee, and expressed our wish that letter should be submitted to the Sub-Committee for consideration. I do not find in the Report any reference to that letter, and I was informed by Lord Sankey that letter was not placed before the Sub-Committee, but was sent to you, Sir, as Prime Minister. I do not think that was quite a proper way of dealing with it.

The letter was submitted to the Chairman of the Sub-Committee, for the Sub-Committee's use and it expressed certain definite views we held on the question of Federation. I am bound to make this comment because, speaking for myself, the Report as drawn up is so much at variance with the principles expressed in the letter that I find we shall have at some stage to raise a debate on this question, and I should like to know what steps the Lord Chancellor proposes to take.

Lord Sankey: I am very much obliged to Dr. Ambedkar for raising the point he has done, because I should have liked to have raised it myself, and it gives me the opportunity of saying a few words which I should have said at the beginning........ This is not a complete picture........ soon you are going to be presented with the complete picture, and Dr. Ambedkar, I shall want your assistance,.........Now with regard to the letter. Dr.

Ambedkar, that you were good enough to send to me, I have considered it very carefully, and it will be vital to discuss it when we come to No. 6.

Dr. Ambedkar: All I should like to know, if I may say so, is whether you will place that letter before the Committee. At what stage you may do so is a matter which I must leave to you.

Lord Sankey: One moment, Dr. Ambedkar. I am going to do a good deal more than that; I am not only going to place your letter before the Committee. I am going to draw the Committee's attention to it myself.

Dr. Ambedkar: I am obliged. That is enough for me.

In Subcommittee No. II

(Provincial Constitution)

First Sitting-4th December 1930

Dr. Ambedkar: I propose to divide my remarks under three heads : (1) provincial autonomy, (2) responsibility in the provinces, (3) provincial services. I make a distinction between provincial autonomy and provincial services. It seems to me that the question of provincial autonomy raises the definition of the relations of the provincial Executive and Legislature vis-a-vis the Central Government and the Central Legislature. The first remark I would offer with the attitude of those who hold that the time has arrived when the provincial Governments ought to be left with as complete an autonomy as is possible under the circumstances, and they should be free from such control as the Central Government now exercises.

But, Sir, I cannot help making this further observation, that viewing the problem of provincial autonomy from the standpoint of the particular class I represent in this Conference and of the interests of India as a whole and the working classes in particular, I think that in any future constitution that we propose to devise for endowing the Provinces with provincial autonomy we must take into consideration certain facts which are bound to limit the character of that autonomy.

The first limiting factor in the provincial autonomy is that it must be made subject to such questions of a provincial character which are, although provincial in nature, also of an All-India character. The Provinces may have their say with regard to these subjects, and yet the Central Government should not be excluded from its jurisdiction with regard to them. For instances, I would like to draw an illustration from labour legislation, legislation affecting tenants and affecting agriculture. These, no doubt, in a country like India, must become provincial subjects yet I do not think they can be viewed entirely from such a small compass. They cannot be regarded as entirely provincial and without an All-India character. The Central Government must have some jurisdiction over subjects of this character, notwithstanding that it cuts across provincial autonomy.

Secondly, I should state that in dividing the powers of Government between the Central and the Provincial Governments in the future constitution of India with a view to giving the Provinces as complete an autonomy as possible, it will also be necessary that such powers as remain undefined must be left with the Central Government. Well, I do not think that there is no other view on that point. But I say that in the present situation in India, where the separatist tendency exists to such an extent as we all know it, where provincial and local parochialism is more dominant than national feeling, while we are building up a Federated India with complete autonomy of the units, we still have the problem of making India as a whole a strong and united country. I would make this further observation, namely, that I do not think that the reservation of powers in the Central Government is likely to affect the autonomy of the Provinces. The reservation of powers as interpreted by the Judicial Committee of the Privy Council in the case of Canada has not had this overriding effect. It means a power that comes into existence in an emergency in a field not specifically allotted to the Provinces. I do not think that the Provincial autonomy should be really affected.

The second thing I should like to observe in connection with this question of Provincial autonomy is that autonomy must be limited by the affording of protection for the interests of the minorities and of the Depressed Classes. As I visualise the situation in India as it will result from the new constitution, I find there will be certain Provinces in which some communities will be in a majority, but in all the Provinces the Depressed Classes, whom I represent, will be in a minority. They will be in a minority in every Province. I cannot understand how we can at this state permit the Provincial majorities to have a complete uninterrupted and undiluted sway over the destinies of these poor people, without any right of appeal being given to the latter in regard to mal-administration or neglect of their interests. There must be some authority somewhere, over and above the Provincial Government, which will be in a position to intervene and rescue them from any adverse position in which they may be placed by the Provincial majorities.

These are the three things, which, in my opinion at any rate must limit the autonomy of the future Provincial Governments of India.

Coming to the question of the character of responsibility in the Provincial Governments, my first observation is that the whole question of responsibility in the Provincial Legislature is entirely dependent upon the kind of Legislature that you are going to get in the Provinces. If the Legislature that you are going to get in the Provinces is a Legislature which is going to be a mirror of the whole population of the Province, if it is going to be thoroughly representative and not merely representative as a museum is, where there are a few specimens of every species for the observation of the general onlooker; if every minority and every class which fears its existence will be jeopardised is placed on a position to make its influence felt, then I think in a Legislature of that sort there will be no harm in conceding the principle that Provincial responsibility may be introduced to the fullest extent. That is my first observation.

Making that a condition that the Legislatures shall be fully and adequately representative of all the classes, I see no objection to the subjects, which are now, reserved being transferred to popular control.

Coming to the question of whether the responsibility in the Provinces should be joint or should be individual I have not the slightest hesitation in saying that the responsibility not only should be joint but must be joint. I have been a member of Legislative Council, and I have seen how Ministries in the Provinces have worked. It has been a most painful experience for me, as it has been the experience, I believe, of many of those who have had the misfortune or the good fortune to be members of a Legislative Council, to find that Ministries have been working as a kind of loose confederation, without having any complete or unanimous view on a particular policy which they adopted. There have been divided counsels, and cases of Ministers not being very willing to support each other.

What has been the result? The result is this, that in no instance have we had any considered policy put forward by the Cabinet as a whole, worked out in detail and placed before the Legislative Council. Things have been done by fits and starts, and I do not think we want our responsibility in future to be bungled in that fashion.

Turning now to the question of communal representation in the Cabinets, I must confess that I am not very much drawn to the suggestion, which is often made that there should be communal representation in the Cabinet. I am not, of course, oblivious of the fact; in fact, I am very conscious of it that if the minority communities are not represented in the Cabinet it is very possible, and even very likely, that in matters of administration which affect their daily lives their interests may be affected very prejudicially by the policy of Ministers whose dominant interest is communalism. I do not forget that for a moment, but my submission is that there is a better way of dealing with that sort of evil, and it seems to me that if the minorities could get constitutional and statutory guarantees laid down in the Constitutional Act itself against anything likely to injure their interests being done or left undone by the Cabinet, the danger which most of us apprehend from the fact that the Cabinets may be communally dominated, will vanish, and we shall not have much cause to insist on communal representation in the Cabinet. Although I am very desirous that the Chief Minister, whoever he is, should recognise or should be made to recognise the interest of having most of the important minorities represented in the Cabinet, we cannot for the moment forget that, after all, a Cabinet office is a very responsible office.

A Cabinet Minister has not merely to look after the interests of the minorities; he has to see to the safety and interest of the Province as a whole. That demands ability and competence; it does not merely demand a communal outlook, and it is from that point of view that I look at the matter. I should like to have the interests of the minorities and the Depressed Classes safeguarded in such a manner that constitutionally it would be impossible for Ministers drawn from the majority communities to do anything prejudicial to the minorities or to neglect their interests.

Coming to the question of the relations between the Governor and his Ministry, I think one thing is obvious, namely that no constitution, if it is really to embody full responsible Government and collective responsibility, can permit the Governor the power to interfere in the day-to-day administration of the country. That would run quite across the system of responsible Government and collective responsibility. The Ministry must be allowed to carry on the day-to-day administration on the basis of joint responsibility.

When we come to the question of the emergency powers which it is suggested should be left with the Governor. I find myself in a somewhat difficult position, because I do not understand exactly what is meant. Is it meant that when an emergency arises the Governor should simply dismiss the Ministry and have nothing to do with it, and should promulgate whatever laws, ordinances or measures he thinks are necessary to meet the situation, notwithstanding the fact that they are opposed by the Ministry? I do not know what is wanted. I can quite understand the Governor should have the absolute, undoubted and unrestricted power of dismissing a Ministry which he thinks is not acting in the best interests of the country, but I cannot understand how there can be responsible Government in a Province in which the Governor is allowed to do a thing without a Ministry. It is one thing to say that the Governor should have a Ministry with which he agrees in a particular emergency, but it is quite a different thing to say that when an emergency arises the Governor should simply disregard the Ministry altogether. I think this point will have to be worked out in some deal, for, as I say, I do not quite understand it.

Coming to the question of the Services, there is one observation I am bound to make. I quite agree in principle that with provincial autonomy the power of regulating the Services in a Province should belong to that Province, and that the

Provinces should have full liberty to Indianise the Services as they desire and according to their means and circumstances. The observation which I feel bound to make, however, is this: I cannot forget that Indians are communal minded. We do hope it is only a hope that a time will come when all Indians will cease to look at problems from a communal point of view in administrating matters which are left to their charge, but that is only a hope; it is not a fact. The fact is that Indians do discriminate between class and class, community and community, in administering such discretion as is left to them in their administration of the law. That is a fact I cannot get over; it is a fact from which I have suffered immensely. My fear with regard to the future constitution of India is that having regard to the present position of the depressed classes, having regard to the fact that education is not widely spread amongst them, and having regard to the fact that there is hardly a single individual holding a gazetted post in the Bombay Presidency for instance:

A Member: There is one.

Dr. Ambedkar: Yes, there is one, and that is the exception, which proves the rule. You know how much trouble I had to get him in. I very much fear that this Indianisation may work out as a tyranny, and therefore, from my particular point of view, I should like to emphasise that at any rate for some time it will be necessary to maintain a British element in the Services. I do not say there should be no Indianisation, but I do say that, having regard to our interests, it should be rather slower than some people desire it to be. These are the general remarks that I wish to offer from our point of view.

Third Sitting—8th December 1930

Dr. Ambedkar: May I make a suggestion? It seems to me this question of Second Chambers is so important that it cannot be discussed properly and adequately by being tacked on to the series of heads we are now discussing. In my opinion a special day ought to be allotted to this subject. I see very little connection between the subject of Second Chambers and that of the protection of minorities, or any of the other matters enumerated in items I and 2. It seems to me this is a very important question. I find nothing in this list of heads dealing with the composition of the Legislature; if you were to add a head "Composition of the Legislature" we should have a proper opportunity of discussing the whole subject.

Chairman: I cannot see how you can separate this whole subject and split it up.

Dr. Ambedkar: The question of Second Chambers can certainly be separated from that of minorities.

Chairman: Not entirely. Whether there is to be a Second Chamber or not affects almost every other subject that comes up, the powers of the Governor vis-a-vis the Executive and the Legislature, the powers of the Legislature and so on. I think you had better let us go on, and if at the end we find the discussion has not been adequate, we will try to arrange for a further discussion on this subject by itself.

Fourth Sitting—9th December 1930

Dr. Ambedkar: It may be. But I am taking these two communities for the moment because they are important. It seems to me that any argument, which is based upon that fact is an argument, which leads to a conclusion which, will never enable us to transfer law and order. Therefore it seems to me that is an argument which ought not to be adopted or accepted. It seems to me also that the noble Marquess assumes that although a Mohammedan or a Hindu will be in charge of the department of law and order, he will be entirely subject to the whims of the particular community to which he belongs. My submission, Sir, is this, that assumes that the future of political parties in India will be so constituted that they will be divided on religious lines and not on the lines of political or economic differences. As I view the situation it seems to me that in the future constitution of India the Executive will be so divided that we shall see less of the religious and racial distinctions coming to the surface and we shall find a Hindu Minister having a party and a following containing a large element of Mohammedans, and a Mohammedan Minister with a following of Hindus in his group, if that happens, and I take it is almost a certainty that it will happen, I do not understand how, for instance, a Hindu Minister who is in charge of law and order could administer law and order in such a manner as to offend the susceptibilities of a part of the group which supports him in office. It seems to me therefore that the fears so far as this particular aspect of the matter is concerned are rather unfounded.

The second thing which seems to be agreed upon more or less is this, that not only should the Executive be a unified Executive but that the responsibility of this unified Executive should be joint and not several. With these conclusions, Sir, I agree, but the points of difference that have arisen in the course of the debate to which we have listened largely relate to the composition of the Executive and it seems to me that there arise three different questions for our consideration in connection with the composition of the Executive. The first question is: should the Executive be confined to members of the Legislature or should it be open to individuals who are officials or non-officials and who are outside the Legislature? The second question is: should it consist of members of the minority communities? The third question is: whether the Governor should have the responsibility of appointing the Ministers himself or whether he should appoint the Chief Minister and leave the matter of the selection of his colleagues to that Chief Minister.

Now, Sir, on all these three questions my answer is in the affirmative. Personally, I do not see why the membership of the Cabinet should be rigorously restricted and confined to the members of the Legislature. I also do not see why there should not exist some provisions whereby the Executive should not be made as representative as possible of all the communities that are represented in the Legislature.

Thirdly, regarding the power of the Governor to compose his Ministry, it seems to me that we must admit that it is his prerogative right to constitute the Ministry and that you must have discretion left to him in the matter of selecting his men. But, Sir, when I say that I answer these three questions in the affirmative, namely, that the Executive need not be confined to the members of the Legislature, that some provision should exist whereby different communities may be represented in the Cabinet, and that the Governor should have left with him abundant discretion in order to form his Cabinet, I say when I make these admissions I make them subject to one supreme condition. That supreme condition is that however the Executive is composed, it shall abide by one principle, namely that it shall accept joint responsibility. If, for instance, this principle of joint responsibility is made obligatory upon the Executive, it seems to me that the importation of a foreign element into the Cabinet will not be a disturbing factor as it is supposed to be. If, for instance, the newcomer who does not belong to the Legislative Council comes into the Cabinet and accepts joint responsibility along with the Cabinet, I do not see any reason why such a procedure should not be permitted. It was pointed out that it may so happen that when a Ministry is censured and it goes out, the official or the one who does not belong to the Legislature will remain while the other members of the Cabinet will go out; that when a new Ministry is formed, he will be again tacked on to the Ministry and that he will be perpetually in the Council. It seems to me with all respects that is a somewhat fallacious view, because, unless the members who are drawn from the Legislature to form the Ministry are prepared to take him along with them and are prepared to bear the responsibility of his actions, they will not consent to work with when he accepts their advice and they accept his advice. If, for instance, a Prime Minister were so situated that he could safely take an outsider into his Cabinet and at the same time maintain the confidence of the House, I do not see why the Chief Minister should be prevented from having that privilege accorded to him.

In the same way, Sir, if, for instance, it was found possible that the Governor should have powers to see that the different minority communities are represented in his Cabinet, and if at the same time it is made perfectly clear that whoever is appointed to the Cabinet must accept joint responsibility with the others, then I submit there is no harm in allowing this sort of thing. It seems to me therefore that the point which it is necessary to emphasise is that the Governor may have the power which as I say belongs to him as of right to compose the Ministry in any way he likes provided that the Ministry does not violate in its operation the principle of its being, namely, that it is to work on the principle of joint responsibility.

Now the next question to which I will address myself, Sir, is how best to achieve this result, how best to bring out a responsible and unified Executive. It seems to me there are two ways open to us. One way is to define in the constitution itself the character of the Executive by law; the other is to leave to convention the constitution of the Executive. Both these ways are adopted, as you all know. We all know that in the Dominions of Canada, South Africa and Australia, responsible Government of a unified character is entirely a matter of convention. Everyone of us knows that in the Canadian Act or in the Acts of South Africa or Australia the words "responsible Government "do not arise. It is not even mentioned in the Canadian Act, as I found to my great surprise, that the Ministers who are to advise the Governor are to be members of the Legislature, although as a matter of fact they are. On the other hand, as we know, in the constitutions of Ireland, Malta and Rhodesia this is a subject which is not left to convention, it is something which is incorporated in law. In Ireland we know that the Prime Minister is a creature of statute, the joint responsibility is also defined by law.

I therefore think that we shall have to make our choice between the two, and in making the choice I for one would be guided by two considerations. I fully realise that when a matter is left to convention it is possible that the convention may be wrongly worked, that it may be abused, and may be abused with impunity. The danger of matters being left to convention in a country like India seems to me to be greater because there are no parties in India which have a keen eye on the way in which the constitution works and we may have Ministers less interested in working the constitution in the right spirit than in maintaining their seats in the Cabinet. On the other hand it seems to me that where matters are defined by law it must necessarily take away all the discretion that must necessarily be left to a Governor.

In a country like India where the political field with all its communal and racial difficulties is an absolutely uncharted sea, it seems to me that we must so contrive that sufficient discretion will be left with the Governor. My concrete suggestion therefore is this, that joint responsibility of the Executive should be prescribed by law and that everything else should be left to the discretion of the Governor, so that we shall have satisfied both the conditions: we shall have provided that whatever responsibility there is, is joint responsibility and that the composition of the Executive is at the same time not hampered in such a manner that the communities which do require to be represented in the Cabinet may be represented or that the necessity which Prime Minister may feel of having a non-official, I mean an outsider, in his Cabinet is provided for.

If we do that, if we insist by law, not leaving it to the discretion of the Governor, that the Executive shall be a joint Executive with joint responsibility, I think all other matters may be left without any fear of abuse to the choice of the Governor.

Now Sir, the next topic which I will take for consideration is that of the powers of the Governor vis-a-vis his Executive. The present relations between the Governor and the Minister, as well we all know, are defined in section 52, sub-clause 3. That clause says that in all transferred matters—and all matters will now be transferred, none being reserved—the Governor shall be guided by the advice of his Ministers; and it adds a further proviso that if he sees sufficient cause to dissent from the advice of his Ministers he may cause action to be taken otherwise than in accordance with that advice. With all due respect to those who framed that clause, and they did it with the best intention of providing responsible Government, I cannot help saying that this clause as it now stands is a perversion of responsible Government; it makes responsible Government a matter of convenience, a matter which may be accepted and followed when it suits the Governor, whereas as a matter of fact what we want is that responsible Government should be a matter of obligation. If responsible Government means anything it means this, that in whatever action the Governor takes in any field he has the support of a Ministry which has the confidence of the House. That is a fundamental proposition which we cannot ignore.

It does not of course mean that a Governor must always accept the advice of his Ministry; it leaves it open to the Governor to throw out the Ministry, to say he will not abide by their advice; but then if the Governor chooses to differ from his Ministry his obligation is not to act on his own initiative but to find some other Ministers who will support his action. So that the proposition is that at all times when the Governor takes action he takes action which is in conformity with the views of Ministers who have the confidence of the House. My submission therefore is that this clause, namely section 52, must be so altered as to make it plain that unless specific provision is made to the contrary by statute there may be cases which, I will come to a little later, the Governor shall always act upon the advice of the Ministers.

Now, Sir, I do readily agree that there may be cases in which it is necessary to provide the Governor with overriding powers, powers in respect to which he will not be obliged to follow the advice of his Ministers but will have the right of independent action. Those cases are mentioned in paragraph 50, page 36 of Volume 2 of the Report of the Simon Commission. The first is that he should have overriding powers in order to preserve the safety and tranquillity of the Province; secondly, he should have overriding powers in order to prevent serious prejudice to one or more sections of the community as compared with other sections; and then lastly it mentions certain cases where the Governor may have fixed upon him specific responsibility as apart from the responsibility of the whole of the Executive, in which case it says that he should also have overriding powers.

With regard to these items my first submission is this, that if you are going to give the Governor to over-ride his Ministers to preserve the peace, safety and tranquillity of the Province, it seems to me you are taking away a very large part of responsible Government in the Provinces.

After all, what we are striving for is that the Provinces shall be governed in all matters, including even the peace, safety and tranquillity of the Province, by a Governor on the advice of his Ministers; and, if you reserve powers to the Governor to act contrary to their advice, it seems to me you are to a very large extent nullifying the powers of responsible Government. I should not, therefore, give the Governor overriding powers in a matter of this sort, unless some way could be found whereby this large formula, which seems to me to eat-up the whole situation, might be very narrowly defined.

Coming to the other question, namely prejudice to one section of the community as compared with the others, my own view is that although this is a very salutary thing my preference is that such matters as are likely prejudicial to affect the interests of any particular community should be governed by statute; it should not be left to the sweet will of the Governor. I say that for this very good reason. After all, a Governor has to keep in touch with a Cabinet which is supported by a majority in the Legislature. He can never work at cross purposes with the Cabinet; the greatest amity must prevail between them, and I am not sure the Governor would always be so minded as to quarrel with a Cabinet which represented a majority in the House merely in order to protect a minority which, in his eyes, might not be very important. Although, therefore, I agree with the underlying suggestion there. I rather prefer that the interests of the minorities should be protected in a firmer manner than is suggested, and for myself I should be prepared to delete this clause.

Regarding the other items 3, 4 and 5, I agree that in cases of this sort the Governor must have overriding powers, because they are cases where he personally is made responsible for the administration of those subjects.

Coming to the next subject, the powers of the Governor vis-a-vis the Legislature, I will divide my remarks under three heads. There is first of all budgetary legislation; secondly, ordinary legislation and thirdly, emergency legislation. The Governor has today powers of certification with regard to the provision for reserved subjects, and that will necessarily go with the abolition of anarchy. Secondly, the Governor has authority to authorise expenditure for the safety and tranquillity of the Province.

It seems to me that if you are going to leave questions of peace and tranquillity to be settled by a responsible ministry, the Governor should not possess this power of authorising expenditure for the safety and tranquillity of the Province. In the next place, he has the power of certifying Bills, which are of two sorts. He may certify that a particular Bill which is being discussed in the Legislature shall not be discussed because it affects the safety and tranquillity of the Province, and he has also the power to certify a Bill which is in the interests of the safety and tranquillity of the Province even though the Legislature may not desire to pass it in the ordinary course. It seems to me both these powers should go; they will not be necessary in the future constitution of India.

He has also powers of previous sanction; certain subjects have to be previously sanctioned by him before they can be discussed, and in my opinion this power should go.

Sir Ahmad Sayed Khan: Discriminatory legislation?

Dr. Ambedkar: That should be dealt with by Statute; I should not leave it to the Governor. The Governor must have the power of veto, and in view of the fact that there will be no Second Chamber in those Provinces which do not want it, it is very necessary that the Governor should have the power of veto. The Governor today has also the power of returning a Bill to the House for reconsideration. This is a very useful power which exists in the constitutions of the various Dominions, and I think it should be retained. The Governor has also power to reserve a Bill for the consideration of the Governor-General and the cases in which he should do so are defined by Statute.

That is a matter, I think which might be more conveniently considered when we consider the relations of the Provincial Governments to the Central Government, but I should like to make one observation on this subject. We should so endeavour to contrive our Provincial constitution that it will function independently, as far as possible of the interference of the Central Government in those domains which have been transferred to its control. We must make a constitution under which there will be no occasion for constant intervention by the Central Government, either administratively or legislatively by the reservation of Bills.

With regard to the question of safeguards for Law and Order and for minorities, I have already stated that Law and Order should be transferred, but I am prepared to make one suggestion, for what it is worth. In cases of emergency, when Law and Order are being jeopardised, I suggest the Governor should have power to pass orders finally, without respect to the advice of the Ministry, regarding the posting and transfer of Police officers. I think that is very necessary; it is essential.

Sir Cowasji Jehangir: In case of emergency only?

Dr. Ambedkar: Yes, but not in other cases.

Dr. Paul: Not in normal times?

Dr. Ambedkar: Not in normal times, no, but in cases of emergency when a riot has taken place or a disturbance has occurred, it is very necessary that an impartial officer like the Governor, who is not swayed by what is happening in the Cabinet, should have the ultimate power to see that people are not transferred from one place to another to suit one community or the other community when a riot is actually proceeding. It seems to me that it gives him sufficient power for the purpose of safeguarding the administration of Law and Order.

With regard to the question of minorities, it was suggested by some speakers that a Second Chamber would afford protection to minorities, and my friend Mr. Wood threw out the suggestion that I had not carefully considered the position of the Depressed Classes in relation to a Second Chamber. I should like to assure my friend that I have given the matter most careful consideration, and I thoroughly agree with my friend Mr. Paul that these Second Chambers, far from being a protection to minorities, will be really milestones round their necks.

There is one subject I did not touch on before, but which I should like briefly to mention now, namely, the relation of the Governor to his Cabinet. Should he preside over the Cabinet as a matter of right or should he not? Should there be the system which prevails in this country where the Cabinet holds its meetings without the King being there, and if so what should be the means of communicating the results and decisions arrived at by the Cabinet to the Governor? I do not know if that arises on this item; if it does not, I will not waste time in discussing it.

Chairman: We have generally discussed the whole question, so that if you desire to continue I shall not object.

Dr. Ambedkar: In that connection I want to say one thing. The Simon Commission has suggested that a Cabinet Secretary should be appointed who would be of the same status as an I.C.S. Officer, and who would act as the liaison officer of the Cabinet to the Governor. In throwing out that suggestion the Commission says it has drawn on the practice that has now become prevalent in this country, namely, that the Cabinet now always has a Secretary, which formerly it did not have. I should like to submit, however, that it is one thing to say that the Cabinet should have a Secretary, but it is a totally different thing to say that Secretary should have access to the Governor over the heads of the Ministers.

In this country the practice does exist, probably, of appointing a Secretary, but I do not think any Cabinet or Prime Minister in this country would consent to that Cabinet Secretary having access to His Majesty over the heads of the Ministers or over the head of the Prime Minister; such a thing would be intolerable. We know that in this country the Cabinet throughout all its history has laid emphasis on the fact that the persons who will be near to His Majesty should be persons who will bear the same complexion as the Ministry, and we know that has been carried so far that even the Ladies of the Chamber who wait upon the Queen are required to be nominated by the Prime Minister and the Cabinet. The situation suggested, therefore, seems to me almost impossible. I do not think any Cabinet which is working on the principle of joint responsibility will consent to have a Secretary of this kind attached to it.

On the other hand, if the Governor is given the power, to preside over the Cabinet when it is discussing its policy, I doubt very much whether that will work, because although the Ministry may, and indeed must, communicate to the Governor the decisions at which it has arrived, I do not think the Ministry will consent to disclose to the Governor the reasons which have led it to come to those decisions. The reasons may be very particular and very delicate, and you all know that the Cabinet is very jealous not to let the Governor know the reasons why it has arrived at a particular decision.

The explanation of that is that the Governor holds in his hands a tremendous power for undoing the Ministry for he may not agree to the Ministry's advice to dissolve the House, but may instead of being embodied in a Statute, the matter should be left to the Instrument of Instructions, which may provide that the Governor can attend if he desires to do so, but it should not be obligatory at all. On the other hand, it should be made obligatory for the Cabinet to communicate to the Governor all the recommendations at which it arrives at its meeting. That is all I desire to say on that point.

Dr. Ambedkar: We should like to say one thing on that point that the Second Chamber should not be constituted first, and then its abolition should be left to constitutional resolution requiring a certain majority. What we suggest is that if the situation is such that it should be left as a matter of discretion in certain Provinces, then first of all a resolution might be passed by the Provincial Legislature expressing its desire for a Second Chamber, and then, that the Second Chamber should be constituted. It should not be first imposed on the Provincial Legislature by the constitution.

Fifth Sitting—15th December 1930

Dr. Ambedkar: Sir, I should like to make one or two observations on the amendment which the noble Marquess has moved. I should like to state at once that the position which he has taken up seems to me to be absolutely logical. In this report we are going to provide that certain interests and minority groups may be represented by nomination in the Legislative Council. At the same time we are also making provision in this report that the Governor shall be given an obligation to endeavour to secure that his Cabinet shall be representative of all interests and of all minorities.

Now, Sir, unless you provide that in the making up of this Cabinet, the Governor shall also have the right to include members who represent certain important interests by nomination, it seems to me that you are creating an absolutely illogical position. Either you must provide that there shall be no nomination to the Legislative Council at all, that all interests, no matter how minute, shall be secured by election to the Legislative Council, or, if there is to be nomination then you must provide that a nominated member shall have the right to be in the Cabinet if his colleagues are prepared to work with him on the principle of joint responsibility. There is no escape from one or other of those positions.

Now. Sir, it is stated by friends who are sitting on this side that if we accept this principle, that a nominated member shall be a member of the Cabinet, or at least that there shall be no ban upon him, it will run counter to the principle of responsibility. I really cannot understand that position. These gentlemen who are saying it will run counter to the principle of responsibility are prepared to take the votes of nominated members. I am taking the report as it stands. I do not know what future amendments there will be. Supposing the report as it stands is carried, that there shall be certain members in the Legislative Council who shall be nominated.

Is it the position of these gentlemen that their votes are illegal? If those who form the Cabinet who are drawn from the elected portion of the House can validly use the votes of members who are nominated to the Legislative Council, if those votes can logically become the basis of the policy of a Government, I cannot see how a member who is one of that nominated group should not become a member of that Cabinet. I fail altogether to understand it. If, as I say, they can take these votes of nominated members and utilise them for their own purposes. I cannot understand what objection there can be to the inclusion of a member from the nominated group in the Cabinet. I therefore say the position of the noble Marquess is perfectly logical.

It seems to me we have to make a choice whether we shall make a provision of the sort suggested by the noble Marquess in his amendment, or whether we shall agree to the other proposal which my friends say they will move at a later stage, that there shall be no nominative element in the Legislative Councils at all. Personally I would much rather have the whole Legislative Council elected with no trace of nomination at all. From that point of view I am not very much in favour of the amendment suggested by the noble Marquess; but if in this Committee or at any later stage nomination remains, then I think I shall have to agree with the noble Marquess and accept the amendment he has proposed.

Diwan Bahadur Ramachandra Rao: I must express my surprise at the speech to which I have just listened.

Dr. Ambedkar: You may, but you cannot have it both ways.

Diwan Bahadur Ramachandra Rao: He knows very well that even under the existing system nominated members are not eligible for appointment as ministers. Section 52 clearly lays it down that no minister shall hold office for a longer period than six months unless he is an elected member of the local Legislature.

Dr. Ambedkar: That is in the melting pot.

Opposition to Co-option in Legislature

Dr. Ambedkar: I am afraid I shall have to oppose this amendment. First of all, such experience of co-option as we have had in Bombay is not very encouraging. It has developed into the worst sort of scandal; the amount of corruption and bribery that take place are such that I for one should not like to introduce this principle in the constitution of the Legislature of Bombay.

A further objection is this. If the various communities that do not find themselves elected at the polls are to get representation of a real sort, representation which is independent of the influence of any other community, I think co-option is a principle which is certainly not going to help them, for it may very well happen that when representatives of the various communities stand for co-option only those will be in fact co-opted as may happen to be subservient to and willing to play into the hands of the majority. It seems to me this would be worse than no representation at all, and I am afraid on that ground I must oppose the amendment. But I submit, Sir, that this Sub-Committee ought to make a recommendation that the future constitution of the Provincial Legislatures should be such that there should be no nominated members at all.

Diwan Bahadur Ramachandra Rao: That is far better, of course.

Dr. Ambedkar: That is my own view of the matter. I am certainly opposed to co-option.

Diwan Bahadur Ramachandra Rao: I agree that some statement that the Legislature should be wholly elected ought to be inserted in this report, and unless some such indication is given of the views of this Subcommittee the nominated element will continue, though I believe it is the desire of most of our members that it should disappear.

A statement to that effect ought to find a place in the report. I have no doubt whatsoever that everyone of us is quite alive to the evils of nomination, and we are anxious it should disappear as early as possible. Under these circumstances I am not prepared to support the amendment, and I would favour the proposal made by my friend, Dr. Ambedkar.

Chairman: What was the proposal? I have no words here.

Dr. Ambedkar: We should say it is the view of the Sub-Committee that hereafter the Legislative Councils in the Provinces should be wholly elected. Chairman: That is another amendment altogether, you will have to send it in writing if you want to move that.

Chairman: I will take your decision on this point.

Raja Narendra Nath: I support Sir A. P. Patro. I think the power of nomination should be strictly confined to the representation of interests, which cannot be given by election.

Dr. Shafa'at Ahmad Khan: Yes.

Raja Narendra Nath: There may be in certain Provinces some communities, such as the one to which Dr. Ambedkar belongs, for which it would be impossible to arrange election.

Dr. Ambedkar: I should not have anything to do with a constitution which did not provide the franchise for my community.

Raja Narendra Nath: The franchise will have to be arranged on a very different basis if it is to be provided for the community to which Dr. Ambedkar belongs, and therefore a limited power of nomination should be provided.

Chairman: It seems to me the majority of the Sub-Committee is in favour of clause (c) as it stands in the Report.

In Subcommittee No. III (minorities)

Second Sitting—31st December 1930

Dr. Ambedkar: Mr. Chairman, I am sure you will readily agree that the task which has fallen upon me to represent the case of the Depressed Classes is a heavy one. I think it is for the first time that the case of the Depressed Classes from the political point of view has come to be considered. The disabilities of the Depressed Classes were mentioned in almost every despatch that was recorded by the Government of India in connection with the political advancement of the country; but the despatches only mentioned the difficulties and never attempted to give any solution of those difficulties.

The problem was just allowed to rest there. In view of that, and in view of other matters, namely, that in a Committee consisting of so many members we are only two to voice the grievances of 43 millions of people, and grievances which the Committee will agree are unparalleled by the case of any other community that exists in India, I submit that the task is really an enormous one, and I should have expected more latitude in the matter of time allowed to me for presenting this case. But I anticipated that probably such would be the fate that would befall me, as it did, of course, at the Plenary Session; and, in anticipation of that, I and my colleague, Rao Bahadur Srinivasan, thought it advisable to submit to this Conference a written memorandum giving in clear-cut language what the Depressed Classes desire by way of political safeguards in the future constitution of India.

That memorandum has already been submitted and circulated among the members of this Committee, and I hope everyone of them has received it. In view of this fact, that the case of the Depressed Classes is in the possession of the members of this Committee, I do not wish to ask indulgence from the Chairman for a larger period to present the case. I will therefore summarise, only to emphasize, what I have stated in the memorandum which is already in the hands of the members of the Committee.

Sir, the first observation that I will make is this, that although there are various minority communities in India which require political recognition, it has to be understood that the minorities are not on the same plane, that they differ from each other. They differ in the social standing which each minority occupies vis-a-vis the majority community. We have, for instance, the Parsee community, which is the smallest community in India, and yet, vis-a-vis its social standing with the majority community, it is probably the highest in order of precedence.

On the other hand, if you take the Depressed Classes, they are a minority which comes next to the great Muslim minority in India, and yet their social standard is lower than the social standard of ordinary human beings.

Again, if you take the minorities and classify them on the basis of social and political rights, you will find that there are certain minorities which are in enjoyment of social and political rights, and the fact that they are in a minority does not necessarily stand in the way of their full and free enjoyment of those civic rights. But if you take the case of the Depressed Classes, the position is totally different. They have in certain matters no rights, and, where they have any, the majority community will not permit them to enjoy them.

My first submission to this Committee, then, is that it should realise that although, to use an illustration, the minorities are all in the same boat, yet the most important fact to remember is that they are not all in the same class in the same boat; some are travelling in "A" Class, some in "B" Class and some in "C", and so on. I have not the slightest doubt in my mind that the Depressed Classes, though they are a minority and are to that extent in the same boat as other minorities, are not even in "C" or "D" Class but are actually in the hold.

Starting from that point of view, I agree that, in some respects, the position of the Depressed Classes is similar to that of the other minorities in India.

The Depressed Classes, along with the other minorities; fear that under any future Constitution of India by which majority rule will be established and there can be no shadow of doubt that majority rule will be the rule of the orthodox Hindus—there is great danger of that majority with its orthodox Hindu beliefs and prejudices contravening the dictates of justice, equality and good conscience, there is a great danger that the minorities may be discriminated against either in legislation or administration or in the other public rights of citizenship, and therefore it is necessary to safeguard the position of the minorities in such a manner that the discrimination which is feared shall not take place.

From that point of view, however, what is asked is that the minorities shall have representation in the Legislature and the Executive, that they shall have representation in the public services of the country, and that the constitution shall provide that these shall be imposed on the future legislatures of India, both Central and Provincial, certain limitations on their legislative power which will prevent the majorities from abusing their legislative power in such a manner as to enact laws which would create discrimination between one citizen and another. I say, this circumstance—this danger of discrimination is common to all minorities, and I, as a representative of the Depressed Classes, join with the demand which the other minorities have made in this regard.

Now, Sir, I will come to those circumstances which mark off the Depressed Classes and the other minority communities in India. I will at once say that the way in which the position of the Depressed Classes differs from the position of the other minority communities in India is this, that in the first place the Depressed Classes are not entitled, under present circumstances, to certain civic rights which the other minorities by law enjoy. In other words, in the existing situation the Depressed Classes suffer from what are called civic disabilities. I will give you just one or two illustrations, because I know I have not much time at my disposal.

Take the case of employment in the Police or in the Army. In the Government of India Act it is provided that no subject of His Majesty shall be deprived of the right of being employed in any public service by reason of his caste, creed or colour. Having regard to that, it is obvious that every member of the Depressed Class community who is capable, who is in a position to satisfy the test laid down for employment in any public department, should have the right to enter that public department.

But what do we find? We find this. If a Depressed Class man applies for service in the Police Department today, he is told point blank by the executive officers of the Government that no member of the Depressed Classes can be employed in the Police Service, because he is an untouchable person. In the case of the Military the same situation obtains. Up to 1892 practically the whole of the Madras Army and the whole of the Bombay Army consisted of members drawn from the Depressed Classes.

All the great wars in the history of India have been fought with the help of sepoys drawn from the Depressed Classes, both in the Bombay Presidency and in Madras. Yet in 1892 a rule or regulation was made which debarred the Depressed Classes from entry into the Military Service, and even today, if you ask a question in the Legislative Council as to why this is done, the answer is that the bar of untouchability does create insuperable difficulties in the recruitment of these classes.

I am quite sure that this disability is as effective as it was imposed by law, and the section in the Government of India Act, which says that all His Majesty's subjects shall have free entry into employment provided they are otherwise fit, is altogether set at naught.

I can cite many other cases. For instance, there is the difficulty the Depressed Classes find in getting themselves accommodated in public inn when they are travelling, the difficulty they find in being taken in an omnibus when travelling from one place to another, the difficulty they find in securing entry to public schools to which they have themselves contributed, the difficulty they find in drawing water from a well for the building of which they have paid taxes, and so on.

But I need not go into all these cases. The one circumstance which distinguishes the position of the Depressed Classes from that of the other minorities is that they suffer from civic disabilities which are as effective as though they were imposed by law.

The second and, in my opinion, the most hideous distinction which marks the Depressed Classes is that the Depressed Classes are subject to social persecution unknown in any other part of the world. In that connection I want to read to the Sub-Committee a small extract from the Report of a Committee appointed by the Government of Bombay in the year 1928 to investigate into the position of the Depressed Classes.

That Committee tried to find out whether there were any impediments in the way of the Depressed Classes enjoying such rights as the law gave them in common with other citizens of the State:

> *Although we have recommended various remedies to secure to the Depressed Classes their rights to all public utilities we fear that there will be difficulties in the way of their exercising them for a long time to come. The first difficulty is the fear of open violence against them by the orthodox classes. It must be noted that the Depressed Classes form a small minority in every village, opposed to which is a great majority of the orthodox who are bent on protecting their interests and dignity from any supposed invasion by the Depressed Classes at any cost. The danger of prosecution by the Police has put a limitation upon the use of violence by the orthodox classes and consequently such cases are rare.*

The second difficulty arises from the economic position in which the Depressed Classes are found today. The Depressed Classes have no economic independence in most parts of the Presidency. Some cultivate the lands of the orthodox classes as their tenants at will. Others live on their earnings as farm labourers employed by the orthodox classes and the rest subsist on the food or grain given to them by the orthodox classes in lieu of service rendered to them as village servants. We have heard of numerous instances where the orthodox classes have used their economic power as a weapon against those Depressed Classes in their villages, when the latter have dared to exercise their rights, and have evicted them from their lands, and stopped their employment and discontinued their remuneration as village servants. This boycott is often planned on such an extensive scale as to include the prevention of the Depressed Classes from using the commonly used paths and the stoppage of the necessaries of life by the village Bania. According to the evidence sometimes small causes suffice for the proclamation of a social boycott against the Depressed Classes. Frequently it follows on the exercise by the Depressed Classes of their right to the use of the common well, but cases have been by no means rare where a stringent boycott has been proclaimed simply because a Depressed Class man has put on the sacred thread, has bought a piece of land, has put on good clothes or ornaments, or has carried a marriage procession with the bridegroom on the horse through the public street.

We do not know of any weapon more effective than this social boycott which could have been invented for the suppression of the Depressed Classes. The method of open violence pales away before it, for it has the most far-reaching and deadening effects. It is more dangerous because it passes as a lawful method consistent with the theory of freedom of contact. We agree that this tyranny of the majority must be put down with a firm hand if we are to guarantee the Depressed Classes the freedom of speech and action necessary for their uplift." A third thing which the Depressed Classes fear more than any other community is that whatever representation they may be granted in the new legislature, they will always be in a very small minority, and consequently, having regard to the apathetic attitude of the orthodox classes towards the Depressed Classes, there is always the danger of the interests of the Depressed Classes, being neglected altogether, or some action taken which may ultimately prove to be prejudicial to their interests.

As against these special circumstances which affect the Depressed Classes, we propose the following safeguards. First of all, we want a fundamental right enacted in the constitution which will declare "untouchability" to be illegal for all public purposes. We must be emancipated, so to say, from this social curse before we can at all consent to the constitution; and secondly, this fundamental right must also invalidate and nullify all such disabilities and all such discriminations as may have been made hitherto. Next, we want legislation against the social persecution to which I have drawn your attention just now, and for this we have provided in the document which we have submitted by certain clauses which are based upon an Act, which now prevails in Burma. I need not go into that detail just for the moment. Then what we want is this, that liability of the executive officers of the Crown for acts of tyranny or oppression shall be made effective. Today under sections 110 and 111 of the Government of India Act that liability is not real. And lastly, what we want is a right to appeal against acts of neglect of prejudice to the Central Government and failing that, to the Secretary of State and a Special Department in the Government of India to take charge of our welfare.

This is, in general, the cases for the Depressed Classes, and the safeguards that they want. Let me just say a word or two as regards the most important of them—namely, their right to adequate representation in the legislature. Now, on the question of the granting of representation of the Depressed Classes, we are absolutely unanimous that representation shall be by election and not by nomination. The system of nomination has produced in the case of the Depressed Classes, results which we all say are abdominable. The system has been abused in a manner in which it was never expected that it would be abused, and it has never given the Depressed Classes the real and independent representation which they must have as their safeguard. Under no circumstances, therefore, will the Depressed Classes accept representation by nomination. As to the question of joint or separate electorates, our position is this—that if you give us adult universal suffrage the Depressed Classes, barring a short transitional period which they want for their organisation, will be prepared to accept joint electorates and reserved seats; but if you do not give us adult suffrage, then we must claim representation through separate electorates. That is our position.

Now regarding the question of the number of seats, it is not possible, of course, for us to state definitely what that number should be, except to state that we will not tolerate any invidious discrimination. We insist upon equality of treatment. But the whole question, in my opinion, is entirely a relative question: it is a question that can be determined only in connection with, and by taking into account, the seats that will be allotted to the other minority communities; but I will make two observations in this connection. The first observation that I will make is this—that we, the Depressed Classes, demand a complete partition between ourselves and the Hindus. That is the first thing. We have been called Hindus for political purposes, but we have never been acknowledged socially by the Hindus as their brethren.

They have taken to themselves all the political advantage with our numbers, with our voting strength, have given to them, but in return we have received nothing. All that we have received is a treatment which is worse than the treatment that they themselves have accorded to other communities whom they do not call Hindus. That must be the first thing, therefore, that we want to be done.

The second thing that I will say concerns the question of weightage. Now, this system—I will be plain, to my mind has been abused. I am not against the principle of weightage. I do not accept the principle that in all circumstances every minority must be confined to its population ratio. A minority may be so small that its population ratio may give a representation which may be wholly inadequate for the purpose of its protection. It may be a representation which may be of no consequence at all. If, therefore, you want to protect a minority adequately and really, then in certain circumstances the principle of weightage will have to be conceded. But the distribution of weightage must be subject to some uniform and intelligible principle. In our opinion weightage is to be conceded because a minority is weak, either in numbers, or because its social standing is low, or its educational standing is backward as compared with others, or because its economic strength is not sufficient to place it on a fighting par with other communities.

Member: Quite right.

Dr. Ambedkar: But I cannot understand, for instance, how weightage can be allowed on the ground of political importance, or loyalty, or services rendered either to the Empire or to the British Government. I think if we adopt that principle, we shall land ourselves in very difficult circumstances from which it will be difficult to extricate ourselves.

Regarding the question of the representation of the Depressed Classes in the Central Legislature. If you have again adult suffrage for the election of members of the Central Legislature, then, of course, the Depressed Classes will claim separate representation in the Legislature, such number of seats being allotted to them in conjunction with the seats allotted to other minorities. But if your representation is to be by a suffrage which is higher or much higher, based on property, and so much higher that the Depressed Classes will probably be entirely left out, then I am afraid the Depressed Classes will have to claim indirect election to the Central Legislature, carried on by electoral colleges composed of members of the Depressed Classes, in the Provincial Legislature, in Municipalities, and in district local boards. That is all that I have to say so far as the Depressed Classes are concerned.

Having said all that I need say let me add one thing in conclusion that this whole question of minority representation is really the crux of the whole situation, and if the majority community desire that all minorities should associate with them in having or in claiming, a constitution which will give India what they call Dominion Status, or what we prefer to call Government by the people, for the people and in the name of the people, then I am afraid that the majority community must see to it that all fears of the minorities are set at rest. Otherwise it may not be possible for us to take what I do not conceal from myself is the risk that most of us are taking in claiming Dominion Status.

Fifth Sitting—14th January 1931

Chairman: The proposal that has just been made makes it impossible for us to go on and adopt the Draft Report that is in front of us, because, of course, it changes the whole circumstances.

If you would be agreeable, I should propose to adjourn this Sub-Committee now, and I will also, you being agreeable, propose to remain in the Chair and to ask that those of you who are specially interested should meet and we must include Dr. Ambedkar.

Dr. Ambedkar: I am obliged to you, Sir.

Chairman: Oh, yes, we must include him and see whether by an exchange of opinions across the table we could not come to an agreement.

Sir P. C. Mitter: I should like to join, Sir, in those discussions.

Dr. Ambedkar: We have heard just now these proposals and percentages being disposed of, but really it strikes me that if you add up all these they not only go over 100 per cent but they practically take no notice of many other communities that are existing in the Punjab and Bengal and in other places.

If these communities, the Sikhs, the Mohammedans, the Hindus are going to appropriate 49 and 20 and so on, what is left for the other people? Are they to be taken into account or not? That is a very serious question, Mr. Prime Minister.

Lt. Col. Gidney: May I just raise my humble voice—it is a very small voice. I know—in this conflict? I support what Dr. Ambedkar has just said. Surely you are not going to take the political rupee and give 15 annas and 9 pies to the major communities, leaving 3 pies to be scrambled for by the other minorities. On behalf of the smaller communities I maintain we should have some say in this distribution.

Chairman: That is just the point. I think that we had better discuss this matter with a smaller body and a little but more informally.

Mr. Foot: And no notes taken?

Chairman: And I shall remain in the Chair, you being agreeable, and see what can be done to straighten out the situation that has been opened up by the very hopeful suggestion made by Sir Muhammad Shafi.

Sixth Sitting—16th January 1931

Chairman: "The inclusion in the Constitution of declaration of fundamental rights safeguarding the cultural and religious life of the various communities and securing to every individual, without distinction of race," and so on, "the free exercise," and so on.

Raja Narendra Nath: I propose we say "the free and equal exercise".

Chairman: "of his or her economic, social and civil rights".

Raja Narendra Nath: I do not think we want the "his or her". Cannot we say "the free and equal exercise of economic, social and civil rights by citizens"? I do not insist on it.

Chairman: "equal" is of substance, but I do not think the other matters very much.

Raja Narendra Nath: I suggest we should say "free and equal exercise". Chairman: As a matter of fact, that is a question from Dr. Ambedkar.

Raja Narendra Nath: The word "equal" was used in Dr. Ambedkar's speech.

Sir M. Shafi: I think "free" covers it.

Dr. Shafa'at Ahmad Khan: I think it should remain as it is.

Chairman: It says "and securing to every individual........ the free exercise". You cannot secure the equal exercise, because equal is an attribute of the individual who uses the rights.

Raja Narendra Nath: I mean equality in rights, equal rights.

Mr. Chintamani: I do not see the particular propriety of that objective "equal".

Raja Narendra Nath: It is used in Dr. Ambedkar's draft.

Chairman: You can secure to each individual the Free exercise of his rights, but if he does not exercise them in terms of equality that is his lookout, not the Government's.

Raja Narendra Nath: Very well.

Chairman: "his or her" can come out, I think.

Dr. Ambedkar: After the word "rights" at the end of the paragraph I should like the words "without discrimination" added.

Chairman: It says already "without distinction of race, caste, creed or sex".

Dr. Ambedkar: I should like the word "untouchability". You included there!

***Chairman:*........... "untouchability!" you already have race and caste.

Dr. Moonje: I think it is all right.

Dr. Ambedkar: In order to explain things better I think that word might be included.

Chairman: Do not let us produce a document which people will laugh at on account of the way it is worded.

Dr. Ambedkar: I think we ought to make a distinction between caste and untouchability. Many people who have caste do not suffer from the difficulties of untouchability.

Raja Narendra Nath: Even the Muslims have caste.

Diwan Bahadur Ramachandra Rao: There is caste among the untouchables. "Caste" is a wider expression.

Mr. Foot: Unless an alteration which is substantial is proposed, I understand it is rather late to make an alteration at this stage.

Dr. Ambedkar: I should like to say "social and civil rights on account of untouchability or otherwise".

Chairman: Untouchability is a violation of social rights, and if you pile on words instead of making it more precise it has, as a matter of fact, an exclusive tendency; it narrows the thing if you give a specific application to a general principle. If you keep your general principle sound you are much safer so far as its application is concerned than if you quote it as applying to the one particular grievance.

Dr. Ambedkar: That is true, but I do maintain that the question of interpretation will come in, and I should like whoever is going to handle this Report to understand that the Sub-Committee did mean not to impose any disability on account of untouchability.

Chairman: In a case like that, if there is any doubt about it, I will take the opinion of the Committee and settle it. Do you persist. Dr. Ambedkar?

Dr. Ambedkar: I am afraid, Sir, I shall have to. My dissent might be noted, that I do wish that this should be made clear.

Chairman: There is a suggestion made that the word "distinction" should be substituted by the word "discrimination"", so that it will read "without discrimination as to race, caste" and so on.

Dr. Ambedkar: Yes, that would do it.

Chairman: That will be all right?

Dr. Ambedker: That will be all right. I suggest at the end it should be "without discrimination".

Chairman: Quite then would you make that alteration please. Then it will read without discrimination.

Dr. Ambedkar: Yes.

Chairman: That is a good amendment : the other, I think, would have been a bad one.

Dr. Ambedkar: Sir, as I understand, paragraph 3 summarises the demand put by the different communities before this Committee.

Chairman: Yes.

Dr. Ambedkar: In view of that, I should like to suggest that the other demands made by the Depressed Classes specifically in their own interests, on account of the fact that their position differs somewhat from the position of the other minorities, should be added. I do not mean to say that they should be added as an accepted proposition by this Conference, but for the sake of completeness those demands should be put in. I would therefore suggest the addition of the following paragraph to this paragraph after the word "rights" : "The Depressed Classes also urged that untouchability, with all its consequent disabilities, should be abolished by law, and that they should be guaranteed free and unfettered enjoyment of their rights; and they also claim the right of appeal to the Governor-General and the Secretary of State in cases of prejudices or neglect of their interests."

Chairman: But you see, in so far as these suggestions can be made workable, they will come in the details that will have to be worked out.

Dr. Ambedkar: I quite see that.

Chairman: Partly legislative and partly administrative.

Dr. Ambedkar: But what I would like to say is this, that in view of the fact that the paragraph tries to summarise what was put before this Committee by the different communities, what was put by the Depressed Classes, as something specifically for themselves, apart from what other communities needed, ought to come in by way of completion.

Chairman: But it says "without discrimination" and so on.

Dr. Ambedkar: Mr. Prime Minister, you will excuse me; it is one thing for the constitution to say that no man shall be discriminated against, and that every man shall be guaranteed the free enjoyment, and so on; but I know as a matter of fact that we are hard up against facts, and that people will not allow us to enjoy the rights which are given to us by the constitution. I am as certain of that as I am certain of my existence. I do not want merely a paper guarantee. The whole community will be against us, and we shall certainly never enjoy one-tenth of what is given to us. I therefore desire that the constitution should not only declare that we shall have specific rights that every community will have, but that the constitution should also provide ways and means by which we shall be protected in the exercise of those rights.

Chairman: The point is, supposing a legislature does not pass a law which will suit you, then the constitution has been broken.

Dr. Ambedkar: No. What I suggest is this : That in the memorandum which I have circulated I have suggested certain ways and means by which we think our rights could be protected in the matter of their exercise. The Committee here, for instance, may not agree that is an appropriate way of doing it; the Committee may suggest that there are some other means of doing it. I am quite prepared and open for consideration of these other ways and means; but what I want to submit is this, that this draft ought to report that the Depressed Classes did suggest that they were not satisfied with the mere declaration that they were placed on an equal footing with other communities; but they pressed in that rights be given to them by the constitution. I am not asking for anything more than that. That is by way of completion of the report. In the memorandum which I submitted, you will see I do recommend a certain procedure for that.

Mr. Foot: The only difficulty which occurred to me, with every sympathy for Dr. Ambedkar, was that if you begin to put in a statement of your position, it would have to be a very full statement. Already we have upon the notes the claim that has been made, and the sympathetic adoption of it here referred to again at the end of paragraph 16. It seems to me perhaps there may be the risk that if you are going to put in any claim at all, you will not have it fully stated in this memorandum.

Dr. Ambedkar: I would just like to say as regards paragraph 16, the last two sentences refer to the Depressed Classes, and they are confined to the seats that are to be allotted to them. That is a different matter altogether. What I am stating is this, that the constitution may give me certain rights, but I know that 99 per cent of the people in India are not going to allow me to exercise those rights. What is the use of those paper rights to me unless the constitution provides that if anyone infringes my rights he is liable to certain penalties? What I say is this. I do not press that the meeting should adopt my proposal. What I want is that the constitution should be made to complete as to cover what I have said on behalf of the Depressed Classes on this Sub-Committee.

Chairman: We have every sympathy with your position, and are prepared to support it; but the difference between putting a paragraph in the constitution declaring for fundamental rights and the drafting of laws carrying out those fundamental rights is a real one. You cannot get into a constitutional declaration any details of a law which is going to enforce it. What you have got to do is, when you get your representation, when you get your declaration of rights, not in detail, in your constitution, then, as a representative of your people cooperating with the other people in the Legislature you have to produce the law which you think carries out the declaration in the constitution, because if you put anything more by way of detail into your constitution and the constitution is not carried out in that respect, then the constitution is not carried out at all. So you will never get on in that way.

Dr. Ambedkar: My submission is this. I perfectly agree with you that this declaration of fundamental rights is of no consequence. I attach no importance to it myself personally, because after all, what is important to an individual is not that his rights should be declared but that he should have the remedy in order to enforce those rights. That is the effective guarantee of the rights in the declaration, and therefore I want that the constitution should give me some means whereby I can get redress when I am wrong. It is no use merely saying that there is no "untouchability" and so on.

Chairman: As a matter of fact we have got the point clearly in our minds, so it need not be reiterated; but what Dr. Ambedkar says is that a declaration in the constitution is not good enough for him unless it is enforceable by law. That is so. In order to make it enforceable by law, laws must be passed creating the penalties and the crimes—the crimes first of all, and the penalties. You cannot create a crime of this kind. I think, not safely—I am in the hands of Lord Reading; he is a lawyer, I am not—you cannot, in drafting a general introductory clause to your constitution, create by that a crime which gives you more rights than those that you can claim under the constitution. Under the constitution you have got certain rights given to you, and I am not at all sure what is the position. Supposing a Depressed Class person was actually persecuted in violation of this declaration, could he not move for some redress in the Courts?

Lord Reading: Well, you have got to give him some remedy for it, of course. You must make it a misdemeanour.

Chairman: Can you do that in the constitution?

Lord Reading: No, I do not think so. If you will forgive me for a moment I do not think Dr. Ambedkar was pressing for that. As I understand it, he wants us to make a definite statement that he had put the claim forward, that he was not satisfied merely with the declaration of "free exercise" etc. What he wants also is that he drew special attention to the fact that was no use to him unless he also had protection for an infringement of these rights, and he leaves it there. Then you have to consider what the remedy is hereafter. That is as I understood him.

Dr. Ambedkar: That is my position.

Discussion on Paragraph 4 of the Report

Dr. Ambedkar: I wish to suggest an amendment to the second sub-paragraph of paragraph 4. After the words "Depressed Classes" I should like to have the words added "barring a short initial period". It would read" and would be acceptable to the Depressed Classes barring a short initial period".

Chairman: I understood you accepted it provided there was adult suffrage?

Dr. Ambedkar: I said that for ten years we should have separate electorate whether there was adult suffrage or not.

Chairman: "And would be acceptable to the Depressed Classes after a transition period"?

Dr. Ambedkar: Yes.

Chairman: Do you agree that makes it more accurate?

Mr. Chintamani: Are we to delete the proviso "provided the franchise was based on adult suffrage"?

Chairman: No, we cannot alter the speeches that were made. But what Dr. Ambedkar said—he will correct me if I am wrong—was that if there is to be no adult suffrage then they must claim separate electorates, but if there is adult suffrage then, after a transition period, they would abandon them. I cannot allow the accuracy to be altered. Discussion on paragraph 12 of the Report

Dr. Ambedkar: Sir, I should like to have the following words added to paragraph 12 in the beginning: "The minorities and the Depressed Classes were definite in their assertion that they would not consent to any self-governing constitution for India unless their demands were accepted." And then you can proceed: "There was general agreement with respect to recommendations," and so on. Speaking for myself, I think I made it very clear at the time when I delivered my speech in this Committee that unless we were assured that we were safe in the new constitution, we could give no consent to any constitution involving the principle of responsibility. If other communities do not care to join in this, it would go as my own statement on behalf of the Depressed Classes.

Lt. Col. Gidney: I join in that statement too, Sir.

Chairman: Of course, the statement as a matter of fact was made, and it was made in a representative way, not merely as an individual statement. But if that is put in this report, you will observe the effect of it, that one or two of you will be able to say: "Our claims have not been satisfied." It is not a decision of this Committee, but it does put obstacles in the way of anything being done unless everybody says they are satisfied with what is being done. Whether you think it is wise to take that statement, undoubtedly made to the Committee, and put it in such a position as to make it necessary to record it in the report which the Committee sends to the Conference, is for you to say. I do not object at all, as a matter of record.

Lord Reading: It is rather difficult to see what part it plays in this particular paragraph; this is dealing with the Executive, and the only point which is mentioned about the new constitution is in regard to the successful working of it.

Dr. Ambedkar: My position is this, Sir, that speaking for myself, I do not merely make a statement, and I do not want the record merely to say that I made certain demands; I want the report also to record the strength of feeling that is in my mind behind this; that it is not merely a demand which I made merely to be accepted or rejected, but I said that the acceptance of these demands was conditional on the acceptance of this.

Lord Reading: I do not see how it can come in this paragraph at all.

Dr. Ambedkar: It may come in anywhere. As it was dealing with general agreements, I thought these few lines might come in appropriately at the top of this paragraph. If you do not think it is suitable, I have no objection.

Chairman: I do not think it can come in here; I do not see how you can work that in here. You could raise it again. It is really what we should call in a Bill before the House of Commons a new clause and not an amendment to a clause 12.

Dr. Ambedkar: In the third line it reads in this way: "that the representation on the Provincial Executives of important minority communities, *i.e.* Hindus, Mohammedans and Sikhs, was a matter of the greatest practical importance." My amendment is this, that we should delete the word "important", because I do not want any discriminations made between minorities and minorities, but you should not mention any minority by name, and that if you are going to do so, then you must mention all the minorities.

Dr. Moonje: That is exactly what I was going to say.

Chairman: As a matter of fact, the reason why these words were put in is that they are in the report to which reference is made. What is the amendment? We are not going to put in anything that you do not agree with. "That the representation on the Provincial Executive of minority communities"?

Dr. Ambedkar: Leave it there. Delete "Hindus, Mohammedans and Sikhs".

Chairman: Let us see what it means. It would then read: "that the representation on the Provincial Executives of minority communities was a matter of the greatest practical importance for the successful working", and so on.

Dr. Ambedkar: Yes.

Chairman: That means that every minority community, if it is 8, 9, 10 or 12, must have a representative upon the Executive.

Dr. Ambedkar: No; I would then add: "as far as possible leaving discretion to the Governor". I should not like any community to be specifically mentioned.

Lord Reading: Surely you must look and see what this says: "There was general agreement with the recommendation of Sub-Committee No. II (Provincial Constitution)." Then it goes on to quote it.

Dr. Ambedkar: It should not.

Dr. Moonje: My suggestion was a small one, but perhaps it might meet Dr. Ambedkar's point of view. It was on the same lines : "important minority communities, *i.e.* Mohammedans, Sikhs, Depressed Classes,". That was my small amendment.

Lord Reading: Then the others will have to come in.

Sir A. P. Patro: The Depressed Classes are not Hindus?

Will you cut off the Depressed Classes? With due respect, I say there are Depressed Classes who would simply revolt at the suggestion that they are not Hindus. In Southern India, if Dr. Ambedkar comes and says they are not Hindus, then I do not know what position Dr. Ambedkar will have in Southern India.

Dr. Ambedkar: We are not discussing that here.

Sir A. P. Patro: Therefore I say representation consistent with facts and experiences.

Chairman: I have referred to the report to which reference is made. "Hindus, Mohammedans and others" I am told was put in by way of illustration, and these words do not appear in the report.

Sir Muhammad Shafi: That is what I was going to say.

Chairman: Just one minute. The word "important" does "that the representation on the Provincial Executives of important minority communities". Therefore "important" will have to stand.

Members: Yes.

Chairman: But "Hindus, Mohammedans and Sikhs" will have to go out; they have no business to be there.

Dr. Ambedkar: Just before you go from that, Sir, I should like to draw attention to the words "working of the new constitution and it was also agreed that on the same grounds Mohammedans should be represented on the Federal Executive". The words "important minorities" should replace the word "Mohammedans" there I mean, in keeping with what we are saying in the beginning.

Chairman: Oh, yes! "It was also agreed on the same grounds".

Dr. Ambedkar: "they should be represented also on the Federal Executive".

Chairman: "That important minorities should be represented on the Federal Executive. On behalf of the smaller minorities a claim was put forward for their representation, either individually or collectively, on the Provincial and Federal Executives or that, failing this, in each cabinet, there should be a Minister specially charged," and so on. That is exactly what was put forward.

Lord Reading: Yes.

Chairman: Officially.

Chairman: As a matter of accurate recording, the use of the word "Mohammedans" is perfectly right.

Sir Muhammad Shafi: Federal stands on a special footing.

Chairman: "Mohammedans" stands.

Mr. Joshi: Yes, I agree to that.

Dr. Ambedkar: Then you must add to "Mohammedans", "and other important minorities".

Chairman: No, you cannot. That was the claim.

Dr. Ambedkar: May I not say so for myself? Speaking for myself, I speak on behalf of the Depressed Classes as well.

Mr. Joshi: It is not agreed. You did not make the claim.

Dr. Ambedkar: It is not a question of whether I did or not.

Chairman: Now, we are doing business, and it is two minutes to eleven.

Dr. Moonje: I would ask, instead of the word "agreed," that we should say, "it was also claimed that on the same grounds," and so on.

Sir Muhammad Shafi: No, no, it was agreed. That is a matter of fact.

Dr. Moonje: I do not know what took place in the Federal Structure Committee.

Sir Muhammad Shafi: The record shows it.

Dr. Moonje: But here, of course, I do not agree with that point.

Sir A. P. Patro: That is accepted, and it goes to the next paragraph.

Dr. Moonje: A claim was put in.

Chairman: The statement was made that the Mohammedans should be recognised, and to that, according to the minutes, there was an agreement, and that has just been lifted out of the records.

Mr. Joshi: The records of this Committee?

Lt. Col. Gidney: I made a distinct statement on this matter when we had this before the plenary session, and I made statement to this effect—that it is all very well for the larger communities to demand certain things, but the minorities wanted some representation.

Chairman: That is in.

Lt. Col. Gidney: This is only an alternative.

Chairman: Oh, no, it is not. The sentence gives an alternative, but it says the claim was made that there should be either representation of the minorities direct, or, failing that is, if that is impossible then...

Lt. Col. Gidney: That is all we want.

Rao Bahadur Pannir Selvam: "Failing this" might replaced by "if this should be found impossible".

Chairman: Yes, instead of "failing this", "if that should be found impossible". There is no reason why that should not be substituted, "if this should be found impossible".

Lord Reading: What is the difference? We are spending time over interchangeable phrases, that is all.

Sardar Ujjal Singh: Make provision for any other communities in the Federal Executive, and insert the words "important minorities" there. We might make some provision, somehow or other, not necessarily, but provision must be there.

Chairman: May I bring you up against the hard facts of the situation. You cannot, on a Federal Executive, have every minority.

Dr. Ambedkar: Let me make my position clear. In the Provincial Constitution, what we have done is, we have placed an obligation upon the Governor to endeavour to do it. He is not tied down, but in the endeavour he should certainly be allowed the freedom to select even from other important minorities. We are not tying him hand and foot in the making of the Constitution. All we have done is that we place an obligation on him not to select, but we place an obligation upon him merely to make an endeavour. Surely that is not tying him down hard and fast, and I submit that after the word "Mohammedans" the words "other important minority communities" should come.

Chairman: No, we have passed that point. We are now at the second point.

Sir A. P. Patro: May I refer to paragraph 13?

Dr. Ambedkar: I would suggest that my dissent be recorded from paragraph 12.

Sardar Ujjal Singh: After the word "Mohammedans", "other important minorities" should be added.

Lt. Col. Gidney: Why close it to the other minorities?

Chairman: I really must rule. As I have said already, we are not closing it to the other minorities. I am quite willing to discuss amendments on the words as they are, but really you must not raise false issues. This makes a claim that the other minorities shall also be represented, but if this should be found impossible—that alteration has been made—then there will be a Minister. That is an accurate record of the claims which were made. Paragraph 12 agreed.

Dr. Ambedkar: I think our dissent should be recorded.

Chairman: Very well.

Discussion on paragraph 18 of the Report

Chairman: 17 is deleted. Now 18, which will then become 17. That this Report be presented to the Committee of the Whole Conference, Those in favour? On the contrary? That is carried. Then it will go to the Committee of the Whole Conference.

Dr. Ambedkar: Sir, there is my amendment.

Chairman: I beg your pardon; I am so sorry.

Dr. Ambedkar: I should like to have this amendment put in as a separate paragraph after 16.

Chairman: Then that is the overriding paragraph.

Dr. Ambedkar: My amendment is this: "That the minorities and the Depressed Classes were definite in their assertion that they would not consent to any self-Government constitution for India unless their demands were accepted."

Chairman: As a matter of fact that was said, and it was said in a responsible way; it was not merely an individual expression of opinion.

Dr. Ambedkar: I think it should be in.

Mr. Joshi: I think labour cannot be regarded as a minority for that statement.

Chairman: I cannot rule it out.

Dr. Ambedkar: I would accept the words : "unless their demands are accepted in a reasonable manner".

That makes it meaningless.

Dr. Ambedkar: Or "their reasonable demands are accepted".

Mr. Zafrullah Khan: Does anybody suppose that if the demands are met in a reasonable way they are going to be pleased?

Mr. Foot: It is only the record of a claim.

Chairman: It is only the record of a claim. That paragraph should be added as paragraph 18, a new paragraph.

Political Safeguards

A scheme of political safeguards for the protection of the depressed classes in the future constitution of a self-governing India

Appendix to Report of Sub-Committee No. III (Minorities) (Submitted by Dr. Bhimrao R. Ambedkar and Rao Bahadur R. Srinivasan)

The following are the terms and conditions on which the Depressed Classes will consent to place themselves under a majority rule in a self-governing India:

Condition No. I

Equal Citizenship: The Depressed Classes cannot consent to subject themselves to majority rule in their present state of hereditary bondsmen. Before majority rule is established their emancipation from the system of untouchability must be an accomplished fact. It must not be left to the will of the majority. The Depressed Classes must be made free citizens entitled to all the rights of citizenship in common with other citizens of the State:

(a) To secure the abolition of untouchability and to create the equality of citizenship, it is proposed that the following fundamental right shall be made part of the constitution of India: Fundamental Right U.S.A. Constitution Amendment XIV and Government of Ireland Act, 1920, 10 & 11, Geo. V, Ch. 67, sec. 5 (2).

"All subjects of the State in India are equal below the law and possess equal civic rights. Any existing enactment, regulation, order, custom or interpretation of law by which any, penalty, disadvantage, disability is imposed upon or any discrimination is made against any subject of the State on account of untouchability shall, as from the day on which this Constitution comes into operation, cease to have any effect in India."

(b) To abolish the immunities and exemptions now enjoyed by executive officers by virtue of sections 110 and 111 of the Government of India Act, 1919 and their liability for executive action be made coextensive with what it is in the case of a European British Subject.

Condition No. II

Free enjoyment of Equal Rights: It is no use for the Depressed Classes to have a declaration of equal rights. There can be no doubt that the Depressed Classes will have to face the whole force of orthodox society, if they try to exercise the equal rights of citizenship. The Depressed Classes therefore feel that if these face the whole force of orthodox society if they try to exercise the equal rights of citizenship. The Depressed Classes therefore feel that if these declarations of rights are not to be mere pious pronouncements but are to be realities of everyday life then they should be protected by adequate pains and penalties from interference in the enjoyment of these declared rights.

(a) The Depressed Classes therefore propose that the following section should be added to Part XI of the Government of India Act, 1919, dealing with Offences, Procedure and Penalties:

(i) Offence of Infringement of Citizenship: U. S. Statutes at arge. Civil Rights Protection Acts of April 9,1866 and of March 1, 1875 passed in the interest of the Negroes after their emancipation.

"Whoever denies to any person except for reasons by law applicable to persons of all classes and regardless of any previous condition of untouchability the full enjoyment of any of the accommodations, advantages, facilities, privileges of inns, educational institutions, roads, paths, streets, tanks, wells and other watering places, public conveyances on land, air or water, theatres or other places of public, amusement, resort or convenience whether they are dedicated to or maintained or licensed for the use of the public shall be punished with imprisonment of either description for a term which may extend to five years and shall also be liable to fine."

(b) Obstruction by orthodox individuals is not the only menace to the Depressed Classes in the way of peaceful enjoyment of their rights. The commonest form of obstruction is the social boycott. It is the most formidable weapon in the hands of the orthodox classes with which they beat down any attempt on the part of the Depressed Classes to undertake any activity if it happens to be unpalatable to them. The way it works and the occasions on which it is brought into operation are well described in the Report of the Committee appointed by the Government of Bombay in 1928 'to enquire into the educational, economic and social condition of the Depressed Classes (untouchables) and of the Aboriginal Tribes in the Presidency and to recommend measures for their uplift'. The following is an extract from the same : Depressed Classes and Social Boycott.

Although we have recommended various remedies to secure to the Depressed Classes their rights to all public utilities we fear that there will be difficulties in the way of their exercising them for a long time to come. The first difficulty is the fear of open violence against them by the orthodox classes. It must be noted that the Depressed Classes form a small minority in every village, opposed to which is a great majority of the orthodox who are bent on protecting their interests and dignity from any supposed invasion by the Depressed Classes at any cost. The danger of prosecution by the Police has put a limitation upon the use of violence by the orthodox classes and consequently such cases are rare.

The second difficulty arises from the economic position in which the Depressed Classes are found today. The Depressed Classes have no economic independence in most parts of the Presidency. Some cultivate the lands of the orthodox classes as their tenants at will. Others live on their earnings as farm labourers employed by the orthodox classes and the rest subsist on the food or grain given to them by the orthodox classes in lieu of service rendered to them as village servants. We have heard of numerous instances where the orthodox classes have used their economic power as a weapon against those Depressed Classes in their villages, when the latter have dared to exercise their rights, and have evicted them from their land, and stopped their employment and discontinued their remuneration as village servants.

This boycott is often planned on such an extensive scale as to include the prevention of the Depressed Classes from using the commonly used paths and the stoppage of sale of the necessities of life by the village Bania. According to the evidence sometimes small cause suffice for the proclamation of a social boycott against the Depressed Classes.

Frequently it follows on the exercise by the Depressed Classes of their right to the use of the common well, but cases have been by no means rare where a stringent boycott has been proclaimed simply because a Depressed Class man has put on the sacred thread, has bought a piece of land, has put on good clothes or ornaments, or has carried a marriage procession with the bridegroom on the horse through the public street.

"We do not know of any weapon more effective than this social boycott which could have been invented for the suppression of the Depressed Classes. The method of open violence pales away before it, for it has the most far-reaching and deadening effects. It is the most dangerous because it passes as a lawful method consistent with the theory of freedom of contact. We agree that this tyranny of the majority must be put down with a firm hand if we are to guarantee the Depressed Classes the freedom of speech and action necessary for their uplift. In the opinion of the Depressed Classes the only way to overcome this kind of menace to their rights and liberties is to make social boycott an offence punishable by law. They are therefore bound to insist that the following sections should be added to those included in Part XI of the Government of India Act, 1919, dealing with Offences, Procedure and Penalties:

Offence of Boycott Defined: This and the following legal provisions are bodily taken from Burma Anti-boycott Act, 1922 with a few with a few changes to suit the necessities of the case.

A person shall be deemed to boycott another who—(a) refuses to let or use or occupy any house or land, or to deal with work for hire, or do business with another person, or to render to him or receive from him any service, or refuses to do any of the said things on the terms on which such things should commonly be done in the ordinary course of business, or (b) abstains from such social, professional or business relations as he would, having regard to such existing customs in the Community which are not inconsistent with any fundamental right or other rights of citizenship declared in the Constitution, ordinarily maintain with such person, or (c) in any way injures, annoys or interferes with such other person in the exercise of his lawful rights.

Punishment for Boycotting: Whoever, in consequence of any person having done an act which he was legally entitled to do or of his having omitted to do any act which he was legally entitled to omit to do or with intent to cause any person to do any act which he is not legally bound to do or to omit to do any act which he is legally entitled to do, or with intent to cause harm to such person in body, mind, reputation or property, or in his business or means of living, boycotts such person or any person in whom such person is interested, shall be punished with imprisonment of either description for a term which may extend to seven years or with fine or with both:

> *Provided that no offence shall be deemed to have been committed under this section if the Court is satisfied that the accused person has not acted at the instigation of or in collusion with any other person or in pursuance of or in collusion with any other person or in pursuance of any conspiracy or of any agreement or combination to boycott.*

Punishment for Instigating or Promoting a Boycott: Whoever—(a) publicly makes or publishes or circulates a proposal for, or (b) makes, publishes or circulates any statement, rumour or report with intent to, or which he has reason to believe to be likely to, cause, or (c) in any other way instigates or promotes the boycotting of any person or class of persons, shall be punished with imprisonment which may extend to five years or with fine or with both. Explanation.—An offence under this section shall be deemed to have been committed although the person affected or likely to be affected by any action of the nature referred to herein is not designated by name or class but only by his acting or abstaining from acting in some specified manner.

Punishment for Threatening a Boycott

Whoever, in consequence of any person having done any act which he was legally entitled to do or of his having omitted to do an act which he was legally entitled to omit to do, or with intent to cause any person to do any act which he is not legally bound to do, or to omit to do any act which he is legally entitled to do, threatens to cause such person or any person in whom such person is interested, to be boycotted shall be punished with imprisonment of either description for a term which may extend to five years or with fine or with both.

Exception.—It is not boycott—(i) to do any act in furtherance of a bona fide labour dispute, (ii) to do any act in the ordinary course of business competition.

Condition No. III

Protection Against Discrimination: The Depressed Classes entertain grave fears of discrimination either by legislation or by executive order being made in the future.

They cannot therefore consent to subject themselves to majority rule unless it is rendered impossible in law for the legislature or the executive to make any invidious discrimination against the Depressed Classes. It is therefore proposed that the following Statutory provision be made in the constitutional law of India:

> *It shall not be competent for any Legislature or Executive in India to pass a law or issue an order, rule or regulation so as to violate the rights of the subjects of the State, regardless of any previous condition of untouchability, in all territories subject to the jurisdiction of the dominion of India:*

(1) to make and enforce contracts, to sue, be parties, and give evidence, to inherit, purchase, lease, sell, hold and convey real and personal property,

(2) to be eligible for entry into the civil and military employ

and to-all educational institutions except for such conditions and limitations as may be necessary to provide for the due and adequate representation of all classes of the subjects of the State,

(3) to be entitled to the full and equal enjoyment of the accommodations, advantages, facilities, educational institutions, privileges of inns, rivers, streams, wells, tanks, roads, paths, streets, public conveyances on land, air and water, theatres, and other places of public resort or amusement except for such conditions and limitations applicable alike to all subjects of every race, class, caste, colour or creed,

(4) to be deemed fit for and capable of sharing without distinction the benefits of any religious or charitable trust dedicated to or created, maintained or licensed for the general public or for persons of the same faith and religion,

(5) to claim full and equal benefit of all laws and proceedings for the security of person and property as is enjoyed by other subjects regardless of any previous condition of untouchability and be subject to like punishment, pains and penalties and to none other.

Condition No. IV

Adequate Representation in the Legislatures: The Depressed Classes must be given sufficient political power to influence legislative and executive action for the purpose of securing their welfare. In view of this they demand that the following provisions shall be made in the electoral law so as to give them:

(1) Right to adequate representation in the Legislatures of the Country, Provincial and Central.

(2) Right to elect their own men as their representatives, (a) by adult suffrage, and (b) by separate electorates for the first ten years and thereafter by joint electorates and reserved seats, it being understood that joint electorates shall not be forced upon the Depressed Classes against their will unless such joint electorates are accompanied by adult suffrage.

Adequate Representation in the Services

The Depressed Classes have suffered enormously at the hands of the high caste officers who have monopolized the Public Services by abusing the Law or by misusing the discretion vested in them in administering it to the prejudice of the Depressed Classes and to the advantage of the caste Hindus without any regard to justice, equity or good conscience. This mischief can only be avoided by destroying the monopoly of caste Hindus in the Public Services and by regulating the recruitment to them in such a manner that all communities including the Depressed Classes will have an adequate share in them. For this purpose the Depressed Classes have to make the following proposals for statutory enactment as part of the constitutional law:

(1) There shall be established in India and in each Province in India a Public Service Commission to undertake the recruitment and control of the Public Services.

(2) No member of the Public Service Commission shall be removed except by a resolution passed by the Legislature nor shall he be appointed to any office under the Crown after his retirement.

(3) It shall be the duty of the Public Service Commission subject to the tests of efficiency as may be prescribed—(a) to recruit the Services in such a manner as will secure due and adequate representation of all communities, and (b) to regulate from time to time priority in employment in accordance with the existing extent of the representation of the various communities in any particular service concerned.

Condition No. VI

Redress Against Prejudicial Action or Neglect of Interests: In view of the fact that the Majority Rule of the future will be the rule of the orthodox, the Depressed Classes fear that such a Majority Rule will not be sympathetic to them and that the probability of prejudice to their interests and neglect of their vital needs cannot be overlooked. It must be provided against, particularly because, however adequately represented, the Depressed Classes will be in a minority in all legislatures. The Depressed Classes think it very necessary that they should have the means of redress given to them in the constitution. It is therefore proposed that the following provision should be made in the constitution of India:

(1) In and for each Province and in and for India it shall be the duty and obligation of the Legislature and the Executive or any other Authority established by law to make adequate provision for the education, sanitation, recruitment in Public Services and other matters of social and political advancement of the Depressed Classes and to do nothing that will prejudicially affect them.

(2) Where in any Province or in India the provisions of this section are violated an appeal shall lie to the Governor-General in Council from any act or decision of any Provincial Authority and to the Secretary of State from any act or decision of a Central Authority affecting the matter.

(3) In every such case where it appears to the Governor-General in Council or to the Secretary of State the Provincial Authority or Central Authority does not take steps requisite for the due execution of the provisions of this section then and in every such case, and as far only as the circumstances of each case require, the Governor-General in Council or the Secretary of State acting as an appellate authority may prescribe, for such period as they may deem fit, remedial measures for the due execution of the provisions of this section and of any of its decisions under this section and which shall be binding upon the authority appealed against.

Condition No. VII

Special Departmental Care: The helpless, hapless and sapless condition of the Depressed Classes must be entirely attributed to the dogged and determined opposition of the whole mass of the orthodox population which will not allow the Depressed Classes to have equality of status or equality of treatment. It is not enough to say of their economic condition that they are poverty-stricken or that they are a class of landless labourers, although both these statements are statements of fact.

It has to be noted that the poverty of the Depressed Classes is due largely to the social prejudices in consequence of which many an occupation for earning a living is closed to them. This is a fact, which differentiates the position of the Depressed Classes from that of the ordinary caste labourer and is often a source of trouble between the two. It has also to be borne in mind that the forms of tyranny and oppression practised against the Depressed Classes are very various and the capacity of the Depressed Classes to protect themselves is extremely limited. The facts which obtain in this connection and which are of common occurrence throughout India are well described in the Abstracts of Proceedings of the Board of Revenue of the Government of Madras dated 5th November 1882, No. 723, from which the following is an extract:

There are forms of oppression only hitherto hinted at which must be at least cursorily mentioned. To punish disobedience of Pariahs, their masters:

(a) Bring false cases in the village court or in the criminal courts.

(b) Obtain, on application, from Government, waste lands lying all round the paracheri, so as to impound the Pariahs' cattle or obstruct the way to their temple.

(c) Have mirasi names fraudulently entered in the Government account against the paracheri.

(d) Pull down the huts and destroy the growth in the back-yards.

(e) Deny occupancy right in immemorial sub-tenancies.

(f) Forcibly cut the Pariahs' crops, and on being resisted charge them with theft and rioting.

(g) Under misrepresentations, get them to execute documents by which they are afterwards ruined.

(h) Cut off the flow of water from their fields.

(i) Without legal notice, have the property of sub-tenants attached for the landlords' arrears of revenue.

It will be said there are civil and criminal courts for the redress of any of these injuries. There are the courts indeed; but India does not breed village Hampdens. One must have courage to go to the courts; money to employ legal knowledge, and meet legal expenses; and means to live during the case and the appeals.

Further most cases depend upon the decision of the first court; and these courts are presided over by officials who are sometimes corrupt and who generally, for other reasons, sympathize with the wealthy and landed classes to which they belong.

The influence of these classes with the official world can hardly be exaggerated. It is extreme with natives and great even with Europeans. Every office, from the highest to the lowest, is stocked with their representatives, and there is no proposal affecting their interests but they can bring a score of influence to bear upon it in its course from inception to execution.

There can be no doubt that in view of these circumstances the uplift of the Depressed Classes will remain a pious hope unless the task is placed in the forefront of all governmental activities and unless equalisation of opportunities is realized in practice by a definite policy and determined effort on the part of the Government.

To secure this end the proposal of the Depressed Classes is that the Constitutional Law should impose upon the Government of India a statutory obligation to maintain at all times a department to deal with their problems by the addition of a section in the Government of India Act to the following effect:

1. Simultaneously with the introduction of this Constitution and as part thereof there shall be created in the Government of India a Department to be in-charge of a Minister for the purpose of watching the interests of the Depressed Classes and promoting their welfare.
2. The Minister shall hold office so long as he retains the confidence of the Central Legislature.
3. It shall be the duty of the Minister in the exercise of any powers and duties conferred upon him or transferred to him by law, to take all such steps as may be desirable to secure the preparation, effectively carrying out and coordination of measures preventative of acts of social injustice, tyranny or oppression against the Depressed Classes and conducive to their welfare throughout India.

4. It shall be lawful for the Governor-General:
   (a) to transfer to the Minister all or any powers or duties in respect of the welfare of the Depressed Classes arising from any enactment relating to education, sanitation, etc.,
   (b) to appoint Depressed Classes welfare bureaux in each province to work under the authority of and in cooperation with the Minister.

Condition No. VIII

Depressed Classes and the Cabinet: Just as it is necessary that the Depressed Classes should have the power to influence governmental action by seats in the Legislature so also it is desirable that the Depressed Classes should have the opportunity to frame the general policy of the Government. This they can do only if they can find a seat in the Cabinet. The Depressed Classes therefore claim that in common with other minorities, their moral rights to be represented in the Cabinet should be recognized. With this purpose in view the Depressed Classes propose:

> *That in the Instrument of Instructions an obligation shall be placed upon the Governor and the Governor-General to endeavour to secure the representation of the Depressed Classes in his Cabinet.*

Report on Depressed Classes

Report of Subcommittee No. III (minorities): These are some of the paragraphs of the Report related to the interests of Depressed Classes which have been approved by the Committee of Whole Conference on 19th January, 1931.

One of the Chief proposals brought before the Sub-Committee was the inclusion in the constitution of a declaration of fundamental rights safeguarding the cultural and religious life of the various communities and securing to every individual without discrimination as to race, caste, creed or sex, the free exercise of economic, social and civil rights (Dr. Ambedkar called attention to the necessity of including in the constitution sanctions for the enforcement of the fundamental rights, including a right of redress when they are violated).

Whilst it was generally admitted that a system of joint free electorates was in the abstract consistent with democratic principles as generally understood, and would be acceptable to the Depressed Classes after a short transitional period, provided the franchise was based on adult suffrage, the opinion was expressed that, in view of the distribution of the communities in India and of their unequal economic, social and political effectiveness, there was a real danger that under such a system the representation secured by minorities would be totally inadequate, and that this system would therefore give no communal security.

Claims were therefore advanced by various communities that arrangements should be made for representation and for fixed proportions of seats. It was also urged that the number of seats reserved for a minority community should in no case be less than its proportion in the population. The methods by which this could be secured were mainly three (1) nomination, (2) joint electorates with reservation of seats, and (3) separate electorates.

The discussion made it evident that the demand which remained as the only one which would be generally acceptable was separate electorates. The general objection to this scheme has been subject to much previous discussion in India. It involves what is very difficult problem for solution, *viz.* what should be the amount of communal representation in the various Provinces and in the Centre; that, if the whole, or practically the whole, of the seats in a legislature are to be assigned to communities, there will be no room for the growth of independent political opinion or of true political parties, and this problem received a serious complication by the demand of the representatives of the Depressed Classes that they should be deducted from the Hindu population and be regarded, for electoral purposes, as a separate community.

There was general agreement with the recommendation of Sub-Committee No. II (Provincial Constitution) that the representation on the Provincial Executives of important minority communities was a matter of the greatest practical importance for the successful working of the new constitution, and it was also agreed that on the same grounds Mohammedans should be represented on the Federal Executive (Dr. Ambedkar would add the words, "and other important minorities" after the word "Mohammedans").

On behalf of smaller minorities, a claim was put forward for their representation, either individually or collectively, on the Provincial and Federal Executives, or that, if this should be found impossible in each Cabinet, there should be a Minister specially charged with the duty of protecting minority interests.

As regards the administration, it was agreed that recruitment of both Provincial and Central Services should be entrusted to P.S.Cs., with instructions to recruit the claims of various communities to fair and adequate representation in the Public Services, whilst providing for the maintenance of a proper standard of efficiency.

It has also been made clear that the British Government cannot with any chance of agreement impose upon the communities an electoral principle which, in some feature or other, would be met by their opposition. It was therefore plain that, failing an agreement, separate electorates with all their drawbacks and difficulties, would have to be retained as the basis of the electoral arrangements under the new constitution. From this the question of proportions would arise. Under these circumstances, the claims of the Depressed Classes will have to be considered adequately.

The Minorities and Depressed Classes were definite in their assertion that they would not consent to any self-governing constitution for India unless their demands were met in a reasonable manner.

In Subcommittee No. VI (Franchise)

Second Sitting—22nd December 1930

Dr. Ambedkar: It seems to me that there are only two important questions which this Round Table Conference is going to consider. One question is whether India should have responsible Government, and the second question is to what people that Government should be responsible.

Chairman: We are now discussing the question of the educational qualification. I may just remind you that the second conclusion to which we came was this: "We recommend that in any given area the franchise qualification should be the same for all communities, but we desire that the Expert Franchise Committee, in making their proposals, should bear in mind that the ideal system would as nearly as possible give each community a voting strength proportional to its population and this Committee should so contrive their franchise as so far as practicable to bring about this result."

I am afraid that is rather a counsel of perfection, but at the same time the only way in which we can possibly expect them to carry that out is if we give them a certain latitude; that is manifest. Therefore, in considering all these questions of educational qualifications and so on, you have to remember that unless you authorise the Franchise Committee to take these into account, you are restricting and not enlarging their possibility of action.

Dr. Ambedkar: I should like, if I may, to ask one question with regard to the conclusion which you, Sir, have read out, and at which you said the Sub-Committee had arrived. Does that conclusion imply that the Franchise Committee will have the liberty to consider a variety of franchises for different communities, to arrive at the result that the voting strength shall be proportional to the strength of those communities?

3rd sitting- 30-12-1930

Chairman: I do not think that is it. We have to give guidance to the Franchise Committee; they will fill in the details. We are, as it were, the architects, and they are the masons and builders.

Dr. Ambedkar: I understand that, but what I should like to know is whether that conclusion gives liberty to the Franchise Committee to have a different franchise for the different communities with the object of securing equality.

Chairman: No. The first sentence says that we recommend that in any given area the franchise qualification should be the same for all communities.

We will now proceed with our discussion on the educational qualification.

Mr. Jadhav : Would any Legislative Council have the

power to go back after ten years and restrict the franchise? Some of them might wish to do that.

Chairman: Their powers would be powers of extension, not of diminution.

Dr. Ambedkar: I should like to say a word on this subject, without prejudice to the position we have taken all along. It seems to me that as compared with the alternatives which have been suggested, one by Mr. Joshi that there should be some law providing for automatic extension, and the other, the main proposal, that the matter should be left to the sweet will of the legislatures, the recommendations made by the Simon Commission seems to me to be better and to be more readily acceptable from my point of view.

It might be much better, as I say, to have some authority which will investigate at the end of a definite period exactly what has been the result of the working of the franchise up to that period. That body will be able to see what disparity there has been as between the different provinces. That body will be able to see what is the machinery existing at the end of the ten years, in order to cope with the elections if the franchise were to be altered, and that body, being impartial itself, will be able to deal with the rights of the mass of the people much more readily, in a much more just and equitable way, than the class-conscious people who may be installed as a result of the limited franchise which we are introducing today. For these reasons it seems to me that the proposals of the Simon Commission are better than the alternatives.

Sir Cowasji Jehangir: Who is to set that up?

Dr. Ambedkar: Just as Parliament in the Act suggested that there should be a Public Service Commission, so it could be suggested that there should be the appointment of a Committee.

Sir Cowasji Jehangir: By the Central Government?

Dr. Ambedkar: Yes.

Chairman: I think I know enough now to draft a Report on this subject, but I should like to know what is your view— not that we shall here and now recommend that any Expert Franchise Committee or any other Committee should be set up after 15 years, say, but in view of possibility that one Province might extend its franchise much more generously than another, so that the whole thing might get out of step, ought we to contemplate the possibility of anybody being constituted to look into the matter then, to try and adjust things, or shall we merely content ourselves with leaving things to the Provinces, or ought we to follow Dr. Ambedkar's idea of a Committee? We need not say that it has to come into being, or when it is to come into being, but that it might function if it came into being.

Mr. Basu: At any period when the Central Government desired to appoint a Committee.

Chairman: We will not say how it is to be appointed, but what do you say about the possibility of appointing such a body?

Diwan Bahadur Ramachandra Rao: I think the Government of India should set up such a body, not that Parliament should set up such a body.

Dr. Ambedkar: What difference does it make?

Diwan Bahadur Ramachandra Rao: We are leaving great freedom in all these matters. I would like to eliminate parliamentary control. I should like to know what the proposal is. If you say that after a number of years it shall be competent for the Government of India to appoint a Committee to look into this question in the whole of the Provinces, I shall have no objection, but if it is a question of Parliament going into this question again in ten years, I object to it entirely. I have no objection to the Committee being appointed by which the franchise will be extended, but I should like that power vested entirely in the Government of India and to be exercised at its discretion whenever there is necessity for such a thing within a certain number of years, or after a certain number of years.

Dr. Ambedkar: How has it any bearing on the functions of this Subcommittee whether this Committee is appointed by Parliament or by the Government of India?

Diwan Bahadur Ramachandra Rao: We are devaluating authority to India from Parliament, because in 1919 when this question came up before the Parliamentary Committee, I and several others with me contended that there should be devolution of questions like this to authorities in India; and because such a step was not taken, we are now confronted with the accumulated complaints about franchise which are now being investigated and they could not be investigated because parliamentary permission was required. Therefore I suggest that any step taken in that direction should be devolution of complete power to the Government of India, to be exercised at its discretion to go into the whole question of franchise in a certain number of years. That is a point upon which I really desire to lay some stress.

Dr. Ambedkar: It is now evident, at least to myself and some of my friends, that we shall have to record a note of dissent from certain propositions that will be placed before the Sub-Committee. Will it be permissible for us to submit to you a note of dissent on the various points, which you may be kind enough to append to the; report, or will you allow us some other method?

Chairman: I do not think that up to the present any of the Sub-Committees have appended minority reports, as it were; I think the report of the Sub-Committee has been one report, but has indicated on its face that certain members—naming them if necessary—have dissented.

Dr. Ambedkar: I should like, with your permission to point out one disadvantage which I see in that procedure. If we are not allowed to record our minute of dissent, you do not give us an opportunity to put our suggestions in a concrete form, which we should like to do if we may be allowed to do so. We are allowed the negative liberty of saying we do not agree, and that is all.

Chairman: I am not sure we cannot meet you. I think you have made your objection quite clear. What you want really is adult suffrage, and I think we have got a sentence in to indicate that certain members of our Sub-Committee—naming them—objected to this because they thought the system of adult suffrage was the only satisfactory system. That states the point.

Dr. Ambedkar: What we should do would depend on the report.

Chairman: Let us leave the difficulty until it arises, and then see if we cannot meet you. I think we can.

4th sitting- 1-1-1931

Draft Report—Point 4

Extension of the Franchise: While it was generally held that adult suffrage was the goal which should ultimately be attained, it was agreed that the basis of the franchise could forthwith be broadened and that a large increase was desirable. Some difference of opinion existed as to the extent to which this was practicable in present circumstances, and it was realised that the Subcommittee had not the necessary material to determine the precise limits of the advance. The Statutory Commission suggested such an increase in the number of electors as would bring that number up to ten percent of the population. Some of our members thought that an increase to twenty-five per cent of the adult population was immediately practicable.

We recommend that an expert Franchise Commission should be appointed with instructions to provide for the immediate increase of the electorate so as to enfranchise not less than ten per cent of the total population and indeed a larger number—but not more than twenty-five per cent of the total population—if that should, on a full investigation, be found practicable and desirable.

We recommend that, in addition to providing for this increase the Commission should consider the introduction of a scheme by which all adults not entitled to a direct vote would be grouped together in primary groups of about 20, for the election of one representative member from each group, who would be entitled to vote in the Provincial elections either in the same constituencies as the directly qualified voters or in separate constituencies to be formed for them.

Dr. Ambedkar: I beg to move an amendment to paragraph 4, namely, that in the second section, line 2, to add the following words after the word "practicable"—" with the electoral machinery available in present circumstances". It would then read "Some difference of opinion existed as to the extent to which this was practicable with the electoral machinery available in present circumstances." Several Members: There are other grounds.

Dr. Ambedkar: That is my amendment. I leave it to the Chairman as the best judge to sum up the sense of the Committee, but the impression that was left upon my mind was that the majority of those who opposed universal adult suffrage as being practical politics for the immediate future did so mainly upon the ground that there was not sufficient electoral machinery in India to cope with the situation if everybody was allowed to vote.

Chairman: I do not think myself, Dr. Ambedkar, that was the sole ground on which the matter was put. It was one of the main grounds, but in recording the view of the Committee I do not think we should limit ourselves to saying that was the sole ground. For instance, the difficulty of communications, and the lack of facilities for travel, and so on, were also very much stressed.

Dr. Ambedkar: I would rather like to have it made clear in the Report.

Mr. Joshi: You might put in some such words as "practical electioneering difficulties".

Sir Cawasji Jehangir: But there are other objections.

Mr. Joshi: We are talking of the general majority, and not of those people who do not want to vote on principle.

Chairman: I think what is already stated meets the point. After all, you and Mr. Joshi come in under the note at the end.

Dr. Ambedkar: I have an amendment on page 3. Instead of the words "but not" I should like to have the words "and even substituted".

Chairman: Many of us felt, and I am one of them, that an immediate increase of twenty-five per cent was straining it somewhat, and I do not think we should be asked to strain it further. Again, you come in under your reservation. Dr. Ambedkar.

Dr. Ambedkar: My second amendment is to strike out the words "and desirable". This matter, whatever increase is desirable or not, is really one which must be decided by this Committee. It cannot be decided by the Expert Franchise Commission. That Commission is to be appointed to devise ways and means to carry into effect the decisions we take. How much increase is desirable is certainly a matter which cannot be left to the competence of the new Franchise Commission. From that point of view I think it is necessary to drop these words.

Chairman: It is very difficult to separate what is practicable and what is desirable. "Practicable" is an elastic word. It may be a very difficult thing to achieve or it may be a comparatively easy thing to achieve; but it may be possible of achievement and therefore you will say it is practicable. In considering the desirability, you can hardly shut out of your mind the extent to which the thing is practicable. The two must come in together to a certain extent.

Dr. Ambedkar: We have decided that in our opinion an extension which covers twenty-five per cent of the population is desirable.

Chairman: You use such an elastic word as "practicable". That is the difficulty I feel. You cannot put the two words in completely watertight compartments. What is practicable must react on what is desirable, and you use a very elastic word. I think it would be wiser to keep both there. We give a clear view of our indication by saying at the very outset that we look forward to adult suffrage as an ideal.

Chairman: We had better take it line by line. Will anybody interrupt if they have an amendment to propose: "We recommend that, in addition to providing for this increase, the Commission should consider the introduction of a scheme by which all adults not entitled to a direct vote would be grouped together in primary groups of about 20,"—"then it is proposed to insert "or in some other suitable manner". Is there any objection? For the election of one representative member from each group, who would be entitled to vote in the Provincial elections either in the same constituencies as the directly qualified voters or in separate constituencies to be formed for them.

Dr. Ambedkar: I should like to say that Mr. K. T. Paul was also of the same opinion as ourselves.

Chairman: That will be noted.

Mr. Joshi: I propose that instead of the words "second best" the words "quite inadequate" should be substituted.

Chairman: That is really a matter for you gentlemen. If you prefer those words "quite inadequate" instead of the words "second best", that is a matter for you really. So it will read: "Mr. Joshi, Mr. Shiva Rao, Dr. Ambedkar, Mr. Srinivasan and Mr. K. T. Paul regard these proposals as quite inadequate and consider that the immediate introduction of adult suffrage is both practicable and desirable." Mr. Jadhav: My name also should be added to that list.

Chairman: A note will be made of that. Then it goes on : "Sir Cowasji Jehangir, P. C. Mitter, and Mr. Basu do not assent to the maximum or minimum we have suggested, but desire the discretion of the Franchise Commission to be entirely unfettered." Obviously that is a matter for them to say what they want.

Chairman: The minor communities are really protected, not so much by the number of voters as by the number of representatives they have, whether they have separate electorates or whether they have joint electorates with reservation. That is in the main their protection. But in order to try to get a conclusion could not we say this, instead of using the words "each community"—Mr. Chintamani put it to me— "We desire that the Franchise Commission in making their proposal should bear in mind that the ideal system would as nearly as possible give the major communities a voting strength in proportion," and so on. I think that would do.

Sir C. Jehangir: "The two major communities."

Chairman: His point is, he does not want to confine himself to the major communities, but he wants to put it in this way that he is only recommending with regard to the major communities; the Minor communities are not the subject matter of the recommendation at all. Cannot you meet him on that?

Sir C. Jehangir: It is too dangerous. When you talk about separate electorate, we have no separate electorates and we do not want them.

Dr. Ambedkar: It means this, that in order to maintain the advantage of having a large existing electorate the suffrage should not be extended to the majority of the people. That is what it comes to, that in order that Sir Cowasji Jehangir should maintain the existing ratio of his population to the electoral strength the other people in the country should not be on the electoral strength.

Sir C. Jehangir: All I mean is that the smaller community should not be jeopardised.

Dr. Ambedkar: Your position is bound to be jeopardised in any lowering of the franchise, and if you feel that proportionately to the other voters your position goes down, then your safety lies either in trusting to the majority or in asking for separate electorates. But you cannot say: 'Because we will be thrown down, we will sink, therefore other communities should not be given it." It comes to nothing else but that.

Sir C. Jehangir: I do not say that.

Chairman: I am afraid that we will have to take our conclusion. Bear in mind, if you will, that we are agreeing to adult suffrage as an ideal. We have passed that part of the report. I have suggested the words "would as nearly as possible give at least major communities".

Dr. Ambedkar: If you want to place it before the Franchise Committee we should still like to say that in our view the principle of adult suffrage should be applied to the Depressed Classes. Chairman: We have got that already.

Mr. Foot: Otherwise you would put an addendum to each paragraph.

Chairman: We cannot have that every time.

Mr. Jadhav: Brahmins and non-Brahmins and different communities in Bombay, Depressed Classes and all should be added.

Chairman: We cannot go into that. (Dr. Ambedkar insists for recording his dissent from para. 13.)

Mr. Foot: There is only one point. In view of the general objection based upon the claim for adult suffrage, need you have a note following each paragraph? Would not there be a general note at the end embodying the objection taken by Mr. Joshi and his colleagues?

Chairman: I think that would be better for you, I quite understand your position. Dr. Ambedkar: I leave it to you.

Chairman: If I may say so, I think it might make you appear to be in rather a false position if, for instance, you appeared to be objecting to the women's vote.

Dr. Ambedkar: We have very good ground for doing that. We are quite prepared, in our minds, and we can meet whatever objection may be raised on that ground. We have no theoretical objection to women.

Mr. Jadhav: The maximum of 25 per cent will be taken up by women, and then there will be no necessity of any other lowering of the franchise.

3

'Ambedkar' for the Movement of Dalits

'Ambedkar' for the Dalit movement, first of all, should be shorn of all the sectarian outlook that unfortunately came to be associated with him. He was an iconoclast and therefore should inspire us to break such icons that are imbued with this outlook. Dalits have to demolish all the handiwork of the reactionaries and vested interests. The project of redefinition of Ambedkar should liberate him from the dens of the ruling class and bring him back to the huts in slums and villages where he rightly belongs.

The greatest thing about Ambedkar is his consistent anti-dogmatic stance. He never accepted any thing in name of authority. He hated humbug of every kind. He always approached problems with a student's sincerity and researcher's intellectual honesty. He gave a vision that even the ideologies are bound by the tenet of impermanence and no body should claim them validity beyond their times. His followers therefore can assume absolute liberty to think through things as per their own experience in changing times.

'Ambedkar' against Exploitation

The underscoring vision in Ambedkar's thought and action is to be found in his yearning for the end of all kinds of exploitation. Whenever and wherever he smelt exploitation, he raised his voice against it. The caste system that subjugated more than one fifth of the population to levels worse than animals' for more than two millennia and which represented institutionalisation of the most heinous inequality by the Hindu religion as ordained by its gods, became the prime target of his life. He attacked it from the standpoint of its victims—the untouchables. He waged many battles; initially targeting the citadels of Brahminism—the custodian of the Hindu religious code, and later politicised the battle, realising the ineffectiveness of the former. He did not let this objective out of sight even for a moment and worked incessantly for its achievement. This Herculean task almost completely overshadows the fact that his struggles extend well beyond the caste struggles and rather encompass all other forms of exploitation.

Even the credit for struggling against untouchability was reluctantly granted to him by the establishment which had belittled him initially as merely a leader of his own caste—Mahar. This prejudicial treatment of Ambedkar could itself be taken as a measure of the severity of the problematic of caste. The facts are clear today that not only was his struggle directed towards the emancipation of all the untouchables but also towards annihilation of the entire caste system. It was basically against the systemic exploitation that ran unabated for centuries. The protest against this inhuman system could be articulated only in a concrete situation, not in a vacuum.

He did not theorise the struggle on a hypothetical plane. He built it on the basis of real problems in a concrete situation. Unlike many cases, the motive force for his life mission was provided by his experience itself. Although he pitched his tents against Brahminism, he never bore any enmity against the Brahmins or identified any one for his friend or foe by caste. The Bahishkrit Hitkarini Sabha that was the launch vehicle of his movement had majority from the forward caste people in its executive body. Even later, this intention of having a non-caste base for the organisation could be consistently seen in his movement, be it the Mahad struggle or the Indian Labour Party. He was perceptive enough to say that the Brahminism could exist in all the castes including the untouchables, for that was the essence of the casteism. It is tragic to find his legacy being monopolised today by only the scheduled castes. Although, he considered the magnitude of the problem of emancipation of dalits is such as to warrant his sole attention, he did take cudgels for other oppressed entities like workers, peasants and women. At one occasion in response to the accusation that he did not care for the tribals, he had to squarely admit the fact that he considered the problem at hand big enough to outlast his life and provokedly put that he never claimed to fight for whole humanity. Such instances though disturbing enough could be understood within their specific context. While dealing with the socioeconomic depravation of dalits, he comprehensively exposed certain systemic dimensions that help perpetuate exploitation. For instance, he was well aware of the capitalist and imperialist oppression besides the decadent feudalism within which domain his problem lay.

Capitalism

During the colonial British regime, capitalism started taking root in India with the collaboration of Indian mercantile capital and British capital. Unlike Europe, it did not have to battle against feudalism; rather it was implanted on the trunk of the latter in India. As a result, even in the capitalist institutions in the cities, caste discrimination simultaneously existed. Ambedkar was quite aware of the exploitative potential of capital and hence he had declared capitalism and Brahminism as the twin enemy of his movement. Capitalism was in an infantile stage then but Brahminism encompassed the phases of slavery, feudalism and extended its tentacles as we see to the phase of imperialism. Moreover, he noted the reactionary compradore character of rising capitalism in the contemporary sectors of the economy and the inhuman exploitation of workers that it unleashed.

His, Indian Labour Party (ILP) was an attempt to take up the question of capitalist exploitation, as well as to combine the struggle on both caste and class basis. Various workers' problems were taken up by the ILP, the leadership of combined strike of the mill workers, parliamentary fight for the workers' interest in relation to the Industrial Disputes Act, and various legal reforms that were brought about while he was in the Executive Council of the Viceroy, can be the examples of his concern for workers' exploitation. It cannot be denied that his approach to these contemporary problems was closer to that of the Fabian socialists with whom he was more familiar. But, it was a model adopted out of familiarity and pragmatism, a matter of strategy, never thought out on an ideological plane to be a theoretical plank. Although, there cannot be any doubt that he stood against capitalism, he could not articulate a sound theoretical basis for doing so. Resultantly, his efforts remained constricted with a short view of workers' welfare but could not provide them a vision of their liberation.

Imperialism

Ambedkar's attitude towards imperialism has been projected in a distorted manner right from the beginning, mainly because he refused to take part in the freedom struggle or opposed Gandhi who for certain category of ignoramuses was the anti-imperialism personified. He strategically sought to maintain neutrality vis-a-vis the colonial State. As per him, it would not be possible for the resourceless dalits to fight its mighty foes all together. He did not want to dissipate and squander his extremely limited resources on several fronts. He however knew the basic exploitative character of the colonial regime. At several occasions, he burst out saying that British imperialism and Indian feudalism were the two leaches that clung to Indian people. However, there was a fundamental difference between his and others' viewpoint. For instance, he did not approve equating opposition to imperialism with opposing the British. He noted that the opposition to imperialism couldn't be effective until its supporters within the country are left untouched.

The then leader of the Communist Party of India—Manabendranath Roy once met him at his residence and during discussions insisted that destruction of imperialism had to be the first and foremost objective of Indian politics. Ambedkar's response to him summarised his outlook towards this problem. He replied to Roy in explicit terms that without struggling against the landlords, mill owners, moneylenders—the friends of imperialism within the country, it was not possible to wage an effective fight against imperialism. It may be a matter of research but a priori his anti-imperialist attitude pervades even his writings as a student.

The validation of his stand comes from an entirely unrelated corner and nearly half a century later. Suniti Kumar Ghosh, (1985 and 1995) in his books has shown in great detail how the Congress representing landlords and capitalists had played a compradore role to serve the interest of imperialism during the so-called freedom struggle and how even after the transfer of power in 1947 the grip of imperialism instead of weakening became stronger. Does it not indicate that he was more correct than any of his contemporary politicians? The ones who biasedly wish to pronounce their half baked verdict that Ambedkar was a stooge of British merely on the basis of his acceptance of membership of Viceroy's Executive Council or talking to the Simon Commission, not only display their ignorance of history but also their casteist fangs. They ought to rethink the comparison between Ambedkar who, even being apparently a part of the imperialist apparatus was perhaps striking at its roots by empowering the people and many others, so called nationalists, who after wearing the mask of anti-imperialism were indirectly strengthening its pillars.

In relation to British rule, Ambedkar basically makes two points. The first is that he questions the so-called freedom struggle launched under the leadership of Congress as an anti-imperialist struggle. He contended that the Congress basically represented the class of feudal lords and the urban capitalists—the two some exploiters of Indian masses. Although, it succeeded through the charismatic leadership of Gandhi in galvanising masses in its support, it essentially relied on bargaining with the colonial rulers for securing itself more share of power.

It always throttled the mass spontaneity as in the case of 1942-uprisings and actively opposed the genuine anti-imperialist struggles of the revolutionaries like Bhagat Singh. Ambedkar reflects the understanding of true character of the Congress in his own way, when he says that if Congress was fighting a real anti-imperialist war, he would whole heartedly support it. The rhetoric of such statement apart, for he never appears to even take a note of other truly anti-imperialist struggles like the one referred to above, it is enough to reveal his attitude towards imperialism and understanding of the class character of the Congress. He knew that the class character of the Congress would not permit it to don this role in reality. Ambedkar could see through the anti-imperialist masks the real fangs of an exploiter of masses.

He thus not only saw no point in siding with this more real exploiter of people than perhaps the colonial rulers, but also did not hesitate to openly oppose it when it came in the way of Dalit liberation. He smelt rot in all such struggles that refused to notice existence of inhuman exploitation of some of their own people within their precincts and tended to over-externalise their woes. Here lay his second point when he raised a question of Hindu imperialism perpetrated through its caste system that was certainly seen as more vicious by its victims than the British rule. It may be pertinent to ask of those who raise the issue of Ambedkar's attitude and conduct towards imperialism, to answer as to why the problem of untouchability or caste system that reduced its one—fifth of the population to subhuman levels did not find a mere mention in the lofty discussions of freedom struggle that predated Ambedkar's raising it. The anti-imperialist aspiration also could be seen in the context of the class/caste division in the society.

The battle for the lost kingdom waged by the vanquished lords also could be camouflaged as an anti-imperialist struggle and at the same time the genuine peoples' anti-imperialist aspiration manifested in the form of say anti-feudal struggle could be condemned as the pro-imperialism, merely because it directed its gun towards the props of the imperialism. The real anti-imperialist aspirations belong to the masses of people the manifestation of which is possible only through the peoples' war. Whatever anti-imperialist struggle people waged were soon hijacked by the phoney war whose real intent was to extract political power to native ruling classes. While the scenes of anti-British struggles were being enacted for the 'mother' India of exploiters, Ambedkar busied himself to liberate the other India- the India of the exploited and oppressed.

Oppression of Women

Besides these mainstream forms of exploitation even the subaltern forms like women's exploitation, could not escape his agenda. He viewed them as the most oppressed of all. His approach to the problems was typically that of a liberal democrat constitutionalist. This certainly constrained his articulation of this problem as in many others. This issue will have to be seriously rethought by dalits under the redefinition project. But suffice here to say that at any opportunity, he raised his voice against women's discriminatory situation in the society.

His basic law of social engineering was that the social revolutions must always begin from the standpoint of the most oppressed or the ones on the lowest rung of the society. Right from the days of Mook Nayak and Bahiskrit Bharat, he appears to take cudgels for women. He always involved women in his struggles and tended to give them vanguard positions. For example, about 500 women had marched at the head of the historical procession at Mahad to assert the untouchables' right to drink water from the public tank. He was immensely pained to see the permanent denial of education and religious rights to women ordained in the Shastras of the Hinduism (*e.g.* Manusmriti). His democratic consciousness never reconciled with any thing lesser than the equality of men and women though its expression was acutely constrained perhaps by his anxieties about the possibilities, so much so that it might even be mistaken as the male centric tactic.

While he asked women to be good mothers so as to shape up their son or to be good wives to their husbands or be a carrier of community's cultural baggage, he did struggle for their equal rights as in the case of Hindu Code Bill. He described sacramental marriages (Mathew, 1991) as polygamy for men and perpetual slavery for women because under no circumstances within that system the latter would get liberty from their husbands, however bad or undesirable they may be. He insisted that women should have the freedom to break this contract.

On Revolution

Revolution, on the face of it, appears to be an anathema to Ambedkar who seems to dread it and instead advocates reforms. But it would be disaster to take it at face value. For, like many other terms, his usage of the term 'revolution' does not bear the same meaning as is in vogue, particularly in Marxist circles. What Ambedkar seems to detest in revolution is the violence. At many places he tends to equate rebellion, revolution and revolt with violence. He also seems to disagree with the method of insurrection. He thought that without mass consciousness being ripe enough for revolutionary change, insurrectionary methods would not succeed.

Moreover, he appears to be sceptical of the justness of revolutions as they invariably represent the triumph of the collective over the individual. It may be attributed to the influence of liberal democracy in which he got his indoctrination in his formative days. Liberal democracy always put an individual on a high pedestal and considered it precious. His concern for the individual is not again doctrinaire but emanates from the value that any and every human being is precious and the belief that alone can act as the best guarantee against the collective tyranny and totalitarian excesses any time. In the context of the collapse of erstwhile Soviet block, where the totalitarian states that came into being in the name of dictatorship of proletariat and played havoc with people, this human-centric value assumes importance. One needs to be however reminded that even the values do need to have some material bases. They do not fall from sky. The contradiction between collective and individual has thus to be resolved in the concrete situation. As for Ambedkar, apart from this scepticism, he does not seem to have any dispute with the general aim and object of revolution.

Revolution, inasmuch as it seeks to bring about a fundamental change in the social relations in the society, will always be opposed by the forces of status quo, whose material interests are directly threatened by this change. In corollary, it becomes imperative for the forces of revolution to overcome this resistance whatever be the means. Whereas, the antagonist camp will always project codes of ethics and morality for their tactical defence in face of the onslaught of revolution, the revolutionaries discard them as decadent; for them revolution itself represents the highest value. Being the upsurge of the suppressed ones, revolutions do have a tendency to be bloody, but it is always in response to the resistance of its opponents.

Therefore it is a representation only by the vested interest to associate violence or moral turpitude with revolutions. On the contrary, it would be more logical to say about the revolutionaries that being propelled by an external motivation to deliver mankind from the existing traps at the risk of their own lives; they cannot be bloodthirsty people. The revolutionary violence is almost an inevitability that arises at the instance of the oppressors.

In that sense Marx called "violence as the midwife of history", emphasising its inevitability. It is the inevitability that marks the compulsion of the vast majority of people to resist the antirevolutionary violence of the minority. The prerequisite here is that the revolution truly represents the majority consciousness. If it does not, then the violence of the few exercised with howsoever a lofty objective could transform into its antithesis, fortifying itself against the majority will. In this sense and insofar as the recent history showed the scepticism that revolutions trample upon individual's rights therefore cannot be dismissed as baseless.

Historically, revolution is the process of identifying and destroying the obstacles in the existing order to take productive forces to the qualitatively next higher level, for the overall progress of human race. The progress achieved by mankind so far is basically due to the qualitative transformation from quantitative continuum that characterises revolutions. The qualitative transformations always need concentrated inputs, akin to latent heat in the case of phase transformation of water. In social transformation it takes the form of revolutionary energy that in turn may manifest into violence. Ambedkar does not neglect the necessity of violence. As he himself said that if dalits wanted to be effective they would need the canons.

It is erroneous to construe that his opposition to violence was idealistic or doctrinaire. Violence was not a taboo for him; it could be practised when it was absolutely necessary. Even his mentor Buddha, who is respected as the greatest apostle of non-violence had the same pragmatic approach towards violence. Ambedkar was not obsessed either with the idea of non-violence or the value of individualism professed by the classical school of liberal democracy. His reservations were against the possibility of the cunning of a few overriding the will of majority as had happened in the case of caste institution. He would hate to see any thing like caste getting institutionalised again. In his scheme of things he therefore was not ready to compromise the value of democracy, the will of majority of people, whatever may be the end.

Ambedkar did not juxtapose reform against revolution, as many people tend to do. He does not reflect comprehension of technicality of dialectical materialism in his usage of these terms. Often his revolution is the violent overthrow of the existing rule and establishment of the new rule. Likewise, he does not seem to mean that reforms will not entail a qualitative transformation. What he certainly means by revolution is the change brought about in a 'big bang' manner. Notwithstanding what Ambedkar said about his own work, revolution does not always entail a 'big bang'; it is not a point concept as mistakenly regarded in common parlance, but a line concept. Mao's Great Proletarian Cultural Revolution may be a good example of this.

There could be many bits of work, which contributes to taking society to a qualitatively higher rung in the ladder of progress that qualify to be the revolutionary work. The qualitative change itself occurs over a discrete time horizon and not a moment. The moment that marks out transformation of power and looks like a 'big bang', alone is not the revolution. The particular phase of history puts constraints on the kind of changes that can be conceived in its womb. Some one dreaming of a socialist revolution in the slave society would only at best be a daydreamer; a romanticist but he cannot be a revolutionary. Likewise, certain phase of history demands a lot of quantitative preparation before a revolutionary change can be planned for. Ambedkar largely reflects these kinds of concerns while dealing with the issue of revolution. He did not see Indian situation ripe enough for any revolutionary change. Any change without resolution of the caste question, according to him, would not only be detrimental to dalits but also be an extremely short-lived.

The importance of Ambedkar's work can be gauged in relation to contemporary social situation and its transitional social context. Indian society was ridden with a peculiar brand of feudalism, the most prominent feature of which was caste. Caste had incapacitated over 15 per cent of its population and maintained them at the subhuman level. The large part of the balance population also suffered the degradation in a varying degree. This decadent institution had far outlived its minimal utility and as a result for centuries kept Indian society in a fossilised form. It served the material needs of a handful of people but all perceived varying stakes in the system on account of its hierarchical structure and faithfully practised it because they internalised it as their *Dharma* ordained by none other than God.

The possible exception in generic terms were dalits who were placed at the lowest rung of the caste ladder and had hardly anything to their share. However, in particular terms only a few castes from the Dalit castes, who did not have any specific caste profession and hence little stake in the system and consequently who as the general workmen of villages had better exposure to the changing urban life than any one else came out of the hegemony of Brahmins to articulate the challenge to the system. The hierarchy among dalits however prevented them to come together and consequently this challenge had to be articulated caste by caste. Capitalism that took root in India in big cities also had struck compromise with the caste institution like its harbingers, the British imperialism. It was an arduous task, as it still is, to conceive a model for this struggle and still more difficult to build.

During the colonial times for various reasons these struggles had germinated largely in Maharashtra and Southern states where the social structure reflected sharper polarisation between dalits and balance society. Ambedkar's advent in the Indian sociopolitical scene marked their zenith. It articulated its attack on Brahminism and capitalism that accepted its alliance, focused its organisation on dalits and gave a clarion call for annihilation of castes for achieving the ultimate aim of society based on Liberty, Equality and Fraternity to provide wider umbrella for all progressive forces to work. It reflects the distinct historical need to democratise Indian society without which it was bound to suffer constriction of its productive forces. This work had to have large content in the sociocultural realm; it is a credit to Ambedkar's acumen that he gave it a political dimension.

It had to be approached as reform. Ambedkar clearly found the talks of communist revolution as out of phase with the history although he never fully accepted the tenets of historical materialism as he thought it negatived human ingenuity and carried it through a predetermined channel. He insisted that India did not provide congenial soil for germination of class-consciousness because of castes. Their annihilation therefore constituted the first task in the revolutionary agenda. It is unfortunate that many communist revolutionaries still parrot the same characterisation of his work as in years back their predecessors proclaimed using the spoon fed theories from the West. One day it is hoped that the contributions of all the caste struggles to democratisation of Indian society would be restored as a native revolutionary heritage by these well meaning people. Till then it will always sound puerile to pigeonhole the historical work as reform or revolution merely on the basis of syntax and not the content. However, it is much more unfortunate for Ambedkarite dalits to deny themselves the credit for this historical contributions by dissociating from the revolutionary agenda, mistakenly thinking that it something alien to them. Effectively, not only they are denying themselves a historical opportunity to contribute to revolution but also delaying their own emancipation.

Dalits have to rethink their position vis a vis revolution. Ambedkar's dream of a society based on liberty, equality and fraternity cannot be realised except through revolution. They will have to understand Ambedkar's life and mission only from this perspective. His contribution to Indian revolution lies in the fact that he tried to comprehend Indian reality independently and tried to contribute to the resolution of its contradictions in his own way. Indian history held out the gauntlet of fossilised Indian feudalism for so long to the Indian revolutionaries but every one conveniently wished it away, initially as a superstructural matter that would disappear automatically when the material base is revolutionised and now after seven decades as a problem belonging to both structure and superstructure, that could be solved through revolutionary practice. It still lacks the clarity and courage to hold the bull by horn.

Ambedkar did not confuse issues, he saw clearly that the annihilation of caste will have to be consciously worked for before taking up any revolutionary project. He went beyond and found out the institutional base of castes in the Indian village whose economic support lay in the land-relations and caste division of labour. But, unlike many communists who still use the stereotype of land reform—a slogan of land to the tiller as the only revolutionary programme, he did not hamper on it because he knew that firstly it was economically impossible to satisfy the land hunger of the landless in the country, secondly the likely transformation of landless to a marginal farmer through land reforms was unlikely to solve the problems of dalits and thirdly, as the later empirical data showed, contrary to expectations the land reforms could aggravate the problem of caste. Instead, he proposed nationalisation of land and co-operativisation of farming. He realised the necessity of detaching substantial village population from land and absorbing it into the industrial sector that was to be mainly under State sector. Even in retrospect, these points could have constituted a viable agenda for democratic revolution. As one naxalite scholar—(Ashok Kumar, 1995) perceptively puts it, for having independently seen the question of annihilation of castes linked with the question of land one could unhesitatingly call Ambedkar as the torchbearer of the people's democratic revolution.

'Ambedkar' as Thinker

Dalits are never tired of projecting Ambedkar as the greatest of all the leaders. That unfortunately smacks of sectarian attitude and of their blind devotion to him. They need to understand that the measure of greatness of any person could only be her / his contribution to better the human situation, in terms of correct understanding of its ailment and contribution to cure it. What Ambedkar did could be seen in relation to the broad five currents in Indian politics of his times:

- The Reformists current that wanted to bring about development on the western pattern, possibly with the support of British imperialism,
- Congress, that represented Indian capital and which demanded self-rule under the domination of British imperialism,
- The Terrorist Nationalists who had taken up arms in their fight for freedom against British imperialism,
- The Communists who were trying to implant Bolshevik revolution in India, and
- The Muslim League which opened up a separatist front of Muslims.

All of them scarcely reflected an understanding of the Indian situation. For instance, none showed even a cursory concern about the problems of one fourth of their countrymen who were forced to live worse than animals as ordained by their decadent religion. It was indeed surprising that although all craved for self-rule from the British, none concerned with the caste-system which basically was responsible in pushing the country repeatedly into slavery. None seemed to attempt an objective analysis of either the history or the present of this country. It could circumstantially be said that their motivations came from their narrow class-caste interests. These movements were motivated by the desire of an abstract freedom for country and a refusal to see the concrete slavery of their own people. Granted that the problems before the country were really intricate, still no one would dare say that the need for democratisation was in anyway subordinate.

The real people's movement in the country was required to wage simultaneous war against imperialism, internal compradore bourgeoisie, landlords and Brahminism. It was only Ambedkar who clearly indicated this requirement. In this light, he was certainly ahead of all others. His own bitter experiences with untouchability had stood him in good stead in seeing this more clearly than any other. He strove to build his movement along this understanding but unfortunately it was neither in his power to deal comprehensively with all the issues, nor was there an ideological and programmatic clarity required therefore.

He inevitably had to focus his attention on dalits who were the worst victims of this multifaceted oppression. It was the misfortune of Indian history that this struggle progressed in a constricted manner and eventually got dissolved into regressive statist politics. It reflected both the limitation of Ambedkar as well the situational compulsion on him.

The anti-caste movements before Ambedkar were mainly welfare oriented. Some wanted a higher rank for their own caste in the caste hierarchy and some taking the inferior culture of their caste to be the reason for their suffering, aimed at improving the same. Mahatma Phuley's movement was an exception to this trend insofar as it attempted to unite the Sudra and Ati-Sudra castes against the exploitation by the parasitic castes of Shetjis (capitalists) and Bhatjis (priests). While Ambedkar accepted the lineage/inheritance of this movement and held Phuley in greatest esteem as his one of the three *Gurus*, he went beyond to declare annihilation of caste to be the object of his movement in the direction of the goal of 'liberty, equality and fraternity'. In the historical context it certainly was a radical step. He rightly diagnosed that the caste system is basically sustained by the peculiar economic constitution of the Indian village of which the land relations were the main features. Towards breaking this link he toyed with an idea of separate settlement for dalits at one time and at another exhorted them to leave villages for cities.

He had clearly understood that castes stood on multiple props, *viz.*, the religio-cultural relations, feudal relations in village setting of which land relations constituted the crux and the sociopolitical nexus with the State. Annihilation of castes thus needed destruction of all of them. He soon realised the necessity of political power for this multi-fronged attack. Even to bring about the residual change in the belief system either through the cultural or religious route, he stressed the necessity of political power. In this way, for the first time he brought the problem of untouchability and caste out of the confines of culture to the political agenda.

Unfortunately, this political agenda got lost into the maze of parliamentary politics that soon became be-all-end-all with Dalit leaders. Even during Ambedkar's times the economic aspects of the problem remained largely untouched giving the impression to his followers as though they did not count. In the overall context it can be seen that they could not be as easily dealt with as the religio-cultural and political aspects of the problem. Moreover, it meant direct confrontation with the State for which Ambedkar was certainly not prepared. Alternately, the feudal relations in villages could be destroyed only if the private ownership of land is abolished and co-operativisation of farming is introduced. He thought, this structural change could be effected through the Constitution. It was a folly that he would soon realise when even as the 'chief architect' of the Constitution he failed so much as to bring this point on the agenda of the Constituent Assembly.

Conception of an Ideal

Babasaheb Ambedkar envisioned his ideal in the famous three principles: liberty, equality and fraternity. They were the basis for the ideal society of his conception. He denied that he had adopted them from the French Revolution. He said he had derived them from the teachings of Buddha. These principles were the clarion call of the French Revolution but later became the ideological props of the liberal bourgeoisie in Europe. Since Marx had ridiculed these principles as the fantasy of the bourgeois society, many people tended to stereotype Ambedkar as the petty-bourgeois liberal democrat. As according to Ambedkar the source of these principles is different from the French Revolution, familiar to Marx, there is a prima facie scope to argue that Marx's ridicule does not apply to him. His conception of these principles is indeed substantially different from that associated with the liberal bourgeoisie. Actually, what Marx refers to are the slogans of liberty and equality of the bourgeois parliamentary democracy.

There, 'liberty' is the liberty to contract and 'equality' refers to equality in market. Ambedkar insists that the conception of the ideal society ought to have them all the three together. Absence of any would not be acceptable to him. The ideal society of his dream could only be seen within a kind of spiritual frame. It would be interesting to compare this society with the communist society of Marx's conception. Marx reached his inference following the dialectical track of historical materialism. In Ambedkar' case it was just his vision. Inevitably, he had to attribute the origin of them to some spiritual source.

For Ambedkar they meant to denote the State of society sans exploitation and with an emotive ambience of fellow feeling. It was beyond him to describe this State further in concrete terms and much so to indicate the forms of struggle to reach it. Known for his obsession with pragmatism and belief that any definitive laws could not bind the flow of human history, he would avoid the speculative construction of this distant stage of human society.

Not even Marx could describe what his dream communist society would be like beyond that it would be freed of the familiar contradictions. It essentially reflected a contradiction between human desire and material reality. It would be disaster to derive the meaning of this ideal State of Ambedkar's conception from what he did. He left that to posterity to decide as per their circumstances. But, rationally there could be little doubt that the vision of Ambedkar can only be realised in the communist society of Marx's conception where most (not all) of the contradictions in human society would have been resolved.

Dalits ought to internalise this vision and strive for its realisation. Ambedkar had a radical enough interpretation of his principles of liberty, equality and fraternity so as to feel inadequacy even in Marxism. He said that Marxism supported only equality. He was in need of a body of thought that would give equal importance to all these three principles. He met it with a convenient conceptualisation of religion. It is paradoxical that a person who is rational enough not to bind the posterity with his vision volitionally binds himself with what is said more than 25 centuries before.

It is natural to find ideals better articulated in spiritual spheres but it is equally true that these dream worlds are incapable to provide any clue for their realisation on the earth except for their pet prescription to ignore the material reality and imagine it happened in the mind. They run away from the fact that the evil humans suffer from are the attributes of the divisions in human society, and their abolition essentially calls for struggles by the sufferers against those who perpetrate sufferings. Howsoever, inherently rational the religion may be or radical its interpretation may be it cannot fully escape these limitations.

It can be seen in relation to Buddhism handed down by Babasaheb Ambedkar with his radical interpretation. Notwithstanding the familiar quibbling around the Dhamma and Dhamma among dalits, what remained of Buddhism with them is what would happen to any religion. It is a different question whether Marxism embodied Ambedkar's ideals or not but it is certain that they are neither realisable neither through any kind of constitutional acrobatics nor through any religious practice.

State

Ambedkar's conception of State reflects some amount of autonomy from the hegemony of the ruling classes. It is why he expected it to act as per the constitutional structure and endeavoured to incorporate the pro-Dalit bias into the Constitution. He must have realised the true nature of it, the boundaries of the autonomy and basic class bias of the State, when he actually reached not only the Constituent Assembly but also became the chairman of its Drafting Committee.

In his anxiety to secure some provisions in favour of dalits, he accepted to be the 'hack' to write what was acceptable to the ruling caste-class representatives. He must have thought that within the given constraints he had done a good job of making the Constitution responsive to the needs of the downtrodden people. Indeed, many of the provisions in the directive principles and elsewhere apparently bear clear imprint of his zeal and owe their existence to him. But, even they had to be within the strategic space provided by the rulers.

His realisation of the folly was near complete when he had to burst out in utter dejection at its ineffectual implementation, that he would be the first man to burn the Constitution as it was of no good to any one. He was inaccurate, as the Constitution had proved good enough to the upper caste-class combine who had hegemonised complete political space in post-1947 India. He attributed it to the 'devils' in the Congressmen who had occupied the constitutional 'temple' he and others had built.

Ambedkar could not reach the point of understanding that the State is a mere instrument in the hands of the ruling classes to coerce the ruled ones into submission to their interests. Until the downtrodden themselves become the ruling class, they cannot expect the State to do good to them. Whatever good that appears to come to their share, in ultimate balance accrues to the other side in multiple measure.

The post-1947 State, which has never tired of propagandising its concern for dalits and poor, has in fact been singularly instrumental in aggravating the caste problem with its policies. Even the apparently progressive policies in the form of Land Ceiling Act, Green Revolution, Programme of Removal of Poverty, Reservations to Dalits in Services and Mandal Commission etc. have resulted against their professed objectives. The effect of the Land Ceiling Act, has been in creating a layer of the middle castes farmers which could be consolidated in caste terms to constitute a formidable constituency. In its new incarnation, this group that has traditionally been the immediate upper caste layer to dalits, assumed virtual custody of Brahminism in order to coerce Dalit landless labourers to serve their socioeconomic interests and suppress their assertive expression in the bud. The Green Revolution was the main instrument to introduce capitalisation in agrarian sector. It reinforced the innate hunger of the landlords and big farmers for land as this State sponsored revolution produced huge surplus for them. It resulted in creating geographical imbalance and promoting unequal terms of trade in favour of urban areas. Its resultant impact on dalits has been far more excruciating than that of the Land Ceiling Act. The much publicised programme for Removal of Poverty has aggravated the gap between the heightened hopes and aspirations of dalits on one hand and the feelings of depravation among the poorer sections of non-dalits in the context of the special programmes especially launched for upliftment of dalits. The tension that ensued culminated in increasingly strengthening the caste—based demands and further aggravating the caste-divide.

The reservations in services for dalits, notwithstanding its benefits, have caused incalculable damage in political terms. Reservations created hope, notional stake in the system and thus dampened the alienation; those who availed of its benefit got politically emasculated and in course consciously or unconsciously served as the props of the system. The context of scarcity of jobs provided ample opportunity to reactionary forces to divide the youth along caste lines. Mandal Commission, that enthused many progressive parties and people to upheld its extension of reservation to the backward castes, has greatly contributed to strengthen the caste identities of people. Inasmuch as it empowers the backward castes, actually their richer sections, it is bound to worsen the relative standing of dalits in villages. Thus, the State, its welfare mask notwithstanding, has viciously and consistently acted against dalits and poor people. It is a complete contra-evidence to hopes of Ambedkar who strove to maximise and make use of the autonomous space of the State for the benefits of the have-nots, particularly dalits. It is one thing to assume autonomous space but quite another to equate it with caste-class neutrality. Unfortunately, the Dalit political behaviour always reflected this erroneous notion of caste-class neutrality of the State. It has already caused great damage to the Dalit interests. The radical Ambedkar might have strategy to use State for Dalit cause but would never see it as caste-class neutral.

Socialism

Despite his ambivalence and reservations about the emphasis on the economic dimension in socialism, Ambedkar broadly remained a socialist. Some scholars do find little scope for suspecting his socialist credentials because of his disapproval of Russell's criticism of property, his non-acceptance of Marxian formulations and his placement of social issues higher than the economic and political issues. He called the complaint against love of money as 'philosophy of sour grapes' and ridiculed materialism as 'the ideology of pigs'. This impression is moreover strengthened by his reservations to accept the economic interpretation of history. But, in all fairness it may be said that what he appears to mean is the integrative consideration of all the factors that are needed for any society to be based on liberty, equality and fraternity. Notwithstanding his variant conception, there should not be any doubt about his socialistic antecedents.

His conception of socialism also underwent evolution. Once he had stated that there was hardly any difference between his socialism and communism. As such, his disagreement with the communists was about the means and not about the aim. He warns the communists that the classless society can emerge only after the emergence of a casteless society. It implies that his quarrel with the then communists was over the stages of revolution. In the 1920s and 30s, these people had borrowed the communist dogma and parroted class struggle in utter disregard of the reality.

Ambedkar, on the contrary, was firmly rooted in it. They believed that the soviet Russian model of revolution was importable for bringing about a socialist revolution into India whereas Ambedkar realistically postulated that unless the consciousness of the working class was congenial for revolution, there was no question of it materializing. And, unless the caste system is destroyed, creation of the pro-revolution consciousness was out of question. His annoyance with the Bombay communists was largely because of their dogmatic behaviour. It is unfortunate that the ideal of classlessness that was latent in his agenda never really surfaced during his lifetime.

Ambedkar relies on the concept of 'State' for materialisation of his conception of socialism. His conception of State is largely idealist. He wanted the State to intervene in the economic structure and its monitoring. He wanted to constitutionalise this State intervention so that it would not be subject to change any time with the whims of simple majority vote in the legislation. Ambedkar who taught, "The lost rights cannot be regained by making appeals or requests to the robbers; it needs struggles"; did not say anything on how the oppressed people will get such strength as to create the constitutional provisions, that would put the class structure upside down. On behalf of his party—Scheduled Caste Federation, he had submitted a draft for the future constitution to the Constituent Assembly for the independent India. It was published later as "States and Minorities". This book has really aided students in understanding some aspects of his conception of socialism.

Nevertheless, one cannot afford to forget the constraints placed by the context in which it was written. The context was that he had failed to get into the Constituent Assembly and was therefore anxious to strike a feasible and still radical note that could find the support of the vast majority of the have-nots which might then create some pressure either for its inclusion in the Constitution or for his entry into the Constituent Assembly. For some years, during the preceding turbulence of negotiations for transfer of power, he found himself totally marginalised. Notwithstanding the probable limitations of this draft, its provisions in operational terms were still very radical. The main provisions are:

- All important industries and services shall belong to the nation.
- Insurance industry shall be in public sector and insurance will be compulsory for every citizen.
- Private sector and entrepreneurs shall have a role in the economy but it shall not be dominating.
- Nationalisation of land and promotion of cooperative farming on a collective principle.

These provisions, if implemented, would have gone a long way towards supporting democratic revolution in the country. It would have limited inequality and exploitation in the economic and political sphere. Politically, it would have had far-reaching impact.

Ambedkar till the end could not completely remove the Fabian influence (which he might have gathered while in England) on him. In his times, particularly before World War II, few people in India were well versed in Marxist philosophy. The knowledge of Marxism seldom exceeded some broad principles and 'Stalin's dictatorship' painted by imperialists or the 'revolt of the workers, the insurgency of the poor. Ambedkar also does not seem to have gone very far from this point. Without indulging into the debate of ifs and buts, there should not be any iota of doubt that the ideal society of his conception could materialise only through socialism.

Democracy

Ambedkar had unshakeable faith in democracy. In his conception of an exploitation-less society, democracy has an extraordinary role. Democracy means 'one person, one vote'; and 'one vote, one value'. Democracy means empowerment of any person for participating in the process of decision-making relating to her/him, democracy means liberty, equality and fraternity—Ambedkar's definition of democracy had such a tone. Because he presided over making of the Constitution and is being projected as its chief architect, there is a misunderstanding that parliamentary democracy is what he wanted. But nothing could be farther from the truth than this. He himself spoke against parliamentary democracy. For instance, he defined parliamentary democracy as "voting by the people in favour of their owners and handing over the rights of ruling over themselves". This provides a glimpse of the expanse of his ideal, which certainly was much beyond the Indian Constitution or any common place understanding about him.

His conception of democracy appears to be purely people oriented. He showed that the bookish concepts of equality are detrimental to the disabled sections of society in the prevailing social setting and proposed a fundamental change in the concept of equality. It envisaged complete abolition of inequality. His principle of positive discrimination is based on this very concept of equality. But the operational aspects of this concept involved the need for some kind of autonomous institution, which was met by 'State' and 'religion'. It is necessary to stress that his greatness lies in the radicality of his conceptions, his vision of a human society sans any kind of exploitation; not in the remedies or apparatus he proposed in the circumstances prevailing in his time.

Aspects of the Strategy and Tactics

In the context of strategy, some of Ambedkar's contributions are really noteworthy. He brought the struggle against Brahminism into the political battlefield. He inferred that without political power the social and religious structures will collapse and motivated his followers to capture political power. But his conception of political power being acutely constrained by the parliamentary framework where bargaining is the predominant medium of securing political power, inevitably it made way for all kinds of aberrations and perversities to creep in. The prevailing politics being the game of possibilities, he was soon sucked into its vortex. Politics came to dominate the other aspects of his personality. Slowly, the impact of politics started becoming visible everywhere. This phase significantly contributed to multiplication of his inconsistencies out of tactical imperatives. Dalits have taken this legacy of parliamentary politics very seriously, almost as the be all and end all of their political being. It may be, interesting to probe how much damage this kind of political orientation inflicted on the Dalit movement.

It is altogether a different question whether Ambedkar had any other alternative to parliamentary politics for political practice. It may be argued that in the context of his resources, adversarial environment and to some extent his personal limitations, he had none. Even if it is taken as correct, it should not be forgotten that it was a matter of strategy and tactic that presuppose contextual variables: it cannot be taken as the lasting value.

The fundamental source of most of Ambedkar's political thoughts and action is his conception of State and religion, that he had adopted as the extraneous instruments to reconcile the state of flux of things and the necessity of order in them. It is necessary to understand that both, the State as well as religion, are the products of the evolutionary process of the human society. There is nothing inevitable about them. Marx took State as the instrument of coercion in the hands of ruling classes and religion as the opium of the masses. Dalits have a long experience of nearly five decades with the so-called welfare State of Ambedkar's design. What does it say? Does the State side with them in their conflict with the landlords? Does it come to their rescue when every day three or four of their daughters are raped?

Does it come to save the shame of their women when they are paraded naked in the streets? Does it take their side when they come in conflict with landlords, moneylenders in villages or with management in the modern settings? Does it really ensure they get their dues as provided in the Constitution or punish the defaulting management for noncompliance? To all of such questions the answer could only be in the negative. It is not a matter of 'devils occupying the temples' as Ambedkar lamented seeing the people occupying the Constitutional positions. The State possesses the characteristics of its master class. In India the upper caste capitalists, landlords, top bureaucrats, etc. being the ruling class, the State can never have saints who would favour dalits. It is a fact that even the government by a Dalit party like the BSP could not transform it into a Dalit State.

Religion, in Ambedkar's conception is necessary to maintain the moral order of the society. It may be interesting to examine to what extent it conforms to this idealistic expectation. Buddhism, which undoubtedly is the most rational of all the religions, does not have any evidence of having created over its near millennium long tenure in India such an order of the society which could claim liberty, equality and fraternity of Ambedkar's conception. Ambedkar's argument that the Bhikku Sangha in Buddhism was the prototype of this kind of society becomes invalid once we call into question the role of Sangha in the production process.

Before that, the order that envisaged nostalgically to recreate the value of the vanishing *Gana Rajya* in microcosm against the evil of rising monarchies, cannot just sublimate to the era of capitalism without being an alley of exploiters unless it transforms itself in some way as a catalyst for the revolution. The moral tenets of Buddhism likewise cannot submerge the lure of surplus extraction, that is its dominating ethos. If at all, it may help it become more pronounced by weakening the resistance of the exploited masses. As we empirically see, the Buddhism of his conception could not produce even a trace of morality in its adherents. On the contrary, for the masses it presents the distorted, if not inverted, worldview; it orients them to look inwards for their misery and be blind to the reality that some one exploits him. He could certainly derive mental peace and pleasure but it is a state of an intoxicated mind. Keeping in mind the causal links in Ambedkar's adoption of these instruments, the redefinition project needs to address these issues afresh.

The strategy of the ruling class always stresses on diversion of peoples' attention from their real problems and their disarmament—both in physical and ideological terms. They invariably have a multilayered strategy in place for this purpose. The vanguard parties of the ruling classes open up sentimental fronts and attempt to divert the attention of people as their real problems get aggravated. Secondly, their time-tested methods of adulterating radical ideas with the masses are always in operation. Towards this end, we see all the ruling parties vying with each other in co-opting Ambedkar. 'Ambedkar' represents a potentially dangerous ideological weapon in the hands of the Indian proletariat and so the ruling class will be hell bent on blunting its edge. They will do everything to eulogise him not only for wooing dalits for their immediate electoral gains but also to neutralise him as the radical ideological force by propagandising a distorted version of the latter. Dalits will have to exercise vigil over their ideological assets even after redefining Ambedkar.

Conclusion

For at least over last four decades Dalits have devotedly followed Ambedkar as their ideal, as a virtual God and zealously practised, as they claim, his teachings. Their social being could be seen to be totally imbued with what they call Ambedkarism—the veritable science of their emancipation. If it is true, and no one would deny it is not, it should be pertinent to ask why despite this flawless following of Ambedkar they continue to be in a pathetic state in every sense. Barring a handful dalits in the government and public sector services and of course politicians, they continue to occupy the lowest rung in the social as well as economic hierarchy of Indian society. Their politics, notwithstanding the media hype, gauged by the measure of general empowerment, continues to be in shambles. Over these decades, their relative situation either shows stagnation or decline. The insinuation to relate this State with their faith in Ambedkar itself would be distasteful for many dalits. But, it is vital for ones that are committed to their liberation to squarely face the facts and dispassionately find out where the rot lay.

Generally, beyond the first burst of anger in reaction to this question, one would face the defensive arguments to discount this relationship. Typically, they tend to attribute their miserable situation to the lack of competent leadership after Babasaheb Ambedkar, to the educated dalits who they think have become Dalit Brahmins and have deserted the community; and sometimes to the people themselves for their extreme self-centredness. Sometimes, the finger is raised at the high caste hegemony that has neutralised the impact of the Constitution that Ambedkar created. Some, particularly the leadership, even would dismiss the basic premise itself that there is something wrong with the Dalit movement. They might even go so far as to claim net achievements indicating the prosperity of themselves or some others of their like. More sober may argue that what is seen is the transition state. Conceding them all some amount of validity even would not erase the stark fact that the general situation of the vast majority of Dalit masses remains still alarmingly pathetic. Externalisation of the reasons for this state has not helped dalits wee bit. The time has come for dalits to self-critically see whether anything was wrong with their ideology and / or with their practice thereof.

Reviewing the post-Ambedkar Dalit movement at some significant milestones, one finds a queer underscoring behaviour, believed to be in accordance with the teachings of Babasaheb Ambedkar, that is certainly incongruent with the essence of what he taught. This dichotomy between the essential Ambedkar and the 'Ambedkar' in the faith of Dalit masses—the icon of Ambedkar, comes out as the problematic in this review. In relation to almost every aspect of his teaching there emerged an icon that represented varying amount of distortion.

Insofar as they constituted the ideology that gripped the masses, these icons can be seen to be at the root of the Dalit pathos. Among the myriad sources for these icons, Ambedkar himself might come out as the major source. Because, even a myth can not sustain for long without some material base. The icons of Ambedkar thus could be linked to some such bases, howsoever tenuous, within his own life. The rationalist in Ambedkar never hesitated to change his opinions and behaviour if the facts so warranted. They appear to be inconsistencies to the ones who see it sans context.

His distance from the focus of control in his sociopolitical environment, the vastly varying target audience (ranging from the Englishmen to the illiterate dalits) to whom he had to communicate, the exigency to respond to the dynamics of communities set in motion by the pre-independence politics, his anxiety to accomplish as many gains for dalits as he could in his life time, the exigencies for 'short' actions at the expense of 'long' vision inevitably led to mark patterns that could support array of behaviours. The first to take advantage of it were his own lieutenants for serving their personal ambitions that set the trends of distortion of Ambedkar in the minds of gullible Dalit masses.

The ruling classes that always look for the grounds to divide masses had severally reinforced this distortion and accelerated fragmentation of dalits in every field. They, along with willing collaboration of Dalit politicians and emerging elite, promoted and sustained the particular icons of Ambedkar that would prevent political coalescence of dalits and suck them into the vortex of parliamentary politics in order to bring the establishment much needed legitimacy. Dalits failed to note this cunning and let themselves flow in the currents of confusion the ruling classes deliberately created. Today, with increasing political crises the ruling classes seem vying with each other in co-opting Ambedkar, as though that may be their last chance of survival. If dalits stood their grounds well, that might have proved to be their last act.

But, unfortunately dalits are giving them new leases of life by blinding themselves to the reality. Not only that they have not resisted these ruling class machinations but on the contrary they are curiously seen to swell the cadres of these castiest, communalist and anti-poor groups and parties. These parties who openly profess the ideology of Hindu revivalism and represent all that is decadent in Indian tradition show the temerity to project Ambedkar among their ideologies. Apart from the reasons of security that propel Dalit youth into their fold, the compradore behaviour of Dalit elite certainly has influenced the phenomenon. What is common in all the attempts by the ruling classes is to sap 'Ambedkar' of its rebellious content.

It is advantageous for them to show that he was the chief architect of the Indian Constitution, committed to parliamentary democracy and opposed to any ideology that propagates violence or revolution. He is projected to favour gradual change implying that dalits should patiently wait and strive persuasively to better their own lives. He is projected as the Bodhisatva that inspires *nirvana*—the State of total detachment from worldly matters. All these images have caused significant damage to the emancipatory struggles of dalits.

Some of these images might be the purposeful and blatant disfiguring of Ambedkar but some of them represent genuine dilemma arising from Ambedkar's own stands on various issues. From the viewpoint of the comprehensive pro-people change in the present historical phase a democratic revolution is an imperative. The motive force for this revolution ought to sprout from dalits. The history provides a strong testimony that any radical movement in the country could be sustained by dalits and tribals at its base. Ambedkar as a symbol for Dalit aspirations holds a key to the barrage that has so far bound the revolutionary upsurge in India below the alarming levels. If one concedes that Ambedkar's framework is going to haunt revolutionary commitment till the Indian Democratic Revolution actually happens and that Ambedkar represents the ideological weaponry in the hands of dalits who along with other oppressed people are going to be the axis of this revolution, then one would clearly see the need to redefine Ambedkar in radical terms commensurate with this purpose.

Many aspects of confusion with regard to the facts could be cleared with rational interpretation of his thoughts. But much might need the logical extrapolation of his basic thinking which for some reason appears to have settled in erroneous forms. As he himself showed the way in the case of his redefinition of Buddha's Dhamma, dalits will have to undertake this task, for giving themselves a powerful ideology. Their future as a social group almost hinges on this task. There are enough clues left behind by Ambedkar himself that point to this need. There is no doubt that he was frustrated at the end of his life seeing the undesired aftermath of his lifelong struggle. He had to lament over the betrayal of the educated dalits in whom he had seen the crusaders of his mission. He had to weep with remorse that he could not do anything for his people in the villages. He had to disown the Constitution for working on which he had cut short his life at least by a few years. He had to swallow the frustration of not being able to pilot the Constitution of his conception (States and Minorities). He had to regret the anti-people State that emerged in republican India. He obviously lacked the analytical tools to see through the reasons for these happenings. His excessive religiosity and spirituality at the fag end of his life perhaps could be taken as the manifestation of this frustration.

The social engineer could only be busy with problems; he is unlikely to come to grip with the design defects in the system. Almost every thing that Ambedkar pinned his hopes on can be found today in antithetical shambles. His educational society, his vision of Buddhism, the political party of his conception, the social reforms could be some of the examples. These tragic aftermaths also would denote the necessity of a critical review of Ambedkar's thoughts if they were to be used as the ideology to further the Dalit movement towards its logical end. If this process is sincerely followed, there cannot be any doubt that this 'redefined Ambedkar' would be a revolutionary icon, organically linking the Dalit struggle to the revolutionary struggle in the world. It will truly globalize the Dalit struggle.

Political Career

Between 1941 and 1945, he published a large number of highly controversial books and pamphlets, including *Thoughts on Pakistan*, in which he criticized the Muslim League's demand for a separate Muslims state of Pakistan. With *What Congress and Gandhi have Done to the Untouchables*, Ambedkar intensified his attacks on Gandhi and the Congress, charging them with hypocrisy. In his work *Who were the Sudras?*, Ambedkar attempted to explain the formation of the Sudras *i.e.* the lowest caste in hierarchy of Hindu caste system. He also emphasised that how Sudras are separate from Untouchables. Ambedkar oversaw the transition of his political party into the All India Scheduled Castes Federation, although it performed poorly in the elections held in 1946 for the Constituent Assembly of India. In writing a sequel to *Who were the Sudras?* in 1948, Ambedkar lambasted Hinduism in the *The Untouchables: a Thesis on the Origins of Untouchability*:

> *Ambedkar was also critical of Islam and its practices in South Asia. While justifying the Partition of India, he condemned practices of Child-Marriage in Muslim society, as well as the mistreatment of women. He also condemned the Caste practices carried out by Muslims in South Asia. He was also critical of slavery in Muslim communities. He said:*
>
> *"No words can adequately express the great and many evils of polygamy and concubinage, and especially as a source of misery to a Muslim woman." "Take the caste system. Everybody infers that Islam must be free from slavery and caste. While slavery existed, much of its support was derived from Islam and Islamic countries. While the prescriptions by the Prophet regarding the just and humane treatment of slaves contained in the Koran are praiseworthy, there is nothing whatever in Islam that lends support to the abolition of this curse. But if slavery has gone, caste among Musalmans has remained."*

He wrote that Muslim Society is "even more full of social evils than Hindu Society is" and criticized Muslims for sugar-coating their sectarian Caste System with euphemisms like "brotherhood". He also criticized the discrimination against the Arzal classes among Muslims who were regarded as "degraded", as well as the oppression of women in Muslim society through the oppressive *purdah* system. He alleged that while Purdah was also practised among Hindus, only in Muslims was it sanctioned by religion. He criticized their fanaticism to Islam on the grounds that their literalist interpretations of Islamic doctrine made their society very rigid and impermeable to change. He further wrote that Indian Muslims have failed to reform their society unlike Muslims in other countries like Turkey.

In a "communal malaise," both groups [Hindus and Muslims] ignore the urgent claims of social justice. While he was extremely critical of Muhammad Ali Jinnah and the communally divisive strategies of the Muslim League, he argued that Hindus and Muslims should segregate and the State of Pakistan be formed, as ethnic nationalism within the same country would only lead to more violence. He cited precedent with historical events like the dissolution of the Ottoman Empire and Czechoslovakia to bolster his views regarding the Hindu-Muslim communal divide.

However, he questioned as to whether the need for Pakistan was sufficient and it might be possible to resolve Hindu-Muslim differences in a less drastic way. He wrote that Pakistan must "justify its existence" accordingly. Since other countries such as Canada also have had communal issues with the French and English and have lived together, it may not be impossible for Hindus and Muslims to live together.

He warned that the actual implementation of a two state solution would be extremely problematic with massive population transfers and border disputes. This claim was almost prophetic in its realization with the violent Partition of India after independence.

Architect of India's constitution despite his increasing unpopularity, controversial views and intense criticism of Gandhi and the Congress, Ambedkar was by reputation an exemplary jurist and scholar. Upon India's independence on August 15, 1947, the new Congress-led government invited Ambedkar to serve as the nation's first law minister, which he accepted. On August 29, Ambedkar was appointed chairman of the constitution drafting committee, charged by the Assembly to write free India's constitution. Ambedkar won great praise from his colleagues and contemporary observers for his drafting work.

The text prepared by Ambedkar provided constitutional guarantees and protections for a wide range of civil liberties for individual citizens, including freedom of religion, the abolition of untouchability and the outlawing of all forms of discrimination. Ambedkar argued for extensive economic and social rights for women, and also won the Assembly's support for introducing a system of reservations of jobs in the civil services, schools and colleges for members of scheduled castes and scheduled tribes, a system akin to affirmative action. India's lawmakers hoped to eradicate the socioeconomic inequalities and lack of opportunities for India's depressed classes through this measure, which had been originally envisioned as temporary on a need basis. The constitution was adopted on November 26, 1949 by the Constituent Assembly. Speaking after the completion of his work, Ambedkar said:

> *Ambedkar resigned from the cabinet in 1951 following the stalling in parliament of his draft of the Hindu Code Bill, which sought to expound gender equality in the laws of inheritance, marriage and the economy. Although supported by Prime Minister Nehru, the cabinet and many other Congress leaders, it received criticism from a large number of parliament members. Ambedkar independently contested an election in 1952 to the lower house of parliament, the Lok Sabha but was defeated. He was appointed to the upper house of parliament, the Rajya Sabha in March 1952 and would remain its member until his death.*

4

Dalit Movements after Ambedkar

A review of the significant events and episodes in the dalit movement after the demise of Babasaheb Ambedkar is attempted here in order to identify the icons behind them and assess their characteristics.

Gaikwad vs. Others

After the death of Babasaheb Ambedkar, the mantle of leadership fell upon the shoulders of Dadasaheb Gaikwad. He appeared to be the natural choice, by virtue of his stature in the movement as well as his age. He had grown up to be Ambedkar's trusted lieutenant through frontline participation in all the battles, right from the days of Mahad. He represented a typical activist of the Ambedkarian movement and had a mass identity. He seemed to know the exact pulse of dalit masses. It is interesting to note that the question of land that by and large constitutes the crux of the dalit problem (as recognised by innumerable scholars even today) was and could only be taken up by Gaikwad. It was the biggest and by far the most glorious event in the post-Ambedkar dalit movement. Even during the days of Babasaheb Ambedkar, the mass struggle for land had never materialised in direct terms and at such a scale. At the most, it could be said to have materialised symbolically in the form of a struggle for abolition of 'Khoti'- a kind of landlordism that prevailed in the Konkan region of Maharashtra. At any rate, as a mass struggle for land at the national level, it did not have any parallel in Indian history. It was the first time that the economic dimension of the dalit problem was effectively integrated with their social oppression. It had gained an overwhelming support from the masses all over the country. Scores of dalit families went to jail and many dalit hamlets remained deserted for days.

However, although it had caught the fancy of dalit masses, the rest of the dalit leadership thought otherwise. They disproved Gaikwad's struggle as being communist and declared that it had no place in Ambedkarian agenda. They highlighted Ambedkar's statement that mass struggles were the grammar of anarchy in the constitutional regime and should not have any place in a parliamentary democracy. They argued that if the land question was at all important, it could have been taken up judicially in the Supreme Court of India. Fortunately, none suggested parliamentary solution. It was perhaps considered infeasible as none could muster requisite majority to effect the people oriented fundamental changes after the Poona Pact. In tacit terms, the other leaders were accusing Gaikwad of being intellectually incapable of comprehending the subtleties of Ambedkar's ideology and hence unsuitable to step into his shoes.

Gaikwad, a rustic in the common man's Dhoti - Kurta attire, and not embellished with university degrees, could not be accepted by these people. They considered themselves the true heirs to the leadership after Ambedkar on the sole criterion that they fitted the Ambedkarian mould (as they conceived it) better than Gaikwad. This mould was based on the contemporary middle class cultural norms that Ambedkar displayed in his attire and general demeanour.

They would conveniently forget that that his western attire was basically a counter to Gandhi's belaboured austerity and a representation of modernity as against Gandhi's anti-modern views. Instead, they aped him in all appearances. They wore trousers and shirts, were suited and booted, had university degrees and could command better sophistry than Gaikwad. They would exhibit their law books as the key to the treasure left behind by Ambedkar. They could thus project themselves as better clones of Ambedkar to the gullible dalit masses. Gaikwad and the people of his ilk could be activists but not the leaders! The first attempt to iconise Babasaheb Ambedkar and considerably successfully so, as the later times proved, is apparent in this early post-Ambedkar episode. That was the icon of a '*saheb*'- the epitaph used for an Englishman but later used as an honorific for natives, who were educated, westernised and placed in bureaucratic authority. It denoted someone far above the masses, one who was endowed with authority and power.

It was the icon of a saviour. It projected leader as the saviour incarnate who would liberate them from their bondage and lead them to prosperity. All that masses had to do was to stand solidly behind him. They did not have any specific role in the project of their own emancipation other than being meek followers of the leader. This particular icon distanced the dalit leadership from the masses in every way in terms of physical attributes like appearance, clothes, language and lifestyle.

It promoted blind following and servile notions. The leaders were to be treated as their quasi-monarch (a la *Bhim Raja*). They could not be questioned on equal terms. They bestowed favours by their very existence. Without leaders the masses could not exist. It obfuscated, mystified and externalised the problems of dalits, if not their very existence. The saheb syndrome that curiously settled among dalits as the general honorific, almost devoid of any attribute association, got significant reinforcement by this icon. Moreover, in so far as this syndrome reflected middle class aspirations and value associations, this icon helped petty-bourgeoisize the entire dalit movement.

Although, later the Dalit Panthers brought in a change in this leadership model, certainly in its physical attributes and so made it more people friendly, it approximately recoiled back to the old RPI (Republican Party of India) model with the demise of the spirit behind Panthers. This leadership model was certainly regressive as it reproduced the decadent feudal structure that dalits were so familiar with in real life; perhaps it was both, its cause as well as its effect. Paradoxically, its protagonists and promoters were the very people who seemed to claim a larger share of modernity. Gaikwad's equation with the masses and his charisma would not be easily swept away by their attempts but it is a fact that he could not take up mass based struggles thereafter and rather chose to fall prey to the enticements of power and pelf form Congress circle. Thus, this early icon of

Ambedkar certainly blocked the emerging mass orientation of the dalit movement.

Tailist Pursuit of Power

The importance of dalits in the scheme of post-1947 politics was duly recognised by the ruling classes, then predominantly represented by the Congress party. It was vital for them to tie dalits to the parliamentary alternative. Hypothetically speaking, if the latent alienation and the proletarian consciousness of dalits were allowed to grow in an unhindered manner, revolutionary prospects for India would have been closer than in any other conceivable place in the world. However, no ruling class would allow this to happen, much less the Indian one, which had impeccable credentials in its adeptness at keeping its victims within the institutional bondage for millenniums with mere soft strategies. Whatever the other motivations, there was certainly this element of strategy at work in making Ambedkar the chairman of the drafting committee for the Indian Constitution.

It is said that it was done at the instance of none other than Mahatma Gandhi. For Gandhi - the super-strategist of the Congress, the Poona Pact with which he effectively blocked the political voice of dalits within the parliamentary framework, it was necessary to commit them to the latter for a long period. Could there be a better method to achieve this than getting Ambedkar- the undisputed leader of dalits, who had come to regard him as their Messiah, to author the Constitution! It is a tribute to Gandhi's farsightedness and cunning that he prompted Nehru to make it happen. Gandhi and Nehru knew that the composition of the Constituent Assembly, surfeit with representation of the propertied classes by design, provided enough fortification not to let Ambedkar's ideology penetrate the Constitutional draft. But, at the same time, Ambedkar could be eulogised as its maker. The strategy killed several birds with one stone. It won the dalit commitment to the Constitution; it projected a progressive facet of the Indian ruling class to the world and planted false consciousness among dalits. Thus, although the content of the Constitution was decided by the ruling classes, the ruled ones were made to own it up. It was a feat of strategy certainly comparable in its import to that behind the caste institution. Behind its generosity and progressive veneer was hidden the trap which would effectively incapacitate the dalits for a long time to come. Once trapped they would stay in perpetual fragmentation in the turbulence of electoral game played by various sections of the ruling classes. Dalits constituting over 15 per cent of the total population are a significant factor in the number game of electoral politics. Their spread prevented them from winning any election on their own steam but at the same time none other could possibly win it without their support. Every ruling class political party would vie with each other to get them as a vote block on its side and still collectively prevent their coalescence into a class.

The mass struggle that materialised under the leadership of Gaikwad certainly shook the ruling classes. They had to devise special strategies to contain the threat of the emerging dalit challenge. It was a challenge indeed, although inadequately articulated, that had exactly touched the most sensitive nerve of the feudal structure, which still lay at the base of everything that mattered to dalits. The implementation of this strategy was soon seen in Gaikwad being befriended by Yashavantrao Chawhan, the then chief minister of Maharashtra and later the Deputy Prime Minister of the country. It culminated in the first alliance between the RPI and the Congress, which helped Gaikwad, and a few others reach the Parliament and Legislative Assemblies. The inauguration of the era of unprincipled alliances could be discerned right here. The Congress was undisputedly a representative party of the Indian ruling classes comprising the high caste capitalists and landlords. The alliance between this party and the party of the most exploited in the land, to say the least, could only be termed unholy.

In the face of it, it appears difficult to associate this phenomenon with Ambedkar who for the best part of his life had fought the Congress tooth and nail, criticised it ruthlessly and ultimately warned his followers to be away from it as it was the 'burning house'. It is interesting to note him standing out among his contemporaries, including the communists and socialists of all hues, in unambiguously characterising the Congress party as the representative of the capitalists and landlords and unmask its fake anti-imperialist facade.

However, as it always happened, in this case too his life-saga left enough strands to be picked up by the vested interests in support of the seemingly contrary act. Whatever the situational contexts and strategic compulsions, but it could be cited that the same Ambedkar had joined the Congress government at the centre under Nehru's Prime Ministership, had accepted the chairmanship of the drafting committee for the Indian Constitution on the basis of support from the Congress majority, and had accepted the Congress support for getting re-elected to the Constituent Assembly after the partition of the country. Whatever might have been his strategy in relenting his stand in accepting the Congress offers, it cannot be ignored that it eventually got subsumed in the universal strategy of the ruling classes to neutralise resistance struggles of the oppressed people.

Whenever the oppressed masses organised their resistance against the oppression, repression and co-option have been the age-old twin strategic tools in the repertoire of the ruling classes. Contrary to the general feeling that the latter is the recent phenomenon, associated with the spread of liberalism, these strategies have been iteratively used by the rulers from time immemorial, depending upon their perception of the intensity of peoples' struggles.

One of the native examples of co-option could be had in the form of Buddha who symbolised a rebellion against the *Brahmin Dharma*, being projected as the ninth incarnation of the God Vishnu. More often than not, co-option being the low cost option is preferred by the ruling classes. What Congress had done in allying with RPI was precisely implementation of this strategy. On the side of RPI, the motivation to ally with any party flowed from, as it seems, the clarion call given by Ambedkar to dalits to become 'the ruling race'. It was supposed to mean the rule of the dalits, the have-nots - the rule of the working classes. It was however conveniently taken to mean being part of the ruling team, the ruling class, by the dalit leaders. Any pursuit of power, regardless of means, thus became a quasi-sacred obsession for the dalit leaders.

In absence of any explanation of the strategic contexts in which Ambedkar had accepted support from the Congress, it provided good enough grounds to sustain the de-shaped icon of Ambedkar in the minds of gullible masses. This icon froze the alternative of parliamentary structure as the only alternative for dalits and consequently impelled them to rely on electoral methods to gain power. The Poona Pact had already eliminated the possibility of shaping up their truly representative leadership through the electoral means and in corollary laid foundation for the proliferation of irresponsible leaders. It had permanently ordained the necessity for dalits to be in alliance with some or the other ruling class party for their political survival. This icon thus fortified the emasculation of dalits in the political sphere. It approved the in-camera parleys of the leaders for their tailist pursuit of power shorn of the mass line and established the bourgeois model of politicking. Dalit movement thus became permanently an adjunct of the ruling class.

Splits and Schism: Imperative of Electoral Commerce

Then came the era of disintegration. The RPI split and further split till people lost count of its factions. Three predominant reasons could be discerned for this disintegration: (i) The ruling class strategy of 'divide and rule', (ii) the lack of ideological coherence in the dalit movement and (iii) the petty-bourgeoisie aspirations of its leadership. Apparently, these reasons reinforced each other and in that sense were not exclusive.

'Divide and Rule' is the well-known strategy of the ruling classes world over to basically weaken the ruled people. Indians generally attributed it to the colonial British policy but the fact is that more than any one else, it is ingrained in the blood of their own ruling class. It underlay their caste system in the form of a continuum of hierarchies that kept the people perpetually divided. This caste continuum has certainly played its obnoxious role even in avowedly 'caste annihilating' dalit movement in terms of providing potential fissures to crack along. As explained above, the post-independence reality, comprising mainly the 'Poona Pact' and enslavement of dalits within the framework of parliamentary democracy exposed dalits to ruling class enticements and resultantly led to their perpetual division. The strong dalit movement even if co-opted for the time being, posed the threat of re-emergence and challenge.

It had to be simultaneously weakened to perpetuate their political subordination. The petty-bourgeoisie aspirations of dalit leaders made operationalisation of this strategy easy. Its feasibility was further enhanced by the ambivalence reflected in Ambedkar's sayings and doings from time to time, which provided scope for any one to interpret him the way one liked. It was his icon as the demi-god of dalits that was used up by the competing commanders of his army to do whatever they liked. This deification that he himself severally warned against and abhorred but which paradoxically had started well during his life time (celebration of his *Jayantis*) and grew after his death with an accelerated pace particularly because he himself became an essential icon in the neo-Buddhist rituals after his embracement of Buddhism less than two months ago. The mass *Dharmantar* - (change in religion), unprecedented in modern times and considered by many as the culmination of his life mission, released the flood of dalit religiosity that overwhelmed every other thing. It imparted him a quasi-spiritual aura as *Bodhisatva*. Many enthusiastically added a *sarana* in his name (*Bhimam saranam gachhami*) to the original *trisarana* of Buddhism. Thereafter the display of devotion towards Ambedkar became a surrogate for one's ideological allegiance to him. Everyone vied with another to display his kind of devotion and in turn to emphasise superiority of his ideological ware for justifying his separate shop. The process of establishing the shop invariably relied upon the collection of clientele from one's own sub-caste and building up subordinate political nexus with some section of the ruling class. The ideological pretensions through the display of devotion to Ambedkar continued thereafter with the aim of expanding the clientele.

The ruling classes of course played their cards well in catalysing this divide in their pursuit of buying the dalit support. This electoral commerce paid off handsomely and created its own rationale and motivation for the permanent division of dalit leaders. Through this process, some of the leaders of the wretched, while serving their cause, amassed wealth worth crores of rupees, became industrialists, maintained fleets of cars, roamed around by air and taxis, without any evidence of the basic source of their prosperity. It is a tribute to the political consciousness of dalits that while they starved and bled themselves over the issue of unity of these leaders, it never occurred to them to ask, even in a whisper, a question about the source of their material well being! Many blatantly indulged in the acts contrary to their profession for amassing wealth-some set up liquor factories and still remained the front rank leaders of the Buddhists, some allied with the rank castiest and communalist and still claimed to be ardent Ambedkarites. What counted was money and power. Paradoxically, the more affluent ones seemed to fit the bill better as they looked bigger 'sahebs', adding an additional aura to their leadership. Apart from the naked might of money in the electoral politics that tended to situate the moneyed men at the pedestal of power, the leadership model outlined above certainly contributed to their sustenance. With the money power they could invest into cultivation of their cronies and in turn command a better return in the wake of electoral parleys.

The splits were in a way a corollary of the leadership model and the over-reliance on the electoral politics sanctioned by the above-indicated icons. The leaders were always seen endowed with an uncommon wisdom that was really beyond the reach of masses. Leaders thus could do whatever they wanted without any scruples and they did it even breaking away from the party. As a result, the so-called giants who claimed the legacy of Ambedkar became contented with the identity of the parenthesised alphabets of their names after the RPI.

They did not even worry about the fact that the formations represented by these parenthesised identities were basically a mere coagulation of their own sub-castes, in their respective geographical areas. It was a qualitative leap backwards for the ones who had proudly launched upon the annihilation of castes as their mission. Every one claimed to be a better follower of Ambedkar than the other is, and in the process, proliferated his icons by projecting one's proprietary models.

Dalit Panthers: The Sparklet that was not to be

The degeneration that set in continued unabated till the birth of Dalit Panthers in early 1970s. There could be varied explanations for the paradigm shift in dalit politics (movement) marked by Dalit Panthers. Remarkably, they spoke the language of defiance and militancy, which created waves. These waves had shaken the foundations of the established order in the country and in essence demonstrated what the wrath of the wretched could be! It provided a valuable insight that was pathetically missing in the dalit politics. Going by their manifesto, dalit panthers had broken many new grounds in terms of radicalising the political space for the dalit movement. They imparted the proletarian - radical class identity to dalits and linked their struggles to the struggles of all oppressed people over the globe. The clear cut leftist stand reflected by this document undoubtedly ran counter to the accepted legacy of Ambedkar as projected by the various icons, although it was sold in his name as an awkward tactic.

It reflected a historical dilemma characteristic of the Indian situation. The pathos of casteism integral with the dalit experience essentially brought in Ambedkar, as his was the only articulate framework that took cognisance of it. But, for the other contemporary problems of depravations Marxism provided a scientific framework to bring about a revolutionary change. Although, have-nots from both dalits and non-dalits craved for a fundamental change, the former adhered to what appeared to be Ambedkarian methods of socio-political change and the latter to what came to be the Marxian method which tended to see every social process as the reflection of the material reality. Both caused erroneous interpretations. It is to the credit of Panthers that the assimilation of these two ideologies was attempted for the first time in the country but unfortunately it proved abortive in absence of the efforts to rid each of them of its obfuscating influence and stress their non-contradictory essence. Neither, there was theoretical effort to integrate these two ideologies, nor was there any practice combining social aspects of caste with say, the land question in the village setting. Essentially, it remained an emotional and a poetic negation of the status quo, craving for the broad revolutionary change and on ideological plane inevitably reflected an amalgam of Ambedkar and Marx. This ideological amalgam could not be acceptable to those under the spell of the prevailing Ambedkar-icons and therefore this revolutionary seedling in the dalit movement died a still death.

The possibility of the radical shift in the paradigm of dalit politics indicated by the manifesto was totally submerged by the reactionary upsurge of the new version of orthodox Ambedkarism. The reactionaries objected to the radical content of the programme alleging that the manifesto was doctored by the radicals - the Naxalites. There is no denying the fact that the Naxalite movement which had erupted quite like the Dalit Panther, as a disenchantment with and negation of the established politics, saw a potential ally in the Panthers and tried to forge a bond right at the level of formulation of policies and programme of the latter. But even if the Panthers had chosen to pattern their programme on the ten-point programme of the Black Panther Party (BPP) in the USA, which had been the basic inspiration for their formation, it would not have been any less radical.

The amount of emphasis on the material aspects of life that one finds in the party programme of the BPP could still have been inimical to the established icon of Ambedkar. Radicalism was the premise for the very existence of the Dalit Panther and hence the quarrel over its programme basically reflected the clash between the established icon of Ambedkar and his radical version proposed in the programme. The fact that for the first time the Dalit Panther exposed dalits to a radical Ambedkar and brought a section of dalit youth nearer to accepting it certainly marks its positive contribution to the dalit movement.

There were material reasons for the emergence of Dalit Panthers, as there are for any episode or event. Children of the Ambedkarian movement had started coming out of universities in large numbers in the later part of 1960s, just to face the blank future staring at them. The much-publicised Constitutional provisions for them turned out to be a mirage. Their political vehicle was getting deeper and deeper into the marsh of parliamentarism. It ceased to see the real problems of people. The air of militant insurgency that had blown all over the world during those days also provided them the source material to articulate their anger. Unfortunately, quite like the BPP, they lacked the suitable ideology to channel this anger for achieving their goal. Interestingly, as they reflected the positive aspects of the BPP's contributions in terms of self-defence, mass organising techniques, propaganda techniques and radical orientation, they did so in the case of BPP's negative aspects too. (See Acoli, Sundiata, a Brief history of the Black Panther Party and its Place in the Black liberation Movement for details). Like Black Panthers they also reflected 'TV mentality' (to think of a revolutionary struggle like a quick-paced TV programme), dogmatism, neglect of economic foundation needed for the organisation, lumpen tendencies, rhetoric outstripping capabilities, lack of clarity about the form of struggle and eventually corruptibility of the leadership.

The Panthers' militancy by and large remained confined to their speeches and writings. One of the reasons for its stagnation was certainly its incapability to escape the petit bourgeois ideological trap built up with the icons of Ambedkar. It would not get over the ideological ambivalence represented by them. Eventually, the petit-bourgeoise 'icon' of Ambedkar prevailed and extinguished the sparklet of new revolutionary challenge. It was completely sapped of its rebellious image and its vitality and soon got corrupted with a ridiculous prefix 'Bharatiya' to it. It survived as another living monument to the ideological bankruptcy and the degeneration of the dalit leadership. It went the RPI way and what remained of it were the numerous fractions engaged in internecine squabbles under the sly hands of the ruling classes.

The Dalit Panther phase represented the clash of two icons: one, that of a radical 'Ambedkar', as a committed rationalist, perpetually striving for the deliverance of the most oppressed people in the world. He granted all the freedom to his followers to search out the truth using the rationalist methodology as he did. He abhorred all kinds of humbug and hated to be bound by any dogma. He desired his followers to do the same. Like his mentor, the Buddha, he would exhort his followers not to take any thing for granted until their own experience corroborated it or their intellect supported it. The other is of the 'Ambedkar' who has forbidden the violent methods and advocated the constitutional ways for his followers, who was a staunch anti-Communist, ardent Buddhist, nay, Bodhisatva, who has given a permanent doctrine that was infallible. As it turned out, the radical icon of Ambedkar was projected without adequate conviction. It was implanted in an alien soil. There was no one committed to propagating such an image of Ambedkar, neither communists nor dalits. Eventually it remained as a veritable hodgepodge compared to the familiar set of icons coming from the other camp.

Phenomenon of Kanshiram: A Culmination of a Kind

The movement of Kanshiram markedly reflected a different strategy, which coined the 'Bahujan' identity encompassing all the SCs, STs, BCs, OBCs and religious minorities than 'dalit', which practically represented only the scheduled castes. Kanshiram started off with an avowedly apolitical organisation of government employees belonging to Bahujana, identifying them to be the main resource of these communities. It later catalysed the formation of an agitating political group creatively coined as DS4 - the Dalit Shoshit Samaj Sangharsh Samiti, which eventually became a full-fledged political party - the Bahujan Samaj Party (BSP).

Purely, in terms of electoral politics, which has some how become a major obsession with all the dalit parties, Kanshiram's strategy has proved quite effective, though in only certain parts of the country. He has given a qualitative impetus to the moribund dalit politics, locating itself into a wider space peopled by all the downtrodden of India. But he identified these people only in terms of their castes and communities. It may be said to his credit that he reflected the culmination of what common place icon of Ambedkar stood for. Kanshiram shrewdly grasped the political efficacy of this icon that sanctioned the pursuit of power in the name of downtrodden castes. The religious minorities which potentially rears the sense of suffering marginalisation from the majority community could be easily added to it to make a formidable constituency in parliamentary parlance. Every one knew it but none did how to implement. Kanshiram has seemingly succeeded in this task at least in certain pockets. The careful analysis will show that the combination of certain historical developments and situational factors has been behind this success. As Kanshiram has amply experienced, it is not replicable elsewhere. It is bound to be short-lived and illusory unless this success is utilised to implement a revolutionary programme to forge a class identity among its constituents.

If not, one will have to constantly exert to recreate the compulsions for their togetherness and allegiance. In absence of any class-agenda, which is certainly the case of BSP, these compulsions could only be created through manipulative politics for which political power is an essential resource. BSP's unprincipled pursuit of power is basically driven by this exigency. It is futile to see in this game a process of empowerment of the subject people as could be seen (although not conclusively) from the statistical evidence of the cases of atrocities, and of overall situation of the poor people under its rule. There should be no lament over this as essentially it is where any kind of political acrobatics is destined to end in the prevailing system. The imperatives of this kind of strategy necessarily catapult the movement into the camp of the ruling classes as has exactly happened with BSP. BSP's electoral parleys with Congress, BJP, Akali Dal (Mann) that reached the stage of directly sharing State power in UP recently, essentially reflect this process of degeneration and expose its class characteristics today.

It seems to have sustaining support from the icon that BSP itself created, where Ambedkar was painted as the intelligent strategist who could turn any situation to his advantage, who used every opportunity to grab political power to achieve his objective. He is the person who saw in political power, a key to the woes of dalits and therefore exhorted them to grab it at any cost. He did not think highly of mass struggles except for tactical reasons to demonstrate the might of the leaders. For him, there existed only means not the values for securing one's goals. He did not see any permanent friend or foe in politics and joined even the Congress whom he had once declared as the enemy. He is seen as the person endowed with State authority (as a member of the Viceroy's Executive Council, Law Minister, and Chairman of the Drafting Committee for the Indian Constitution) - the sole source of his power to benefit his people. He was the sole arbiter of the interests of his people. Of course, he had disdain for all shades of communism.

Kanshiram's reading of Ambedkar ignores the fact that Ambedkar had to carve out space for his movement in the crevices left by the contradictions between various Indian political parties and groups on one side and the colonial power on the other. For most of his time, he sought maximisation of this space from the contending Muslim League and Congress, to name the predominant players, and eventually brought dalit issue to the national political agenda. Kanshiram stuffs his Ambedkar icon entirely with such kind of superfluity that it would look credible to the gullible dalit masses. This icon approves of his sole ideology that political power to his party (read him) could solve all dalit problems. His strategy till then has been to be in vantage position to decide who would be the king and thereby leverage his bargaining power. He did not care for democracy. To some extent this non-democratic stance spells his compulsions to have unitary command over his party structure as without it, his adversaries would gobble it up.

He did not have any utility for any programme or manifesto, no concern for any issue howsoever burning, no qualms about policy or principles because, his sole obsession is to maximise his power by whatever means. In the rhetoric of empowering Bahujans, he does not even feel it necessary to demonstrate what exactly this empowering means and what benefits it would entail them. He never even spelt out what precisely ails his Bahujans except for highlighting their prejudiced social identities in worn-out casteist phraseology. That explains his entries into and exits from political alliances with any one with the same alacrity. The obsession with capturing power robbed him of certain fundamental values that Ambedkar never compromised.

The underlying value of the movement of Ambedkar was represented by liberty, equality and fraternity. Kanshiram does not seem to respect any value than the political and money power. In Ambedkar, one cannot miss an overflowing concern for the oppressed and wrath against the perpetrators of oppression. Kanshiram's concern scarcely transcended his speeches in his electoral rallies. It was with this concern and commitment that Ambedkar kept on referring to Marx and Marxism till his end, something as a touchstone to test his alternatives. Kanshiram simply abhorred it.

Ambedkar struggled to formulate the dalit problem. Kanshiram either took it for granted or did not care for it at all. He never tried to articulate the nature of his Bahujanas' ailment except for the rhetorical reference to their subordination by the minority upper caste Hindus. For Ambedkar certain values, moral code etc. were paramount, Kanshiram never seemed to be bothered by these issues. Ambedkar always foresaw plans and programmes; visualised appropriate structures for the downtrodden. Kanshiram expressed clear disdain for such things. For Ambedkar political power was a means, to Kanshiram it appears to be the end. Notwithstanding these broad differences, he has succeeded in luring the dalit masses in certain pockets of the country by projecting an Ambedkar icon that sanctioned his unscrupulous pursuits of power.

The crux of Kanshiram can be traced to his superfluous attempt to replicate Ambedkar's movement of 1920s as if the times had stood still for the bygone five decades. Ambedkar's mobilisation of dalit masses through struggles is vulgarised by him as the 'agit-prop' tool to collect people behind him. When Ambedkar realised the potency of political power, he launched his Indian Labour Party that reflected his urge to bring together the working class, transcending the caste lines. It is only when the political polarisation took communal turn that he abandoned his ILP project and launched the Scheduled Caste Federation.

For Kanshiram, the talk sans caste and communities is perhaps an anathema. His casteist platform as such appears preordained by his ambition for power. Ambedkar joined hands with a few political parties - one the communists (while joining the strike of mill workers) and the other is the Praja Samajwadi Party of Ashok Mehta in the 1952 elections. Although, he accepted the Congress support and offered to work in their government, he never tied up his political outfit to the Congress. It always appeared a politically expedient step for him as an individual without any organisational implication. Kanshiram's record so far clearly shows that he is ready to join hands with any one promising him the share of political power. Declaredly he would avoid the leftists of all hues and accept the friendship of the rank reactionaries of every kind. Ambedkar pointed at the capitalism and Brahminism as the twin enemy for his movement but Kanshiram enthusiastically embraced them without any pinch to his conscience. Ambedkar, in his own way, has been in search of suitable ideological carrier for the dalit movement. Kanshiram has no utility for such a thing.

Multiplicity of Brands, Little Differentiation

Apart from these broad political trends, there are many regional outfits like Dalit Mahasabha in Andhra Pradesh, Mass Movement in Maharashtra, Dalit Sena in Bihar and elsewhere, etc., some of which dabble directly into electoral politics and some of them do not. So far, none of them have a radically different icon of Ambedkar from the ones described above. They offer some proprietary ware claiming to be a shade better than that of others.

Hinduised Buddhism: Turning the Wheel Backward

Another trend in the dalit movement emphasises the spread of Buddhism as its goal. As in politics, there are numerous organisations devoted to this task. According to them, Buddhism was the culmination of Ambedkar's mission and hence, the true Ambedkarite not only had to be a Buddhist but also had to work for the spread of Buddhism. Ambedakr's declared vision of making India a Buddhist country spells a mission statement to them.

Their activities revolve around building Buddhist viharas, becoming *Shramners and Bhikkus*; imbibing religious mode of living and engaging in quasi-studious pursuits like learning Pali, reading Buddhist scriptures, rewriting the episodes in history. At the renaissance some amount of excavation of skeletons is inevitable but it had become an obsession with the dalit intellectuals, who squandered considerable energies in desecting the Hindu mythology to expose its cunning and rediscovering the Buddhist glories as their own legacy. One of the underlying motives in this enterprise was to project superiority of Buddhism and in turn their own as they believed that they were the original Buddhists. Paradoxically, all of them quibble over the distinction between 'Dharma' and 'Dhamma', claiming that Buddhism is Dhamma whereas others are the Dharmas. Unlike other religions, Buddhism does not have any place for rituals, gods or any permanent entity like soul, and is just a practicable moral code for living.

However, in practice, all kinds of mumbo jumbo that some times appears to be exceeding the familiar but on-the-wane rituals of Hinduism, are followed, so much so that not only Buddha but even Ambedkar is not spared from the godhood (*Bhim Bhagawan*). Of late, the relatively upwardly mobile (middle class) among dalits are increasingly getting attracted towards 'Vipasyana' - a kind of meditation that is said to have been practised by Buddha himself to get his enlightenment and so is 'prescribed' in Buddhism to be a good Buddhist. Many of them lately claim that it is the essence of Buddhism. It is amusing to see this mind-centric trend growing among dalits.

In all this, Ambedkar's attempts at rationalisation and redefinition of Buddhism are completely forgotten. What rather is remembered is that he himself had given them the '*vidhi*' for marriage and for such other occasions; that he himself had devotedly said the three precepts and five oaths and stood through the long winding *Gathas* in the language of antiquity, that how he got into spiritual trance in front of the Buddha's statue when he visited Sarnath.

The icon they follow is that of a man incarnate of Buddha who analysed the problem of humanity and ultimately prescribed *nirvana* - a indescribable State marked by the extinction of all kind of craving. One who after Ashoka made greatest contributions to the revival and spread of Buddhism. It shows Ambedkar as a spiritual person who ultimately finds the roots of all the problems in the world within oneself and therefore preaches the virtue of moral rearmament and inner purity. The essence of being was to attain *nirvana*, the State of total contentment. It implied the futility of struggling against the material exploitation of dalits as their real salvation. It lay rather in extinguishing their own craving. It tended to internalise all their problems to themselves and stressed the need to cleanse their minds. Inevitably, it envisaged typical religious conduct from the followers with the highly pitched religious benchmarks available anywhere.

The sphere of religions abounds in such paradoxes. Its idiom basically promotes them. Buddhism could very well be conceived as the rebellion against the predominant creed of the establishment that prevailed more than 25 centuries ago, quite like Marxism in our times. Buddha was the first philosopher who forsook the futility of sterile philosophising and stressed the need to change the world. It is interesting to see in him as the first dialectician, some one in the same lineage as Hegel and Marx. It is ahistorical to expect Buddha to give a solution to the problems of our times but it is important to appreciate the underscoring rational approach followed by him in his search. His conclusions are not important, as they are essentially constrained by the State of knowledge and overall development of the physical sciences during his times. What is important is to see the expanse of positive things that he could postulate at that time. Significantly, Buddha discarded the concept of God and soul and spoke against all kinds of rituals; he asked people to accept things only if it corresponded with their own experience or passed the test of their own intellect. He gave complete freedom to people to make amends to the *Dhamma* as per the needs of time. But, it could not escape the pressures of institutionalisation, which transformed it into a religion. They made him a God, wove stories that well competed with any mythology, built elaborate rituals to be followed and sapped it of its essential zeal of changing the world.

The paradox would be better illustrated by the responses of ardent Ambedkarites to the recent news about one Islamic Taliban commander threatening to dynamite two fourth-century monuments - 1500-years-old statues of Buddha in central Afghanistan. The response came from highly educated non-resident Indian Ambedkarites. It was interesting inasmuch as they reveal what havoc the religious mindset that owes allegiance to Buddhism can play with even its human-centric tenets. They said that the dalits in India should immediately take out a massive procession to the consulate of Afghanistan and threaten them that no Afghan would be spared in India if they carried out destruction of the Buddha statues in Afghanistan. It was a burst of anger at the first hearing of the news and was not to be meant but nonetheless it revealed the consciousness, the consciousness of Khomini or of any Hindu fundamentalist at work. It is one thing to speak against the fundamentalist vandalism and condemn it or even punish the responsible people in whatever way but it is quite another to don reverse fundamentalism to kill innocents to save dead stone statues in some distant land. It is important to realise the fact that even the Buddha's *Dhamma* whose roots are firmly in the soil of rationality and whose sole raison de etre' is the human suffering, could be mutilated to be its exact opposite by the very followers of Ambedkar who consciously cleansed it of the dust of irrationality and mysticism gathered over millennia.

SC/ST Associations: Facing a Dead End Ahead

One more significant trend in the dalit movement has its source in the policy of reservations in services of the State. Apart from the central and State governments, the large number of public sector undertakings that were floated by them, and other institutions established and promoted with public money, also came to be the State, attracting the constitutional provisions regarding reservations for the SCs and STs in services. The dalits in these sectors represented the collective investment and achievements of the dalit community, as reservations were the only hope for them to secure material well being. Although, they found themselves catapulted to modern sectors of economy, they found there were newer traps already in place, which clearly communicated the caste code for the modern organisations.

The dalits had to conform their behaviour to this code for their survival. It reflected all the familiar prejudices against them. Their experience of the blatant violations of these provisions generally manifested in terms of backlogs in filling reservation posts, denial of promotions and general discriminatory treatment meted out in postings, transfers and other aspects of organisational life. The trade unions and management associations would not address their woes because they involved a contradiction between the interests of dalits and non-dalits. Thus were born the SC/ST associations. Even after their countrywide proliferation, these associations do not have any locus standi with managements except for the ritualistic interviews during the annual visits of parliamentary committees on the welfare of SCs and STs.

It is a sad commentary on the functioning of the Constitution that over the last four decades it has driven these collectives to a State of hopelessness. The constitutional provisions regarding the reservations flow in the form of various circulars issued by the Government of India that are supposed to be implemented by its executive machinery. Over the years there has been a plethora of these circulars each written in such a convoluted language that even the highest court of law also felt it an arduous task to interpret them. One of the deliberate lacunae that exist in this scheme is that there is no effective onus on any one for the implementation of these provisions. The executive can blatantly refuse to implement them under the plea of variant interpretation and drive the SC/ST employee or his association to the courts of law. Even if the poor employee or the SC/ST association could last the long winding court process over the years and succeed in getting the favourable verdict (a remote possibility though) the employer can still persist with his negative attitude. There are scores of cases of this kind where the petitioner employee or his association had to launch contempt proceeding against the employers and end up being bankrupt in the process. The helplessness of dalit employees in the services, in a way is the reflection of the sorry State of dalit politics. Since, there was no way these associations could effectively struggle, they landed up seeking petty favours from managements and in return being a black sheep during anti-management struggles.

The typical activities of these associations comprise celebration of the birth anniversaries of Ambedkar, representing dalit employees to the management or administration, and doing certain philanthropic and community service, depending upon the degree of their own organisation and resources. The icon that they seem to be following is that of a saviour, emancipator, to whom they need to pay their obeisance, to obey his commandments. Their community service for instance could be easily traced to Ambedkar's call to dalits to contribute 20 % of their earnings to the cause of the community. Although, rarely any dalit (save the poorest ones) goes so far as to sacrifice one fifth of his income over the cause of the community, none seem to refuse some symbolic contribution. Some better organised associations distribute notebooks, text books among slum children, run coaching and career counselling classes, organise relief works in the wake of calamities, open eateries in the dalit congregations like the ones at the Dikshyabhumi in Nagpur and Chaityabhumi in Mumbai. These are the gestures of repayment of the social debt.

They see in Ambedkar as the one who struggled to get them so many facilities and it is their bounden duty to take fullest advantage of the same. It was their sacred duty to occupy positions of power in bureaucracy. It is assumed, as Ambedkar appears to have assumed himself, that the educated dalits with bureaucratic authorities will serve the cause of their community in direct proportion to their relative position. The myth is still sustained in spite of heaps of evidence to the contrary. Ambedkar's exhortation to 'agitate' is reduced down to making appeals to various authorities, having meetings with managements submitting memoranda and at the maximum, to filing the writ petitions in the courts - in short all that in the feasible range of the public service - rules. However, the constraints soon constitute the conscience. Ambedkar is reduced to a deity that imparts an identity. It is therefore that one curiously finds dalits celebrating the joint birth anniversaries of Babasaheb Ambedkar and Shivaji along with the Shiv Sena in the so-called den of Ambedkarism - the State of Maharashtra.

Gender Equality: More Noise, Little Substance

It is expected of the people who avowedly fought against their unequal status, to have a congenial attitude towards the victims of other inequalities. Women are one social group who despite constituting half of the human population and contributing equally to the sustenance of human society are being discriminated against all over the world in varying degrees of severity. Gender inequality should have been the foremost issue in the dalit movement. At least this problem could have been approached with the demonstration of a paradigm shift towards a radical culture. But unfortunately, with the rise of petty- bourgeoisie consciousness in dalits, they have adopted the more regressive culture of the forward castes. Traditionally, dalit women had equality of sorts in so far as they worked with their men folk for managing their homestead. But now the cultural preference of relegating them to the background to do the household chores and / or to look after children is increasingly evident in dalit homes. It is a matter of pride that right from the days of Ambedkar, women have played a major role in the dalit movement. Among the poorer folks they still continue to do so. But this historical legacy also could not thwart the onslaught of the regressive culture.

In the din of what Ambedkar did for women, the icon that guides action is of the exponent of legal and coded equality of women, something like equality on the statutes (a la Hindu Code Bill). Culturally, dalits have not transcended the boundaries of sanskritisation, in the sense that their women folk have been given the worn out role model of a Brahmin woman; just because Ambedkar had once exhorted them to emulate her in the manner of donning their saris and other ornaments. At other times, he had reminded them of the importance of their role in community development as mothers or wives and advised them to perform it better. Thus, it may be said that the approach towards women even in the glorious days of the struggle also had not gone beyond the men-centric traditional role women donned. Similar observation can be made against Buddhism, that its meta-ideals also could not so much as grant them the absolute equality with men.

It is a well known fact that Buddha had granted his tacit approval for the ladies to enter the Buddhist order as the '*Bhikkunies*', at the instance of Anand -one of his close and favourite disciples, but had prescribed that they will always bow in reverence to a *Bhikku* irrespective of their relative seniority in the order. Although, it is said that the dalit movement scarcely reflected the current shift in favour of equality of women, it would be erroneous to judge the events of the past by present standards. It is not to be forgotten that Ambedkar had to communicate with dalits in their familiar idiom. The cultural change, moreover is an invisible process. What Ambedkar said or did had the limitation of historical possibilities; he would not say anything for the sake of postulating. He craved for change and strove to bring it about with a practicable approach. In relation to women, his approach needs to be understood from this perspective. Unfortunately, dalits seem to have frozen it into an icon and raised fences around themselves from the concept of radical gender equality.

Suicidal Anti-Materialism

It is a sad paradox of history that the movement of dalits, who are undisputedly the biggest sufferer of material depravation, should show an utter disregard for things material in an era characterised by stark materialism. It smacks of its distaste for the real issues of life while displaying excessive enthusiasm for the emotional issues. After the massive movement of landless labourers led by Dadasaheb Gaikwad, incidence of the material questions that afflict most of the people, could be seen as just notional (e.g., the agitation for fallow lands by Samyak Samata Andolan). Even the Panthers could not escape this trend. There have been massive displays of strength of dalit unity but it all has been for emotional issues. The examples abound. The glorious movements for 'Namantar', against the ban on the Riddles of Rama and Krishna, and many others representing the dalit-anger towards the attempts of castiest elements to denigrate and desecrate the statues of Babasaheb Ambedkar, certainly demonstrated potential force of dalits. The material reality that surfaced in the wake of each of these movements in terms of inhuman atrocities perpetrated in vengeance of their assertion, at the same time could not awaken them. In the Namantar case, in response to the Long March by dalits, the local dalit hamlets were burnt down, many people got lynched, many women were raped, and all were ostracised and boycotted. Every time this heinous episode recurs and dalits bear the brunt!

With regard to the neglect of material aspects of living in the dalit movement, the inspiring icon is made up of Ambedkar's much publicised opposition to the vulgar materialism propagated by the then communists. It is stuffed with his thoughts that reflect not necessarily disdain for the material things but a leaning towards a belief that the societal phenomena could well be shaped by the non-material things or processes. It is coloured by the fact that the tone of the struggles he launched has always been in the realm of codes, norms, traditions, and institutional practices that he aimed his struggle against for bringing about the socio-cultural change, a social revolution. The culmination of his mission, as it is seen by dalits, in Buddhism, that predominantly taught the virtue of extinguishing the thirst for material things and reaching indefinable State of mental peace called *Nirvana*, has certainly lent strength to this icon. Dalits always defined their struggle to be for prestige - for *'Asmita'*, for self-respect. The questions of land, remunerative wages, working conditions, government's economic policies etc. never interested them. In the history of four decades at no time any of their leaders or any intellectual cared to look at how the government policies or international happenings influenced the lives of average dalits in villages.

Even in the face of atrocities that dalits suffer day in and day out, never does the realisation dawn on them that much of it could be traced to their State of material depravation. The fact that they cannot organise defence is also related with their material wherewithal. It does not seem to be a question of violence or non-violence. Fortunately, Ambedkar's own stand on violence, as he often declared it in order to expose the futility of Gandhi's obsession with non-violence in the long polemics is well known to dalits. It reflected what according to him, the Buddha said 'to the extent possible, non-violence; if necessary, violence". But the icon of Ambedkar that came before people was conveniently shorn of this practical attribute. This icon seems to obfuscate even Buddha as the impracticable proponent of unqualified compassion and non-violence. It emphasises constitutionalism even in the wake of perpetration of heinous atrocities.

Elections: The incurable Obsession

Barring emotional issues, the dalit movement has been hijacked by the petty warring factions of incompetent leaders whose sole obsession appears to be elections of whatever kind. As roosters wake up crowing at the dawn or frogs surface out of nowhere around water pools formed with the first showers of monsoon, they all surface out of their slumber with any election announcement. Then follow the talks for alliances, allegations and counter allegations of money transactions, threats of splits and actual splits. This process could be preceded by the talks of unification of various factions, if they were not together, essentially engineered by the electoral strategies of some ruling class party. The masses however land up emotionally supporting such unity moves and ultimately fall prey to the machinations of big money. This cycle is seen repeated a number of times at least in Maharashtra, which has historically been assumed as the hub of dalit politics even after losing its provincial relevance. This dalit electioneering has been so shorn of reality and devoid of any political perspective as to seem end in itself, serving the personal interests of leaders.

They would not have any manifesto, no strategy, no agenda or plan; no realistic assessment of their strength and weakness. Participating in elections however was their sacred duty. The Ambedkar-icon that appears to back this strange phenomenon derives its material from the fact that Ambedkar himself relied upon elections for securing power despite his own bitter experiences, that he tended to think of the popular mandate gained through periodical elections as the only legitimate political process in the Constitutional regime and denounce other modes of mass struggle. It is additionally imbued with a hope that despite several defeats Ambedkar rose to occupy seats of power through the electoral process.

Now the people are increasingly getting dejected with the games of dalit leaders and are found to be straying over to other parliamentary parties, even of Brahminical hues. Many of the latter have already co-opted Ambedkar. Some have lent him their veneration by including his name into their list of the *'Pratah smaraniya'*- the memorables at the dawn. They have launched the class assimilative drives like Rashtriya Samarasata Manch. Today, there is a sort of clamour for claiming Ambedkar's legacy among all the parliamentary parties. In the face of disintegration of the dalit block and increasing political crises faced by these parties, they all need Ambedkar for their survival. Essentially, the icon of Ambedkar they promote is customised to serve their own interests. Even the BJP, the party that swears by Hindu religion and glorious Hindu tradition and culture, has put up Ambedkar to serve its ideology and politics, with fairly encouraging results. The icon they project is that of a staunch nationalist, of one who was proud of 'Indian' (read Hindu) culture and tradition minus evils like untouchability and of one who was against communism.

The election mania is so deep entrenched in the minds of dalits that they ceased to think of any other alternative. There is no appreciation of the fact that they have been squarely cheated in this intoxicating game. At the first place, the resource sensitive game does not gel with the starkly resourceless players. Second, so far they do not transcend their caste confines, their constituency remains acutely constrained by the numbers of their own caste. Third, even if one succeeded overcoming these odds in the election, there may essentially lie series of compromises ahead for basic survival in the houses. The system ensures that a true representative of dalits does not reach the portals of power, and if reached, he or she is soon neutralised. It is amazing that the simple empirical evidence of the systemic failure does not get across dalits. The constant strength of dalit representation in the Indian Parliament and legislative Assemblies by virtue of the reservation policy, has been utterly ineffective simply because the various identities in addition to the caste never let them come together. Electoral dalit politics pre-supposes alliances and compromises invariably with the ruling class parties who may satisfy the thirst for power of its leaders but certainly not support the dalit empowerment.

Ambedkar: Need for a Review

Various icons that the post-Ambedkar movement of dalits appear to have built up, characterise Ambedkar as the maker of the Indian Constitution, provider of the present order, a Bodhisatva, a constitutionalist, a messiah, a saviour, an SC leader, a liberal democrat, a staunch anti-Communist, a social engineer who believed in the reform process and disliked revolutions. It is heavily sculpted by the petty-bourgeoisie outlook that has completely hegemonised the dalit movement. It rarely reflects the dreamer in him who was perpetually in search of ways and means to see the human society sans exploitation, injustice and humbug. Many students of the dalit movement are influenced by these post-Ambedkar reflections in characterising Ambedkar as the bourgeoisie liberal democrat. Does it really project what Ambedkar stood for? Does it capture the full essence of his movement? More importantly, is that the Ambedkar whom we are going to use as the weapon in the emancipatory struggle of dalits?

Dalits as a social group, are still the poorest of poor. A negligible minority has managed to escape poverty limits and to locate itself on to a continuum ranging up to a reasonable level of prosperity with the help of certain State policies like reservation and political patronage. In social terms however, all dalits, irrespective of their economic standing, still suffer oppression. This social oppression varies from the crudest variety of untouchability, still being practised in rural areas, to the sophisticated forms of discrimination encountered even in the modern sectors of urban life. Although, the statistics indicate that dalits have made significant progress on almost all parameters during the last five decades, the relative distance between them and non-dalits seems to have remained the same or has increased. More than 75 per cent of the dalit workers are still connected with land; 25 per cent being the marginal and small farmers and the balance 50 per cent being landless labourers. The proportion of dalits landless labourers to the total labourers has shown a steady rising trend. In urban areas, they work mainly in the unorganised sector where the exploitation compares well with that of a feudal rural setting. Out of the total dalit population of 138 million, the number of dalits in services falling in the domain of reservations does not exceed 1.3 million including sweepers; less than even a percent. And this too would be grossly misleading, as out of this 1.3 million the relatively well-off group A and B officers (in which most of the clerical staff of the PSUs also come), count only 72,212 as against 131,841sweepers.

With the new politico-economic order emerging in the world, the grammar of the dalit liberation struggle is going to be totally different from that familiar to dalits. The onslaught of the adversarial forces is being felt world over by all the oppressed people and it would be folly for dalits not to feel a part of the latter. Their objective situation as a social block is not represented by the minuscule minority that managed to find themselves in the organised sectors of economy, but by the vast majority who are left behind in the villages or the numbers who toil in the unorganised sectors in towns and cities. They need the weaponry for battling out their salvation. This battle is to be waged simultaneously on two fronts, marked by the caste and class. These terms under segmented and sectarian usage came to bear an erroneous exclusivity. Since, Ambedkar still provides a better framework for their problems than any other, and since he commands an unchangeable place in their hearts, the weapons in his armoury needs dusting and sharpening. They will need a review for their effective application in the changing context and possibly, substantial supplementation and replenishment. Ambedkar, quite similar to Buddha in his own hands, needs redefinition.

The folklore 'Ambedkar' needs to be replaced by the radical 'Ambedkar', who would inspire people to claim the whole world as theirs and not to beg for petty favours from the robbers. It is the responsibility of all those who are capable of seeing the reality, to contribute to this task. For, without such a redefinition, Ambedkar could be fossilised as god but would fail in the emancipation project; he might be raised to the highest pedestal by the vested interests but then he would be unable to reach out to where he is most needed; he would lose out to the parody of history.

Redefining Ambedkar

Ambedkar's thoughts are variously presented by scholars. Some tend to put them in familiar academic slots, viz.: social, political, economic, religious etc. The other method may be bracketed as biographical. The problem with the former is that it tends to discretise his thoughts within the artificial compartments of academic disciplines. The latter tends to be narrational, eulogical and scarcely analytical. Both of them are likely to miss out the underscoring vision and more so the futuristic dimension, which are essentially the attributes of the holistic conception.

Visions and Icons of Great Person

Every great person has a vision that impels all her/his works. Its discernibility may vary from case to case, generally being the function of the degree of turbulence around her/him, her/his relative position within the power structure in the given environment, her/his own equipment and conception of self-role. Marx, for instance, offers an articulate vision in clearest terms as he assumed the primary role of a philosopher to bring about revolutionary change, whereas Ambedkar had donned the mantle of mass-leadership in his primary role to spearhead the change; the degree of turbulence in the work domain of Marx had been minimal as he basically struggled in the realm of thought spanning complete human history whereas Ambedkar situated himself in the political turbulence that obtained in India as his strategy; Ambedkar's position in the power structure that bounded his work domain was certainly weak relative to Marx's.

This is neither to undermine the role of Marx as the activist constantly trying out his philosophy in the realm of practice nor to belittle the problems he suffered in life. With regard to personal equipment, both Ambedkar as well as Marx, could be taken to be equally equipped to undertake their respective tasks that they had undertaken. Marx had started off with philosophy and adopted the class-consciousness of the proletariat quite unlike Ambedkar, in whose case it was his own consciousness - the consciousness of an untouchable built up through concrete experience that had propelled his philosophical search. Marx was well aware of his role in the revolutionary project, that he had to provide requisite tools and tackles for the working class for bringing about a change in the overall interest of humanity. But, Ambedkar was always loaded with anxiety as he had to strategize his way through the political maze around him, winning for dalits the maximum he could in a short span of time. In process, his role also underwent transformation with the expanse of the battleground. Inevitably, his thoughts and action always remained context-laden, polemical and pragmatically purposeful. It is therefore a relatively difficult task to discern a coherent vision underscoring the life work of Babsaheb Ambedkar.

It is a moot point as to what extent a great person, who is essentially anchored in her/his space and time, could transcend these barriers and be equally effective in a different situation. A great person basically is the product of prevailing social relations. It is a particular moment in history that reflects an acute demand for such a person. Depending upon her/his location in the social setting, s/he imparts her/his individual feature to the historical moments and movements in terms of working out specific means for resolving contradictions that engender them and releasing the forces of history in a specific direction. The masses whose cause she / he espouses throng around her/him in this process, depending upon the level of their collective consciousness. The longevity of the ideas a great person propounds in a historical setting depends upon the nature of contradictions, the size and expanse of problems and the time domain in which they are situated. Generally, the classes that share the vision and ideology of such persons tend to iconise them with specific attributes of their class choice, in an attempt to institutionalise the latter.

In this process, they would de-contextise some of the ideas and proffer them as universal theorems, if they perceive a pay-off for themselves in the sphere hegemonised by them. This phenomenon becomes clear only over a long time horizon. For instance, the religious principles that were sprouted in the soil of certain specific social relations have basically blossomed in an alien soil with the help of the nutrients of class interests. Very broadly speaking, the trend of iconisation of great persons and the attempt of institutionalising their ideas is a gauge to assess the forces of status quo in the society.

Ambedkar: Commitment and Constraint

In the case of Babasaheb Ambedkar, iconisation was inevitable. The combination of factors like his high stature, his devotion to the cause of his people; the historical setting in which he lived, the low level of literacy and political consciousness in masses; and the vested interests of internal as well as external people have been its cause. The problem is not with iconisation as it is with its multiplicity. A question may be pertinently asked can Ambedkar be uniquely represented by a single icon? As Prof. Upendra Bakshi had outlined in one of his articles during the centenary year of his birth anniversary that there were many Ambedkars and had questioned as to which Ambedkar do we commemorate? When he said so, Prof. Bakshi was referring to different facets of Ambedkar's personality that could be virtually segregated. One can even periodise some of them. For example, the pre-1942 Ambedkar as a young, untouchable man endowed with highest scholastic distinctions, struggling within and without for the emancipation of his people is a grossly different personality than the Ambedkar as a member of the viceroy's Executive Council or the Ambedkar as the law minister in the Nehru cabinet in the post-independence India or the Ambedkar as the chairman of the drafting committee for the Indian Constitution or even the Ambedkar of still later years who had completely identified himself with Buddhism and in a way completely spiritualised himself.

What comes clearly however, from this review is that the changes in his outlook and role were essentially driven by his unstilted commitment to the cause of emancipation of oppressed humanity in general and dalits in particular. He might not have had appropriate methodological tools to deal with the problem at hand. With the equipment that basically belonged to a school of social engineers, he tried to dissect history. Paradoxically, he attempted to demolish the establishment with the very tools that were forged to serve the ruling classes. By training he did not have the facility to look at history as the continuum of human struggle with a certain inherent logic. He did use history as a repertoire of human episodes and attributed even logic to it but its source was externalised.

Non-Dialectical Solution: State and Religion

It appears that Babasaheb Ambedkar had really internalised the doctrine of momentariness (*Anityatawad* and later *Kshanikwad*) of Buddha and therefore even refused to care for consistency in his views and opinions. This doctrine states that every thing changes every moment, that things are constantly becoming. It follows that in this situation of flux not even mental processes could be static, they had essentially to match the dynamicity of the material world. He thus never hesitated in changing his thoughts or strategy as per the unfolding situation. Viewed another way, these changes can be understood in relation to foci of control. The degree of consistency in thought and action is generally inversely proportional to the distance of the subject from the foci of control of its surrounding. Ambedkar had nil or little control over his situation. He had to consistently create space for himself and strategize to influence the situation to his advantage. (The dynamics of the situation was propelled by the forces that were variously placed in the adversary camps.) The framework within which he conceived his struggle had exposed him to his lot to respond to this dynamics. The hallmark of Ambedkar's thoughts is the dynamic rationale, which he has consistently employed to comprehend situations and to strategize his response thereto. 'Ambedkar' therefore cannot be captured in static terms. His icon will have to represent the dynamism that he lived. Since, this is an infeasible proposition; we will have to discern the underscoring vision behind his works, the intransient essence of his entire mission to create a suitable icon. This icon, even if it does not resemble the familiar Ambedkar, alone could be the beacon of the dalit movement.

The concept of *Anityawad* in Buddhism essentially belongs to dialectics that has made Buddha an early dialectician philosopher. The dichotomy that creeps in can only be resolved by dialectical method. It may be questioned whether Ambedkar's method was dialectical. It appears that while he accepts constant becoming of things as the principle underscoring the universe, he faces a dilemma with respect to the conception of order in this State. It could be resolved dialectically in terms of systemic attribute of self-regulation—a characteristic of internal control. But the conventional conception of order, essentially a non-dialectical conception, leads to externalisation of control. Ambedkar, having experienced the brutal aspects of history and unbridled exploitation of man by man, appears in need of a control mechanism operating at two levels, viz., internal and external, so as to maintain the societal order in the desired State. His internal control mechanism is the moral code provided by the religion and the one for external control is the State.

If this moral code is internalised by all individuals and in turn by society as the summation of the latter (as the liberal tradition held), society is expected to have an internal order. If however the baser instincts of some people or group of people defy this order, either as a result of conflicting codes they follow or for any other reason, then in such case the State will step in and restore the order. The will of the collective is supposed to be embodied in the State by the Constitution. It is therefore that Ambedkar has reservation in agreeing with Marx that 'religion was the opium of masses' or the 'State shall eventually wither away'. Ambedkar certainly did not know that the order could be the attribute of the system itself. It is only in the sixties that Cybernetics principles came to lime light that the complex probabilistic systems, which the social systems certainly are, do have the inherent capability of self-regulating and self-organising control.

Liberalism and Reformism

By upbringing and training Ambedkar was influenced by western liberalism. The openness and liberal values of the western society had struck him with pleasant surprise by his own admission. There is a reason to believe that he had studied Marxism. His first essay on caste reflects some amount of analytical orientation of Marxism. One of the subjects in his curriculum also happened to be related to Marxian socialism and his guide Prof. Seligman was well versed with the economic interpretation of history. However, as his later work reveals, Ambedkar reflected more closeness with the liberal tradition than Marxism. However, consciously he never identified himself with the Liberalism. Being aware of its pitfalls, he needed to declare that he was not a liberal reformist, although while having reservations with the postulations of Marxism he could never hide his attraction towards it.

The pitfall of his thinking emanates from his conception of the moral force of religion divorced from the material reality. He therefore hopes that without any bloodshed, the society based on liberty, equality and fraternity could be created. Of course as hypothesized above, he conceptualizes the constitutional State based on these principles. With this wishful thinking, he tends to ignore the fact that regardless of the pretensions of ruling classes, the impact of liberal governance in the multi-centric iniquitous society is bound to result in sustaining multi-centricity and inequality. This liberalism rather promotes politics of casteism and communalism, schism among dalits, their use in political power games, subversion of their real problems and protects the interests of the few rich. It was a kind of contradiction in terms to assume that liberal democracy, which is actually the manifestation of the political power of the bourgeois, will do justice to the paupers. It might appear to extend certain concessions to the weaker sections, but its real motive is to maintain the existing rule of the ruling classes. Liberal democracy might appear better than the decadent Hindu caste system but it is incapable of bringing any real change in favor of dalits. It muffles the tension of the exploitative system and kills the revolutionary motivation of its victims.

Redefinition Project

Many of the constructs employed by Babasaheb Ambedkar in his working have a qualified meaning. Firstly, they are not absolute as they appear. They are the derivatives of his thought process, the source of which could be traced to his basic objective of annihilation of castes and creating a society based on equality, liberty and fraternity. Even these three principles that he held so dear to his heart, bear very different meaning from the familiar ones associated with the French Revolution. He said he had them from Buddha. What Buddha said also is to be understood from his interpretation, which could be as different from the accepted version as to be disproved by the Buddhist church. His Buddha and His Dhamma, for instance, had faced this kind of disapproval initially from many Buddhists. Understanding Ambedkar thus essentially demands extra consideration and care about the specific meanings of the constructs and concepts he uses.

The lack of it has already caused much misunderstanding among many people. It is one thing to have a clear understanding of what he said or meant but quite another to extrapolate it to something congruent to his basic objective or vision that may be useable in shaping the future movement. Quite like Marx had said of philosophy, it could be said that the issue is not to understand Ambedkar as he is but to possibly think of him as a weapon in the struggle to which he devoted his life. The redefinition referred to here will have to essentially address both these issues. From the viewpoint of one seeking a revolutionary change, there are indeed many dimensions on which Ambedkar calls for critical interpretation. Many of the concepts that seem to act as the props for his formulations are rooted in the reactionary camp. Paradoxically, he brings them to work for his emancipatory project, which potentially is no less than a revolution. Predominant among these concepts are identified as State, religion, liberal democracy, constitutionalism, revolution, socialism, violence and Marxism, that some way or the other have been the cause of misunderstandings about him.

It is important to appreciate that Ambedkar employed the search process that is essentially rational and the underlying objective undoubtedly radical. There could be flaws in the specific design or the application of the search process, depending upon the State of his knowledge and complexity of the situation to which it is applied. Besides this, the end result depends upon the repertoire of alternatives used for the search. What it means is that the specific method, thought or action of Ambedkar may constitute the historical facts but they cannot be taken in their face value if one wants to comprehend the ideological aspects of Ambedkar. In his usage of the above concepts for instance he does not always exercise the academic rigour. Besides the reason that much of his usage was addressed to the un-academic lot, most of the times he tended to impart his own meanings to the terms he used. With the changed contexts or with the change in information, he readily changed his opinions. For, hypothetically speaking, if Ambedkar had lived longer he would have certainly changed his views, looking at more information available or experiencing the undesired aftermath of some of his own beliefs and opinions. Had he not disowned the Constitution, which he had so laboriously written and so forcefully defended, saying that he was used as the hack to write it? Whatever he had done had several limitations. He never hesitated to change his opinion or stand if he was convinced that it was right. The redefinition project proposed here, in a way, is something, which he has done himself, all his life and would have continued doing if he had been alive. It is essentially something in the nature of continuing his unfinished task.

The methodological aspects of this exercise consists in the process of conceptualisation of the core vision and ideological proclivities of Ambedkar through the analytical study of his life within its contextual parameters, oriented towards capturing its intransient content. It should reflect the basic purpose, that is, to see whether and how he could catalyse the emancipatory movement of dalits and in turn democratise the Indian society. This process may not be free from bias. The bias could be in favour of the change craved for by the have-nots, not of the ruling classes that has necessarily been colouring the history so far. It cannot escape the viewpoint of the latter. The viewpoint is rather embodied in the basic intention to forge Ambedkar as the weapon for the future struggles of dalits. The process of conceptualisation may be formalised by drawing out multiple ideological patterns based upon the constituent parameters of the hypothesised vision and testing them with the facts in their macro and micro settings. The test results could be used to refine the definition of the parameters and repeating the exercise until they can no more be improved. The iterative process will eliminate the tactic-based episodes and increasingly highlight the intransient dimensions. The radicalisation consists in derivation of the programme from these dimensions with any scientific methodology.

It is not possible to demonstrate adoption of this methodology within the space of this paper. The following discussion therefore directly deals with the salient dimensions of Ambedkar's life in order to capture its intransient essence.

'Ambedkar' for The Movement of Dalits

'Ambedkar' for the dalit movement, first of all, should be shorn of all the sectarian outlook that unfortunately came to be associated with him. He was an iconoclast and therefore should inspire us to break such icons that are imbued with this outlook. Dalits have to demolish all the handiwork of the reactionaries and vested interests. The project of redefinition of Ambedkar should liberate him from the dens of the ruling class and bring him back to the huts in slums and villages where he rightly belongs.

The greatest thing about Ambedkar is his consistent anti-dogmatic stance. He never accepted any thing in name of authority. He hated humbug of every kind. He always approached problems with a student's sincerity and researcher's intellectual honesty. He gave a vision that even the ideologies are bound by the tenet of impermanence and no body should claim them validity beyond their times. His followers therefore can assume absolute liberty to think through things as per their own experience in changing times.

Here, we can discuss certain issues, clarity on which may contribute to this task.

'Ambedkar' against Exploitation

The underscoring vision in Ambedkar's thought and action is to be found in his yearning for the end of all kinds of exploitation. Whenever and wherever he smelt exploitation, he raised his voice against it. The caste system that subjugated more than one fifth of the population to levels worse than animals' for more than two millennia and which represented institutionalisation of the most heinous inequality by the Hindu religion as ordained by its gods, became the prime target of his life. He attacked it from the standpoint of its victims - the untouchables. He waged many battles; initially targeting the citadels of Brahminism - the custodian of the Hindu religious code, and later politicised the battle, realising the ineffectiveness of the former. He did not let this objective out of sight even for a moment and worked incessantly for its achievement. This Herculean task almost completely overshadows the fact that his struggles extend well beyond the caste struggles and rather encompass all other forms of exploitation.

Even the credit for struggling against untouchability was reluctantly granted to him by the establishment which had belittled him initially as merely a leader of his own caste - Mahar. This prejudicial treatment of Ambedkar could itself be taken as a measure of the severity of the problematic of caste. The facts are clear today that not only was his struggle directed towards the emancipation of all the untouchables but also towards annihilation of the entire caste system. It was basically against the systemic exploitation that ran unabated for centuries. The protest against this inhuman system could be articulated only in a concrete situation, not in a vacuum. He did not theorise the struggle on a hypothetical plane. He built it on the basis of real problems in a concrete situation. Unlike many cases, the motive force for his life mission was provided by his experience itself. Although he pitched his tents against Brahminism, he never bore any enmity against the Brahmins or identified any one for his friend or foe by caste. The Bahishkrit Hitkarini Sabha that was the launch vehicle of his movement had majority from the forward caste people in its executive body. Even later, this intention of having a non-caste base for the organisation could be consistently seen in his movement, be it the Mahad struggle or the Indian Labour Party. He was perceptive enough to say that the Brahminism could exist in all the castes including the untouchables, for that was the essence of the casteism. It is tragic to find his legacy being monopolised today by only the scheduled castes.

Although, he considered the magnitude of the problem of emancipation of dalits is such as to warrant his sole attention, he did take cudgels for other oppressed entities like workers, peasants and women. At one occasion in response to the accusation that he did not care for the tribals, he had to squarely admit the fact that he considered the problem at hand big enough to outlast his life and provokedly put that he never claimed to fight for whole humanity. Such instances though disturbing enough could be understood within their specific context. While dealing with the socio-economic depravation of dalits, he comprehensively exposed certain systemic dimensions that help perpetuate exploitation. For instance, he was well aware of the capitalist and imperialist oppression besides the decadent feudalism within which domain his problem lay.

Capitalism

During the colonial British regime, capitalism started taking root in India with the collaboration of Indian mercantile capital and British capital. Unlike Europe, it did not have to battle against feudalism; rather it was implanted on the trunk of the latter in India. As a result, even in the capitalist institutions in the cities, caste discrimination simultaneously existed. Ambedkar was quite aware of the exploitative potential of capital and hence he had declared capitalism and Brahminism as the twin enemy of his movement. Capitalism was in an infantile stage then but Brahminism encompassed the phases of slavery, feudalism and extended its tentacles as we see to the phase of imperialism. Moreover, he noted the reactionary compradore character of rising capitalism in the contemporary sectors of the economy and the inhuman exploitation of workers that it unleashed. His, Indian Labour Party (ILP) was an attempt to take up the question of capitalist exploitation, as well as to combine the struggle on both caste and class basis. Various workers' problems were taken up by the ILP, the leadership of combined strike of the mill workers, parliamentary fight for the workers' interest in relation to the Industrial Disputes Act, and various legal reforms that were brought about while he was in the Executive Council of the Viceroy, can be the examples of his concern for workers' exploitation. It cannot be denied that his approach to these contemporary problems was closer to that of the Fabian socialists with whom he was more familiar. But, it was a model adopted out of familiarity and pragmatism, a matter of strategy, never thought out on an ideological plane to be a theoretical plank. Although, there cannot be any doubt that he stood against capitalism, he could not articulate a sound theoretical basis for doing so. Resultantly, his efforts remained constricted with a short view of workers' welfare but could not provide them a vision of their liberation.

Imperialism

Ambedkar's attitude towards imperialism has been projected in a distorted manner right from the beginning, mainly because he refused to take part in the freedom struggle or opposed Gandhi who for certain category of ignoramuses was the anti-imperialism personified. He strategically sought to maintain neutrality vis-à-vis the colonial State. As per him, it would not be possible for the resourceless dalits to fight its mighty foes all together. He did not want to dissipate and squander his extremely limited resources on several fronts. He however knew the basic exploitative character of the colonial regime. At several occasions, he burst out saying that British imperialism and Indian feudalism were the two leaches that clung to Indian people. (BB, 58 (8)). However, there was a fundamental difference between his and others' viewpoint. For instance, he did not approve equating opposition to imperialism with opposing the British. He noted that the opposition to imperialism couldn't be effective until its supporters within the country are left untouched. The then leader of the Communist Party of India - Manabendranath Roy once met him at his residence and during discussions insisted that destruction of imperialism had to be the first and foremost objective of Indian politics. Ambedkar's response to him summarised his outlook towards this problem. He replied to Roy in explicit terms that without struggling against the landlords, mill owners, moneylenders - the friends of imperialism within the country, it was not possible to wage an effective fight against imperialism. It may be a matter of research but a priori his anti-imperialist attitude pervades even his writings as a student.

The validation of his stand comes from an entirely unrelated corner and nearly half a century later. Suniti Kumar Ghosh, (1985 and 1995) in his books has shown in great detail how the Congress representing landlords and capitalists had played a compradore role to serve the interest of imperialism during the so-called freedom struggle and how even after the transfer of power in 1947 the grip of imperialism instead of weakening became stronger. Does it not indicate that he was more correct than any of his contemporary politicians? The ones who biasedly wish to pronounce their half baked verdict that Ambedkar was a stooge of British merely on the basis of his acceptance of membership of Viceroy's Executive Council or talking to the Simon Commission, not only display their ignorance of history but also their casteist fangs. They ought to rethink the comparison between Ambedkar who, even being apparently a part of the imperialist apparatus was perhaps striking at its roots by empowering the people and many others, so called nationalists, who after wearing the mask of anti-imperialism were indirectly strengthening its pillars.

In relation to British rule, Ambedkar basically makes two points. The first is that he questions the so-called freedom struggle launched under the leadership of Congress as an anti-imperialist struggle. He contended that the Congress basically represented the class of feudal lords and the urban capitalists - the twosome exploiters of Indian masses. Although, it succeeded through the charismatic leadership of Gandhi in galvanising masses in its support, it essentially relied on bargaining with the colonial rulers for securing itself more share of power. It always throttled the mass spontaneity as in the case of 1942-uprisings and actively opposed the genuine anti-imperialist struggles of the revolutionaries like Bhagat Singh. Ambedkar reflects the understanding of true character of the Congress in his own way, when he says that if Congress was fighting a real anti-imperialist war, he would whole heartedly support it.

The rhetoric of such statement apart, for he never appears to even take a note of other truly anti-imperialist struggles like the one referred to above, it is enough to reveal his attitude towards imperialism and understanding of the class character of the Congress. He knew that the class character of the Congress would not permit it to don this role in reality. Ambedkar could see through the anti-imperialist masks the real fangs of an exploiter of masses.

He thus not only saw no point in siding with this more real exploiter of people than perhaps the colonial rulers, but also did not hesitate to openly oppose it when it came in the way of dalit liberation. He smelt rot in all such struggles that refused to notice existence of inhuman exploitation of some of their own people within their precincts and tended to over-externalise their woes. Here lay his second point when he raised a question of Hindu imperialism perpetrated through its caste system that was certainly seen as more vicious by its victims than the British rule. It may be pertinent to ask of those who raise the issue of Ambedkar's attitude and conduct towards imperialism, to answer as to why the problem of untouchability or caste system that reduced its one -fifth of the population to sub-human levels did not find a mere mention in the lofty discussions of freedom struggle that pre-dated Ambedkar's raising it.

The anti-imperialist aspiration also could be seen in the context of the class/caste division in the society. The battle for the lost kingdom waged by the vanquished lords also could be camouflaged as an anti-imperialist struggle and at the same time the genuine peoples' anti-imperialist aspiration manifested in the form of say anti-feudal struggle could be condemned as the pro-imperialism, merely because it directed its gun towards the props of the imperialism. The real anti-imperialist aspirations belong to the masses of people the manifestation of which is possible only through the peoples' war. Whatever anti-imperialist struggle people waged were soon hijacked by the phoney war whose real intent was to extract political power to native ruling classes. While the scenes of anti-British struggles were being enacted for the 'mother' India of exploiters, Ambedkar busied himself to liberate the other India- the India of the exploited and oppressed.

Oppression of Women

Besides these mainstream forms of exploitation even the subaltern forms like women's exploitation, could not escape his agenda. He viewed them as the most oppressed of all. His approach to the problems was typically that of a liberal democrat constitutionalist. This certainly constrained his articulation of this problem as in many others. This issue will have to be seriously rethought by dalits under the redefinition project. But suffice here to say that at any opportunity, he raised his voice against women's discriminatory situation in the society.

His basic law of social engineering was that the social revolutions must always begin from the standpoint of the most oppressed or the ones on the lowest rung of the society. Right from the days of Mook Nayak and Bahiskrit Bharat, he appears to take cudgels for women. He always involved women in his struggles and tended to give them vanguard positions.

For example, about 500 women had marched at the head of the historical procession at Mahad to assert the untouchables' right to drink water from the public tank. He was immensely pained to see the permanent denial of education and religious rights to women ordained in the Shastras of the Hinduism (e.g. Manusmriti). His democratic consciousness never reconciled with any thing lesser than the equality of men and women though its expression was acutely constrained perhaps by his anxieties about the possibilities, so much so that it might even be mistaken as the male centric tactic. While he asked women to be good mothers so as to shape up their son or to be good wives to their husbands or be a carrier of community's cultural baggage, he did struggle for their equal rights as in the case of Hindu Code Bill. He described sacramental marriages (Mathew, 1991) as polygamy for men and perpetual slavery for women because under no circumstances within that system the latter would get liberty from their husbands, however bad or undesirable they may be. He insisted that women should have the freedom to break this contract.

Constitution: An Exercise in Liberal Democracy

Although, Ambedkar was conscious of the limitations of liberal democracy in the emancipatory project he had undertaken and at times had even declared that he was not a liberal democrat, for many reasons he could not escape its clutches completely. He could not be unaware that liberal democracy basically was born as the ruling class ideology in 19th century Europe. It takes individuals and their groups as basically selfish units as its premise. It holds that individuals and social groups progress only through competition. It had however to take cognizance of weaker sections in the society, paradoxically in a large number, who cannot enter this competition openly and hence could be potentially be spoilers of the game. The French Revolution had demonstrated this potential in ample measure. As the Whigs in the English Liberal party had thought "the best way to ward off revolution was to adopt a liberal generous attitude toward the lower classes.

The upper classes should make concessions gracefully and in good time, and not wait until the lower classes are roused to exact them. If a revolution happens, it doesn't show that the people are bad and should have been repressed more thoroughly... repression is self-defeating. What it shows is that the upper classes were not wise enough and self-confident enough to make reasonable concessions in good time." It accommodates the relatively weaker sections by extending them some concessions or aids for some time, basically to equip them for this universal competition. The State performs the role of a referee in this competition. This State is supposed to be run by the representatives of all the social groups. Notwithstanding his awareness of the above facts, Ambedkar's schema does reflect the expectation that the State would perform the role of independent referee.

The influence of liberalism on Ambedkar is more pronounced after he accepted the role of the chairman of the drafting committee for the Indian Constitution in collaboration with the Congress. In the light of his own proposals of State socialism submitted to the Constituent Assembly on behalf of the Scheduled

Caste Federation, this ideological somersault could only be understood as the situational compulsions acting upon him. Just before entering the Constituent Assembly he had experienced the bitter phase of political oblivion and had seen from closer angles the prospect of his life's mission ending without any result. He had a dire need to enter the Constituent Assembly and include certain provisions for his people in the future Constitution. When Congress offered him this role, he had to perform it within bounds in exchange for his life's ambition to provide for his people. The compulsions are too obvious to be ignored. His States and Minorities envisages most of the productive assets to be the State property. This was against the principle of liberal democracy. The liberal theory of property right from the days of John Locke and Thomas Hobbes in the 17th century stressed on private property and on the duty of the government to protect it. It was the Congress liberalism that he had to submit to and had to plead for property rights that were considered pivotal within the Constitution.

The same holds true for the centralization of power and certain basic rights, which were congenial to the capitalist class. He had to accept all such provisions that considered the existing power structure from status quo viewpoint instead of transformation. He was compelled to accommodate the principles of social democracy, which he has been regarding as the basic soul into the ineffective chapter of the directive principles of the constitution. He himself had to accept the same parliamentary executive that he had always misgivings about as being dangerous to the life and freedom of ex-untouchables.

He could not be unaware of the fact that from the viewpoint of the oppressed and dalits, except for the reservations, the Constitution was not making any material difference. On the contrary, it had made all the arrangements for letting all the benefits of power stay with the wealthy and traditional elite classes while dangling the carrot of Constitutional safeguards and reservations for dalits and the oppressed people. The existing socio-economic structure was kept in tact in the Constitution underneath the western democracy which proclaimed the principle of 'one vote, one value' in political arena. Ambedkar could not hide his discomfort at this dichotomy and had to burst out in his famous warning that if equality in the socio-economic sphere is not achieved within a reasonable time, the disadvantaged people would blast off the structure of the political democracy. He was aware of the fallacy in the assumption that political democracy would catalyze the social revolution through universal franchise and periodic elections. He had himself tested the bitter fruits of this process through the electoral defeats. Politics run on the principles of free market economy can never entail equality. The slogans like socialism, social justice, equality etc. were merely masks to fool the people. The grammar of the game of electoral politics foreordained the politicians serving the interests of big landlords, capitalists and compradore bourgeoisie. They could not survive free political competition without the latter's blessings. Ambedkar should have been aware that liberal values and liberal institutions are incapable of arresting the monopolistic hold of the moneyed classes on political power.

On Revolution

Revolution, on the face of it, appears to be an anathema to Ambedkar who seems to dread it and instead advocates reforms. But it would be disaster to take it at face value. For, like many other terms, his usage of the term 'revolution' does not bear the same meaning as is in vogue, particularly in Marxist circles. What Ambedkar seems to detest in revolution is the violence. At many places he tends to equate rebellion, revolution and revolt with violence. He also seems to disagree with the method of insurrection. He thought that without mass consciousness being ripe enough for revolutionary change, insurrectionary methods would not succeed. Moreover, he appears to be sceptical of the justness of revolutions as they invariably represent the triumph of the collective over the individual. It may be attributed to the influence of liberal democracy in which he got his indoctrination in his formative days. Liberal democracy always put an individual on a high pedestal and considered it precious.

His concern for the individual is not again doctrinaire but emanates from the value that any and every human being is precious and the belief that alone can act as the best guarantee against the collective tyranny and totalitarian excesses any time. In the context of the collapse of erstwhile Soviet block, where the totalitarian states that came into being in the name of dictatorship of proletariat and played havoc with people, this human-centric value assumes importance. One needs to be however reminded that even the values do need to have some material bases. They do not fall from sky. The contradiction between collective and individual has thus to be resolved in the concrete situation. As for Ambedkar, apart from this scepticism, he does not seem to have any dispute with the general aim and object of revolution.

Revolution, inasmuch as it seeks to bring about a fundamental change in the social relations in the society, will always be opposed by the forces of status quo, whose material interests are directly threatened by this change. In corollary, it becomes imperative for the forces of revolution to overcome this resistance whatever be the means. Whereas, the antagonist camp will always project codes of ethics and morality for their tactical defence in face of the onslaught of revolution, the revolutionaries discard them as decadent; for them revolution itself represents the highest value. Being the upsurge of the suppressed ones, revolutions do have a tendency to be bloody, but it is always in response to the resistance of its opponents. Therefore it is a representation only by the vested interest to associate violence or moral turpitude with revolutions. On the contrary, it would be more logical to say about the revolutionaries that being propelled by an external motivation to deliver mankind from the existing traps at the risk of their own lives; they cannot be bloodthirsty people.

The revolutionary violence is almost an inevitability that arises at the instance of the oppressors. In that sense Marx called "violence as the midwife of history", emphasising its inevitability. It is the inevitability that marks the compulsion of the vast majority of people to resist the anti-revolutionary violence of the minority. The pre-requisite here is that the revolution truly represents the majority consciousness. If it does not, then the violence of the few exercised with howsoever a lofty objective could transform into its anti-thesis, fortifying itself against the majority will. In this sense and insofar as the recent history showed the scepticism that revolutions trample upon individual's rights therefore cannot be dismissed as baseless. Historically, revolution is the process of identifying and destroying the obstacles in the existing order to take productive forces to the qualitatively next higher level, for the overall progress of human race. The progress achieved by mankind so far is basically due to the qualitative transformation from quantitative continuum that characterises revolutions. The qualitative transformations always need concentrated inputs, akin to latent heat in the case of phase transformation of water. In social transformation it takes the form of revolutionary energy that in turn may manifest into violence. Ambedkar does not neglect the necessity of violence. As he himself said that if dalits wanted to be effective they would need the canons.

It is erroneous to construe that his opposition to violence was idealistic or doctrinaire. Violence was not a taboo for him; it could be practised when it was absolutely necessary. Even his mentor Buddha, who is respected as the greatest apostle of non-violence had the same pragmatic approach towards violence. Ambedkar was not obsessed either with the idea of non-violence or the value of individualism professed by the classical school of liberal democracy. His reservations were against the possibility of the cunning of a few over-riding the will of majority as had happened in the case of caste institution. He would hate to see any thing like caste getting institutionalised again. In his scheme of things he therefore was not ready to compromise the value of democracy, the will of majority of people, whatever may be the end.

Ambedkar did not juxtapose reform against revolution, as many people tend to do. He does not reflect comprehension of technicality of dialectical materialism in his usage of these terms. Often his revolution is the violent overthrow of the existing rule and establishment of the new rule. Likewise, he does not seem to mean that reforms will not entail a qualitative transformation. What he certainly means by revolution is the change brought about in a 'big bang' manner. Notwithstanding what Ambedkar said about his own work, revolution does not always entail a 'big bang'; it is not a point concept as mistakenly regarded in common parlance, but a line concept. Mao's Great Proletarian Cultural Revolution may be a good example of this. There could be many bits of work, which contributes to taking society to a qualitatively higher rung in the ladder of progress that qualify to be the revolutionary work. The qualitative change itself occurs over a discrete time horizon and not a moment.

The moment that marks out transformation of power and looks like a 'big bang', alone is not the revolution. The particular phase of history puts constraints on the kind of changes that can be conceived in its womb. Some one dreaming of a socialist revolution in the slave society would only at best be a daydreamer; a romanticist but he cannot be a revolutionary. Likewise, certain phase of history demands a lot of quantitative preparation before a revolutionary change can be planned for. Ambedkar largely reflects these kinds of concerns while dealing with the issue of revolution. He did not see Indian situation ripe enough for any revolutionary change. Any change without resolution of the caste question, according to him, would not only be detrimental to dalits but also be an extremely short-lived.

The importance of Ambedkar's work can be gauged in relation to contemporary social situation and its transitional social context. Indian society was ridden with a peculiar brand of feudalism, the most prominent feature of which was caste. Caste had incapacitated over 15 per cent of its population and maintained them at the sub-human level. The large part of the balance population also suffered the degradation in a varying degree. This decadent institution had far outlived its minimal utility and as a result for centuries kept Indian society in a fossilised form. It served the material needs of a handful of people but all perceived varying stakes in the system on account of its hierarchical structure and faithfully practised it because they internalised it as their *Dharma* ordained by none other than God. The possible exception in generic terms were dalits who were placed at the lowest rung of the caste ladder and had hardly anything to their share.

However, in particular terms only a few castes from the dalit castes, who did not have any specific caste profession and hence little stake in the system and consequently who as the general workmen of villages had better exposure to the changing urban life than any one else came out of the hegemony of Brahmins to articulate the challenge to the system. The hierarchy among dalits however prevented them to come together and consequently this challenge had to be articulated caste by caste. Capitalism that took root in India in big cities also had struck compromise with the caste institution like its harbingers, the

British imperialism. It was an arduous task, as it still is, to conceive a model for this struggle and still more difficult to build. During the colonial times for various reasons these struggles had germinated largely in Maharashtra and Southern states where the social structure reflected sharper polarisation between dalits and balance society. Ambedkar's advent in the Indian socio-political scene marked their zenith.

It articulated its attack on Brahminism and capitalism that accepted its alliance, focused its organisation on dalits and gave a clarion call for annihilation of castes for achieving the ultimate aim of society based on Liberty, Equality and Fraternity to provide wider umbrella for all progressive forces to work. It reflects the distinct historical need to democratise Indian society without which it was bound to suffer constriction of its productive forces. This work had to have large content in the socio-cultural realm; it is a credit to Ambedkar's acumen that he gave it a political dimension. It had to be approached as reform. Ambedkar clearly found the talks of communist revolution as out of phase with the history although he never fully accepted the tenets of historical materialism as he thought it negatived human ingenuity and carried it through a pre-determined channel. He insisted that India did not provide congenial soil for germination of class-consciousness because of castes. Their annihilation therefore constituted the first task in the revolutionary agenda.

It is unfortunate that many communist revolutionaries still parrot the same characterisation of his work as in years back their predecessors proclaimed using the spoon fed theories from the West. One day it is hoped that the contributions of all the caste struggles to democratisation of Indian society would be restored as a native revolutionary heritage by these well meaning people. Till then it will always sound puerile to pigeonhole the historical work as reform or revolution merely on the basis of syntax and not the content. However, it is much more unfortunate for Ambedkarite dalits to deny themselves the credit for this historical contributions by dissociating from the revolutionary agenda, mistakenly thinking that it something alien to them. Effectively, not only they are denying themselves a historical opportunity to contribute to revolution but also delaying their own emancipation. Dalits have to rethink their position vis a vis revolution.

Ambedkar's dream of a society based on liberty, equality and fraternity cannot be realised except through revolution. They will have to understand Ambedkar's life and mission only from this perspective. His contribution to Indian revolution lies in the fact that he tried to comprehend Indian reality independently and tried to contribute to the resolution of its contradictions in his own way. Indian history held out the gauntlet of fossilised Indian feudalism for so long to the Indian revolutionaries but every one conveniently wished it away, initially as a superstructural matter that would disappear automatically when the material base is revolutionised and now after seven decades as a problem belonging to both structure and super-structure, that could be solved through revolutionary practice.

It still lacks the clarity and courage to hold the bull by horn. Ambedkar did not confuse issues, he saw clearly that the annihilation of caste will have to be consciously worked for before taking up any revolutionary project. He went beyond and found out the institutional base of castes in the Indian village whose economic support lay in the land-relations and caste division of labour. But, unlike many communists who still use the stereotype of land reform - a slogan of land to the tiller as the only revolutionary programme, he did not hamper on it because he knew that firstly it was economically impossible to satisfy the land hunger of the landless in the country, secondly the likely transformation of landless to a marginal farmer through land reforms was unlikely to solve the problems of dalits and thirdly, as the later empirical data showed, contrary to expectations the land reforms could aggravate the problem of caste.

Instead, he proposed nationalisation of land and co-operativisation of farming. He realised the necessity of detaching substantial village population from land and absorbing it into the industrial sector that was to be mainly under State sector. Even in retrospect, these points could have constituted a viable agenda for democratic revolution. As one naxalite scholar - (Ashok Kumar, 1995) perceptively puts it, for having independently seen the question of annihilation of castes linked with the question of land one could unhesitatingly call Ambedkar as the torchbearer of the people's democratic revolution.

'Ambedkar' as the Radical Thinker

Dalits are never tired of projecting Ambedkar as the greatest of all the leaders. That unfortunately smacks of sectarian attitude and of their blind devotion to him. They need to understand that the measure of greatness of any person could only be her / his contribution to better the human situation, in terms of correct understanding of its ailment and contribution to cure it. What Ambedkar did could be seen in relation to the broad five currents in Indian politics of his times:

- The Reformists current that wanted to bring about development on the western pattern, possibly with the support of British imperialism,
- Congress, that represented Indian capital and which demanded self-rule under the domination of British imperialism,
- The Terrorist Nationalists who had taken up arms in their fight for freedom against British imperialism,
- The Communists who were trying to implant Bolshevik revolution in India, and
- The Muslim League which opened up a separatist front of Muslims.

All of them scarcely reflected an understanding of the Indian situation. For instance, none showed even a cursory concern about the problems of one fourth of their countrymen who were forced to live worse than animals as ordained by their decadent religion. It was indeed surprising that although all craved for self-rule from the British, none concerned with the caste-system which basically was responsible in pushing the country repeatedly into slavery. None seemed to attempt an objective analysis of either the history or the present of this country. It could circumstantially be said that their motivations came from their narrow class-caste interests. These movements were motivated by the desire of an abstract freedom for country and a refusal to see the concrete slavery of their own people. Granted that the problems before the country were really intricate, still no one would dare say that the need for democratisation was in anyway subordinate. The real people's movement in the country was required to wage simultaneous war against imperialism, internal compradore bourgeoisie, landlords and Brahminism. It was only Ambedkar who clearly indicated this requirement. In this light, he was certainly ahead of all others. His own bitter experiences with untouchability had stood him in good stead in seeing this more clearly than any other.

He strove to build his movement along this understanding but unfortunately it was neither in his power to deal comprehensively with all the issues, nor was there an ideological and programmatic clarity required therefor. He inevitably had to focus his attention on dalits who were the worst victims of this multi-faceted oppression. It was the misfortune of Indian history that this struggle progressed in a constricted manner and eventually got dissolved into regressive statist politics. It reflected both the limitation of Ambedkar as well the situational compulsion on him.

The anti-caste movements before Ambedkar were mainly welfare oriented. Some wanted a higher rank for their own caste in the caste hierarchy and some taking the inferior culture of their caste to be the reason for their suffering, aimed at improving the same. Mahatma Phuley's movement was an exception to this trend insofar as it attempted to unite the Shudra and Ati-Shudra castes against the exploitation by the parasitic castes of Shetjis (capitalists) and Bhatjis (priests). While Ambedkar accepted the lineage/inheritance of this movement and held Phuley in greatest esteem as his one of the three *Gurus*, he went beyond to declare annihilation of caste to be the object of his movement in the direction of the goal of 'liberty, equality and fraternity'.

In the historical context it certainly was a radical step. He rightly diagnosed that the caste system is basically sustained by the peculiar economic constitution of the Indian village of which the land relations were the main features. Towards breaking this link he toyed with an idea of separate settlement for dalits at one time and at another exhorted them to leave villages for cities. He had clearly understood that castes stood on multiple props, viz., the religio-cultural relations, feudal relations in village setting of which land relations constituted the crux and the socio-political nexus with the State. Annihilation of castes thus needed destruction of all of them. He soon realised the necessity of political power for this multi-fronged attack. Even to bring about the residual change in the belief system either through the cultural or religious route, he stressed the necessity of political power. In this way, for the first time he brought the problem of untouchability and caste out of the confines of culture to the political agenda.

Unfortunately, this political agenda got lost into the maze of parliamentary politics that soon became be-all-end-all with dalit leaders. Even during Ambedkar's times the economic aspects of the problem remained largely untouched giving the impression to his followers as though they did not count. In the overall context it can be seen that they could not be as easily dealt with as the religio-cultural and political aspects of the problem. Moreover, it meant direct confrontation with the State for which Ambedkar was certainly not prepared. Alternately, the feudal relations in villages could be destroyed only if the private ownership of land is abolished and co-operativisation of farming is introduced. He thought, this structural change could be effected through the Constitution. It was a folly that he would soon realise when even as the 'chief architect' of the Constitution he failed so much as to bring this point on the agenda of the Constituent Assembly.

Conception of an Ideal

Babasaheb Ambedkar envisioned his ideal in the famous three principles: liberty, equality and fraternity. They were the basis for the ideal society of his conception. (BAWS, 1/57). He denied that he had adopted them from the French Revolution. He said he had derived them from the teachings of Buddha. These principles were the clarion call of the French Revolution but later became the ideological props of the liberal bourgeoisie in Europe. Since Marx had ridiculed these principles as the fantasy of the bourgeois society, many people tended to stereotype Ambedkar as the petty-bourgeois liberal democrat. As according to Ambedkar the source of these principles is different from the French Revolution, familiar to Marx, there is a prima facie scope to argue that Marx's ridicule does not apply to him. His conception of these principles is indeed substantially different from that associated with the liberal bourgeoisie. Actually, what Marx refers to are the slogans of liberty and equality of the bourgeois parliamentary democracy. There, 'liberty' is the liberty to contract and 'equality' refers to equality in market. Ambedkar insists that the conception of the ideal society ought to have them all the three together. Absence of any would not be acceptable to him. The ideal society of his dream could only be seen within a kind of spiritual frame. It would be interesting to compare this society with the communist society of Marx's conception. Marx reached his inference following the dialectical track of historical materialism. In Ambedkar' case it was just his vision. Inevitably, he had to attribute the origin of them to some spiritual source.

For Ambedkar they meant to denote the State of society sans exploitation and with an emotive ambience of fellow feeling. It was beyond him to describe this State further in concrete terms and much so to indicate the forms of struggle to reach it. Known for his obsession with pragmatism and belief that any definitive laws could not bind the flow of human history, he would avoid the speculative construction of this distant stage of human society. Not even Marx could describe what his dream communist society would be like beyond that it would be freed of the familiar contradictions. It essentially reflected a contradiction between human desire and material reality. It would be disaster to derive the meaning of this ideal State of Ambedkar's conception from what he did. He left that to posterity to decide as per their circumstances. But, rationally there could be little doubt that the vision of Ambedkar can only be realised in the communist society of Marx's conception where most (not all) of the contradictions in human society would have been resolved.

Dalits ought to internalise this vision and strive for its realisation. Ambedkar had a radical enough interpretation of his principles of liberty, equality and fraternity so as to feel inadequacy even in Marxism. He said that Marxism supported only equality (BAWS, 3/462). He was in need of a body of thought that would give equal importance to all these three principles. He met it with a convenient conceptualisation of religion. It is paradoxical that a person who is rational enough not to bind the posterity with his vision volitionally binds himself with what is said more than 25 centuries before. It is natural to find ideals better articulated in spiritual spheres but it is equally true that these dream worlds are incapable to provide any clue for their realisation on the earth except for their pet prescription to ignore the material reality and imagine it happened in the mind. They run away from the fact that the evil humans suffer from are the attributes of the divisions in human society, and their abolition essentially calls for struggles by the sufferers against those who perpetrate sufferings.

Howsoever, inherently rational the religion may be or radical its interpretation may be it cannot fully escape these limitations. It can be seen in relation to Buddhism handed down by Babasaheb Ambedkar with his radical interpretation. Notwithstanding the familiar quibbling around the Dhamma and Dhamma among dalits, what remained of Buddhism with them is what would happen to any religion. It is a different question whether Marxism embodied Ambedkar's ideals or not but it is certain that they are neither realisable neither through any kind of constitutional acrobatics nor through any religious practice.

State

Ambedkar's conception of State reflects some amount of autonomy from the hegemony of the ruling classes. It is why he expected it to act as per the constitutional structure and endeavoured to incorporate the pro-dalit bias into the Constitution. He must have realised the true nature of it, the boundaries of the autonomy and basic class bias of the State, when he actually reached not only the Constituent Assembly but also became the chairman of its Drafting Committee. In his anxiety to secure some provisions in favour of dalits, he accepted to be the 'hack' to write what was acceptable to the ruling caste-class representatives. He must have thought that within the given constraints he had done a good job of making the Constitution responsive to the needs of the downtrodden people.

Indeed, many of the provisions in the directive principles and elsewhere apparently bear clear imprint of his zeal and owe their existence to him. But, even they had to be within the strategic space provided by the rulers. His realisation of the folly was near complete when he had to burst out in utter dejection at its ineffectual implementation, that he would be the first man to burn the Constitution as it was of no good to any one. He was inaccurate, as the Constitution had proved good enough to the upper caste-class combine who had hegemonised complete political space in post-1947 India. He attributed it to the 'devils' in the Congressmen who had occupied the constitutional 'temple' he and others had built. Had he lived little longer, he would have realised that the ones that he considered his co-workers to build the temple were themselves the agents of the very devils.

He hoped to thwart the devil's march by people's power conceived in the form of a parliamentary party called Republican Party of India. It was within the very precincts of the temple inhabited by devils and therefore it soon proved to be the devil's feast. Ambedkar could not reach the point of understanding that the State is a mere instrument in the hands of the ruling classes to coerce the ruled ones into submission to their interests. Until the downtrodden themselves become the ruling class, they cannot expect the State to do good to them. Whatever good that appears to come to their share, in ultimate balance accrues to the other side in multiple measure.

The post-1947 State, which has never tired of propagandising its concern for dalits and poor, has in fact been singularly instrumental in aggravating the caste problem with its policies. Even the apparently progressive policies in the form of Land Ceiling Act, Green Revolution, Programme of Removal of Poverty, Reservations to Dalits in Services and Mandal Commission etc. have resulted against their professed objectives. The effect of the Land Ceiling Act, has been in creating a layer of the middle castes farmers which could be consolidated in caste terms to constitute a formidable constituency.

In its new incarnation, this group that has traditionally been the immediate upper caste layer to dalits, assumed virtual custody of Brahminism in order to coerce dalit landless labourers to serve their socio-economic interests and suppress their assertive expression in the bud. The Green Revolution was the main instrument to introduce capitalisation in agrarian sector. It reinforced the innate hunger of the landlords and big farmers for land as this State sponsored revolution produced huge surplus for them. It resulted in creating geographical imbalance and promoting unequal terms of trade in favour of urban areas. Its resultant impact on dalits has been far more excruciating than that of the Land Ceiling Act. The much publicised programme for Removal of Poverty has aggravated the gap between the heightened hopes and aspirations of dalits on one hand and the feelings of depravation among the poorer sections of non-dalits in the context of the special programmes especially launched for upliftment of dalits. The tension that ensued culminated in increasingly strengthening the caste - based demands and further aggravating the caste - divide.

The reservations in services for dalits, notwithstanding its benefits, have caused incalculable damage in political terms. Reservations created hope, notional stake in the system and thus dampened the alienation; those who availed of its benefit got politically emasculated and in course consciously or unconsciously served as the props of the system. The context of scarcity of jobs provided ample opportunity to reactionary forces to divide the youth along caste lines. Mandal Commission, that enthused many progressive parties and people to upheld its extension of reservation to the backward castes, has greatly contributed to strengthen the caste identities of people. Inasmuch as it empowers the backward castes, actually their richer sections, it is bound to worsen the relative standing of dalits in villages.

Thus, the State, its welfare mask notwithstanding, has viciously and consistently acted against dalits and poor people. It is a complete contra-evidence to hopes of Ambedkar who strove to maximise and make use of the autonomous space of the State for the benefits of the have-nots, particularly dalits. It is one thing to assume autonomous space but quite another to equate it with caste-class neutrality. Unfortunately, the dalit political behaviour always reflected this erroneous notion of caste-class neutrality of the State. It has already caused great damage to the dalit interests. The radical Ambedkar might have strategy to use State for dalit cause but would never see it as caste-class neutral.

Democracy

Ambedkar had unshakeable faith in democracy. In his conception of an exploitation-less society, democracy has an extra-ordinary role. Democracy means 'one person, one vote'; and 'one vote, one value'. Democracy means empowerment of any person for participating in the process of decision-making relating to her/him, democracy means liberty, equality and fraternity - Ambedkar's definition of democracy had such a tone. Because he presided over making of the Constitution and is being projected as its chief architect, there is a misunderstanding that parliamentary democracy is what he wanted. But nothing could be farther from the truth than this. He himself spoke against parliamentary democracy. For instance, he defined parliamentary democracy as "voting by the people in favour of their owners and handing over the rights of ruling over themselves" (BAWS 10/36). This provides a glimpse of the expanse of his ideal, which certainly was much beyond the Indian Constitution or any common place understanding about him. His conception of democracy appears to be purely people oriented. He showed that the bookish concepts of equality are detrimental to the disabled sections of society in the prevailing social setting and proposed a fundamental change in the concept of equality. It envisaged complete abolition of inequality. His principle of positive discrimination is based on this very concept of equality. But the operational aspects of this concept involved the need for some kind of autonomous institution, which was met by 'State' and 'religion'. It is necessary to stress that his greatness lies in the radicality of his conceptions, his vision of a human society sans any kind of exploitation; not in the remedies or apparatus he proposed in the circumstances prevailing in his time.

Buddhism

Religion was the institution envisaged to control the organisation at the level of an individual and society to curb their latent exploitative instincts. It was a philosophical device that would regulate their lives, including the interface between them at the most primary level. Ambedkar viewed it as a code of behaviour, a way of life that is upheld by the multitude. He insisted that this code should be based on and be compatible with the precepts of modern science. The religion as normally defined or that became a pill of opium for Marx, was not the religion of his concept either. When ultimately he embraced Buddhism he claimed to have used the criteria of modern science. Buddhism, as it was propounded by Gautama the Buddha hardly qualified to be called religion in so far as it did not have even a single of the three necessary features of religion - viz.: belief in God, permanent entity and a set of rituals. But it is a matter of opinion whether its institutionalised form that we are familiar with still retains its uniqueness. Shunning the futile debate, it could be definitely said and has been acknowledged that the Buddhism that he embraced was far more radical than its familiar version. His 'Buddha and His Dhamma' is replete with instances where he reconstructs and redefines Buddhism with a near-scientific approach.

Buddhism, in its purer form, puzzled many people with its radical outlook and rational approach. It did not have a place for God, ritual of any kind or for any permanent entity that characterise all other religions. Morality is said to be its basis and surprisingly a pure democratic criterion of 'happiness and welfare of many' (*Bahujan Hitay, Bahujan Sukhay*) as its motto. He exhorted Bhikkus (monks) and Bhikkunis (nuns) to wander all over the world carrying the Dhamma to people and not to rest at one place. Even by this, he did not mean spread of his creed; it was essentially an expression of the compassion and concern he had for suffering humanity. For, he had repeatedly advised people not to take his word for granted but test it on the touchstone of their experience and intellect before accepting or rejecting it. He never claimed any role in their emancipation asking them to be their own light- " *Atta Deep Bhava*". He treated the Sangha (the order of his Bhikkus and Bhikkunis) as a microcosm of the society. The Bhikkus and Bhikkunis were not allowed to have any private property except for the basic eight things for their personal use. In economic and political sphere, he put forth the ideal of service before the monks and nuns. The people who did not observe this ideal are said to be the parasites, consuming national wealth.

In the realm of philosophy, Buddha's contributions were far reaching. Several centuries before Hegel, he presented full-blown dialectics in his philosophy. Hegel had provided the basis for Marxism, in a sense that Marx had just to make the reality in Hegel upside down. Buddha's reality also had shades of Hegel, although he never explicitly accepted, unlike Hegel, the primacy to the consciousness, but he did not get his Marx to resurrect his dialectical non-materialism. The principle of impermanence is the fundamental tenet of Buddhism. For Buddha, any thing that is not permanent does not exist; its application is all pervading. Somewhat as a corollary of this principle, Buddha proposed the tenet of dependent origination (*Pratit Samutpad*). With regard to materialism, and consciousness, Buddhist philosophy goes quite close to materialism, in the sense that it does not regard independent existence of consciousness without the body. Significantly, Buddha's approach reflects his orientation to help people emancipate themselves and not pontificate on things irrelevant. It is quite the same as Marx insisting on 'changing the world' as the object of philosophy. There are many 'un-knowables' on which he kept his famous silence. His 'middle path' appears to provide for the grey areas where a definite stand could be erroneous.

Ambedkar's attraction to Buddhism is basically on account of its moral base and absence of irrationality. On this account it has been the subject of admiration and awe of scores of intellectual people. A person like Einstein had opined that it was the only religion suitable for the scientific age. Ambedkar must have had multiple motives behind embracing Buddhism. Basically he was in search of a religion as an instrument of internal control on individuals' instincts and social behaviour. He had a social need of an appropriate cultural identity for his people after they had discarded the chains of Hinduism. He was moreover aware of the aberrations that had crept in Buddhism and had to redefine it to present its rational version. Basically, he included many a rational interpretation presented by scholars like Dharmanand Kosambi, and left a mirror to posterity to have a glimpse of his worldview. This worldview, does take cognisance of the material reality of living, subscribes to law of causation, relies on humane rational to interpret the world and finally embodies a craving for changing it. Although, there is no difficulty in understanding or empathising with his decision, the claim that Buddhism could be the substitute for Marxism or a liberating philosophy for the whole world is not only anachronistic but also grossly magnified idealistic hyperbole.

Another notable feature is his repeated reference to Marxism in relation to Buddhism. Many of his disciples misused it as his opposition and even extended it to enmity to Marxism. It is untrue and unfortunate. Like his claims to have checked the consistency of Buddhist tenets with those of modern science, he claimed that his Buddhism was Marxism plus some thing.

It certainly shows that he did not hold Marxism in the same esteem as science, but there is no doubt that he considered Marxism as the near-best and willed that his chosen religion should contain all of it and be superior to it. It is interesting to study what aspects he considers important in Marxism and what methodology he employs to compare them with corresponding contents in Buddhism. What is important is to note that with the amount of information available on Marxism to him, he considered it great enough to serve as a benchmark to assess Buddhism.

On Marx and Communism

Babasaheb Ambedkar thought that the communists while attempting to bring about revolution do not bother about justice or injustice, truth or untruth; atrocities and taboos and if times demand, are prepared for bloodshed to establish the State with soviet methods. It was shocking to his moral philosophy and therefore he always expressed his reservation and even disapproval for these methods. He says "The object of communism is as economic and social as it is political. About social, the revolution in public opinion has not taken place. Moreover, majority of people does not have ability to understand the economic and political aims of communism " (BB, 337 (7)). Elsewhere, he cites the historical examples in the context of historical materialism of Marx and says that the political revolution has always taken place on the background of social revolutions. Howsoever congenial the objective situation for revolution may be, it should be an axiom that till the revolutionary consciousness in people does not impel them to revolt, revolution cannot take place. He could not agree with the communists of his times who reared a mechanistic belief that revolutionary consciousness would automatically be born out of the material reality around. He wanted to stress the importance of the mediation of the conscientisation process in creating the revolutionary consciousness. He had little difficulty in visualising the communist prospects of a stateless and classless society as many people have. But there cannot be any doubt that he wished materialisation of some such 'utopia' where all kinds of exploitation would be deeply buried in the past and all the people would enjoy liberty, equality, and fraternity in their sublimest part in full measure.

One of the main problems with the prevailing icons of Ambedkar is that they project him uniformly as anti-Marx. It is the single saddest aspect for the moribund state of the dalit movement. Ambedkar often referred to Marx in various ways but never discussed him at the philosophical plane where essentially Marx resides. It is notable that he has not much to disagree with Marx on the ideological level except for the derogatory comments on materialism. Any one knowing even the basics of Marxism would say that these comments do not have anything to do with Marxism. They relate with the mechanical materialism and not with the dialectical materialism of Marx. What prompted these comments perhaps was the practice of the then communists who vulgarised materialism in tending to ignore anything not material and have been spiteful of the movements of dalits. Beyond this nowhere he appears to discuss basics of Marxism viz., dialectical materialism, historical materialism and scientific socialism. He did express doubt about the uni-linear flow of human history but unfortunately not in any depth to discern the areas of disagreement. Insofar as it implies that the history can develop divergent streams under certain conditions, the validity of the doubt cannot be dismissed.

Ambedkar and Marx share many common spaces. Both were driven by the same goal of reaching the society sans exploitation. Both had a firm commitment to the most oppressed people (technically not so for Marx, though), and saw them in the vanguard role for bringing about the revolutionary change for overall progress of the mankind. Marx arrived at his formulation by scientific study of history and found that in the era of capitalism the working class would be the vanguard of the socialist revolution. Ambedkar did not see working class in India and any probability of its emergence until the castes were annihilated. He therefore saw the necessity of launching the anti-caste movement with its worst victims - the untouchables in the vanguard role. The language and syntax certainly differed because of different frameworks they came to follow.

Marx laboured on rigorous philosophical formulation and came out with his own body of thought or a science of revolution. Ambedkar got drowned into the turbulence of present and used philosophy for his reassurance or as a support for practice. A large part of his thoughts have a polemical hue and therefore cannot be used shorn of its context without risk. Ambedkar quite like Marx felt that the object of philosophy was to change the world. His statement that he does not believe in any 'ism' can be considered anti-dogma. It is with the same sense he used to say He was a realist. What a coincidence between this and the statement of Karl Max, when he said, "I am not a Marxist "!

Besides these similarities, Marx was always referred to by Ambedkar as a kind of benchmark right up to his last days though unfortunately he never reflected the rigour that is expected in such discussions. It hovered around the superfluous and hearsay features of Marxism. Serious thinkers of Marx are surprised at his conception of Marxism till they are reminded of their location in times. Notwithstanding Ambedkar's claim that he had read more number of books on Marxism than that read by all the communists in India, in those days the philosophical material on Marxism does not seem to be easily available. What was available was the stuff that talked about the Bolshevik revolution and what went in the Soviet Russia. Rarely does one find a purely philosophical discussion even in Marxist circles in those times. The point is that the impression spread by the vested interests that Ambedkar had rejected Marxism after careful consideration is firstly not true. Whatever his understanding of it, his interest in Marxism had never waned. He prophesied that if Buddhism failed to deliver the results, the whole world would go in for Marxism. Secondly, his feeling of inadequacy of Marxism was related to the superfluous picture of Marxism available to him.

Obviously, Marxism did not have what he was looking for, to readily offer. In the realm of practice, the natural possibility of an alliance between him and the communists seems to have been thwarted by the mechanical outlook of the Indian communists who refused even to take cognisance of the problem of castes. Their ostrich like behaviour towards the frozen reality of this land was more unMarxist than anything conceivable. Still, Ambedkar had joined hands with them during the ILP days to protest against the anti-labour bill and had led the historical strike of the workers in Bombay. But this alliance was short-lived. Endowed with the most potent tools for analysing the social phenomena, it was the duty of the communists to understand Ambedkar and not vice versa.

They not only failed in that but also went further to antagonistically oppose him. The Brahminical puritanism that they brought in Marxism was totally misfounded as the times proved. On the sheer consideration that dalits as the most oppressed people of this country did constitute their potential base, their strategy should have had a place for them if they were really committed to revolution. But, it is a fact that dalits just did not exist in their scheme of things. If any one were to be held responsible for betrayal of the revolution in India, it would be these mistaken comrades and not Ambedkar.

Unlike the frontline communist leaders in Bombay, Ambedkar did not need to declass himself to internalise the proletarian class-consciousness. Ambedkar belonged to the working class, he lived in the chawl - the mill workers quarters in Bombay. Even during his stay in USA and Europe, he lived the life of utter depravation, not even having enough food to eat. But for his western attire, which was supposed to reflect disgust for humbug prevalent in those days, he continued to identify himself with the masses and working classes in their trials and tribulations. He did not have any necessity to demonstrate this identity by any extraneous means. The overpowering politician in him in the later days certainly eroded this consciousness and consequently led him increasingly after the short solutions shunning the direct struggles.

The communists basically had their base in the Trade Unions (TU) of the textile mill workers of Bombay. These TUs were tight-lipped on the discrimination faced by dalits in not getting the jobs in better remunerative departments like weaving in textile mills. The economic condition of dalits was much worse than their *savarna* counterparts. Ambedkar observed that the communists used these TUs for their political gains rather than for the welfare of the working class. Whenever they took precipitate action to strike the work, the workers tended to suffer differentially, owing to their castewise placements. Ambedkar's objection to this 'irresponsible' TU behaviour was on two counts: (i) they were driven by raw 'economism' to the detriment of prospects of enhancing the political consciousness of the working class, (ii) they were using them as cannon fodder in the promotion of their political interests. Ambedkar's writing on communism or Marxism is heavily imbued with his annoyance with the Bombay-communists. This legacy to identify Marxism with its self-appointed practitioners still appears to be followed by dalits. They cite examples of the parliamentary communist parties to show the lacuna or inapplicability of Marxism. It is necessary for them to understand that Marxism needs criticism but it presupposes its careful study.

One of the greatest barriers the communists pose to others is their unMarxist and puritanical attitude. In India that was naturally likened to Brahminism with which all were familiar and because by default the communist leadership happened to come from Brahmin and other *dwija* castes. Marxist essence presupposes scientific enquiry, a dynamic understanding of the situations and requisite tolerance for divergent views. But the institutionalised Marxism always appeared ready with the glued labels like renegade, reactionary, revisionist etc. to mark out those who did not toe the official line. These fallen comrades then are treated as the worst class enemies nullifying in one shot their life time contribution to the revolution. This tradition has unconsciously induced a dogmatic behaviour in the Marxist circles. By virtue of the powerful analytical tools of Marxism their analyses still read superior to any one around but it could be generally said that they have not made full use of their potentialities. They are adept at stuffing new facts into the old inferences to demonstrate eternal validity of their dogma. For instance, if they had seen the objective reality in Ambedkar's time as they did now about the problem of castes, the history of this country could have been a bit different! What worries the committed revolutionists is this attitude of the 'official' Marxists. For instance, there does not appear any significant appreciation of the changes in the mode of production under capitalism with the advances in communication and computational (information) technologies. The capitalist organisations have undergone sea change with adoption of them from the Fordist models that constituted the reference for the Marxist schema.

These organisations have re-engineered themselves into delayered, downsized, flexible, decentralised units and are tending to destructure so as to reduce the cycle times with the fullest use of information technology. In place of factories employing huge numbers of workers engaged in monotonous assembly line tasks, alienated from the product of their labour are coming the distributed production units with knowledge workers, fairly autonomous in their work sphere, located in apparently authority neutralised teams, with flexi-times and profit sharing avenues. The policy package of globalisation that is out to increasingly marginalise and crush the people in poorer countries is just the corollary of this paradigm change. Although, contrary to opinion of many, this socalled flexible capitalism does not any way affect the validity of the theory, one worries to note no influence of these changes in the strategy and tactics of the Marxists. The redefinition project will have to take into account this emergent shape of the world.

One of the problems Ambedkar appears to face in accepting Marxism is its prescription of the 'dictatorship of proletariat' during the post-revolutionary transition period to communism. For him any kind of dictatorship was an anathema. He equates it with monarchy. While it is true that he had not understood the basic rationale behind or rather derivation of this concept, his apprehensions cannot be said to be mis-founded as the later developments in the socialist countries revealed. To overcome this lacuna he devises a via media solution of State socialism without demolishing the parliamentary democracy. To cover up the inherent lacunae in the parliamentary democracy, he proposes to incorporate the structure of the economy in the Constitution and limit the sovereignty of the parliament. He visualised this solution as bringing in socialism without 'shedding a drop of blood' or resorting to dictatorship. It is unfortunate that instead of understanding the inherent defect of the framework of the political economy, he strove to propose such unrealistic solutions.

The separation of the dalit and communist movements has caused the greatest loss to the revolution in India. The fact that dalit and oppressed people, who constitute the backbone of this movement were kept away from it, restricted its growth. On the other side, on account of discarding the ideology of class struggle, the dalit movement could never come to grips with the real problem of dalits and comprehend the means to solve them. As a result, the condition of this community went on deteriorating, their movement remained revolving around the trifling, temporary and emotional issues thrown in their front by the cunning of ruling classes and their leaders remained entangled with their self interests and politics of status quo. The project of redefinition of Ambedkar will consist in systematically examining Ambedkar's conceptions and relocating him in relation to Marxism.

Aspects of the Strategy and Tactics

In the context of strategy, some of Ambedkar's contributions are really noteworthy. He brought the struggle against Brahminism into the political battlefield. He inferred that without political power the social and religious structures will collapse and motivated his followers to capture political power. But his conception of political power being acutely constrained by the parliamentary framework where bargaining is the predominant medium of securing political power, inevitably it made way for all kinds of aberrations and perversities to creep in. The prevailing politics being the game of possibilities, he was soon sucked into its vortex. Politics came to dominate the other aspects of his personality. Slowly, the impact of politics started becoming visible everywhere. This phase significantly contributed to multiplication of his inconsistencies out of tactical imperatives. Dalits have taken this legacy of parliamentary politics very seriously, almost as the be all and end all of their political being. It may be, interesting to probe how much damage this kind of political orientation inflicted on the dalit movement.

It is altogether a different question whether Ambedkar had any other alternative to parliamentary politics for political practice. It may be argued that in the context of his resources, adversarial environment and to some extent his personal limitations, he had none. Even if it is taken as correct, it should not be forgotten that it was a matter of strategy and tactic that presuppose contextual variables: it cannot be taken as the lasting value.

The fundamental source of most of Ambedkar's political thoughts and action is his conception of State and religion, that he had adopted as the extraneous instruments to reconcile the state of flux of things and the necessity of order in them. It is necessary to understand that both, the State as well as religion, are the products of the evolutionary process of the human society. There is nothing inevitable about them. Marx took State as the instrument of coercion in the hands of ruling classes and religion as the opium of the masses. Dalits have a long experience of nearly five decades with the so-called welfare State of Ambedkar's design. What does it say? Does the State side with them in their conflict with the landlords? Does it come to their rescue when every day three or four of their daughters are raped? Does it come to save the shame of their women when they are paraded naked in the streets? Does it take their side when they come in conflict with landlords, moneylenders in villages or with management in the modern settings? Does it really ensure they get their dues as provided in the Constitution or punish the defaulting management for non-compliance? To all of such questions the answer could only be in the negative. It is not a matter of 'devils occupying the temples' as Ambedkar lamented seeing the people occupying the Constitutional positions. The State possesses the characteristics of its master class. In India the upper caste capitalists, landlords, top bureaucrats, etc. being the ruling class, the State can never have saints who would favour dalits. It is a fact that even the government by a dalit party like the BSP could not transform it into a dalit State.

Religion, in Ambedkar's conception is necessary to maintain the moral order of the society. It may be interesting to examine to what extent it conforms to this idealistic expectation. Buddhism, which undoubtedly is the most rational of all the religions, does not have any evidence of having created over its near millennium long tenure in India such an order of the society which could claim liberty, equality and fraternity of Ambedkar's conception. Ambedkar's argument that the Bhikku Sangha in Buddhism was the prototype of this kind of society becomes invalid once we call into question the role of Sangha in the production process. Before that, the order that envisaged nostalgically to recreate the value of the vanishing *Gana Rajya* in microcosm against the evil of rising monarchies, cannot just sublimate to the era of capitalism without being an alley of exploiters unless it transforms itself in some way as a catalyst for the revolution. The moral tenets of Buddhism likewise cannot submerge the lure of surplus extraction, that is its dominating ethos. If at all, it may help it become more pronounced by weakening the resistance of the exploited masses. As we empirically see, the Buddhism of his conception could not produce even a trace of morality in its adherents. On the contrary, for the masses it presents the distorted, if not inverted, worldview; it orients them to look inwards for their misery and be blind to the reality that some one exploits him. He could certainly derive mental peace and pleasure but it is a state of an intoxicated mind. Keeping in mind the causal links in Ambedkar's adoption of these instruments, the redefinition project needs to address these issues afresh.

The strategy of the ruling class always stresses on diversion of peoples' attention from their real problems and their disarmament - both in physical and ideological terms. They invariably have a multi-layered strategy in place for this purpose. The vanguard parties of the ruling classes open up sentimental fronts and attempt to divert the attention of people as their real problems get aggravated. Secondly, their time-tested methods of adulterating radical ideas with the masses are always in operation. Towards this end, we see all the ruling parties vying with each other in co-opting Ambedkar. 'Ambedkar' represents a potentially dangerous ideological weapon in the hands of the Indian proletariat and so the ruling class will be hell bent on blunting its edge. They will do everything to eulogise him not only for wooing dalits for their immediate electoral gains but also to neutralise him as the radical ideological force by propagandising a distorted version of the latter. Dalits will have to exercise vigil over their ideological assets even after redefining Ambedkar.

Conclusion

For at least over last four decades Dalits have devotedly followed Ambedkar as their ideal, as a virtual God and zealously practised, as they claim, his teachings. Their social being could be seen to be totally imbued with what they call Ambedkarism - the veritable science of their emancipation. If it is true, and no one would deny it is not, it should be pertinent to ask why despite this flawless following of Ambedkar they continue to be in a pathetic state in every sense. Barring a handful dalits in the government and public sector services and of course politicians, they continue to occupy the lowest rung in the social as well as economic hierarchy of Indian society. Their politics, notwithstanding the media hype, gauged by the measure of general empowerment, continues to be in shambles. Over these decades, their relative situation either shows stagnation or decline. The insinuation to relate this State with their faith in Ambedkar itself would be distasteful for many dalits. But, it is vital for ones that are committed to their liberation to squarely face the facts and dispassionately find out where the rot lay.

Generally, beyond the first burst of anger in reaction to this question, one would face the defensive arguments to discount this relationship. Typically, they tend to attribute their miserable situation to the lack of competent leadership after Babasaheb Ambedkar, to the educated dalits who they think have become dalit Brahmins and have deserted the community; and sometimes to the people themselves for their extreme self- centredness. Sometimes, the finger is raised at the high caste hegemony that has neutralised the impact of the Constitution that Ambedkar created. Some, particularly the leadership, even would dismiss the basic premise itself that there is something wrong with the dalit movement. They might even go so far as to claim net achievements indicating the prosperity of themselves or some others of their ilk. More sober may argue that what is seen is the transition state. Conceding them all some amount of validity even would not erase the stark fact that the general situation of the vast majority of dalit masses remains still alarmingly pathetic. Externalisation of the reasons for this state has not helped dalits any bit. The time has come for dalits to self -critically see whether anything was wrong with their ideology and / or with their practice thereof.

Reviewing the post-Ambedkar dalit movement at some significant milestones, one finds a queer underscoring behaviour, believed to be in accordance with the teachings of Babasaheb Ambedkar, that is certainly incongruent with the essence of what he taught. This dichotomy between the essential Ambedkar and the 'Ambedkar' in the faith of dalit masses - the icon of Ambedkar, comes out as the problematic in this review. In relation to almost every aspect of his teaching there emerged an icon that represented varying amount of distortion. Insofar as they constituted the ideology that gripped the masses, these icons can be seen to be at the root of the dalit pathos. Among the myriad sources for these icons, Ambedkar himself might come out as the major source. Because, even a myth can not sustain for long without some material base.

The icons of Ambedkar thus could be linked to some such bases, howsoever tenuous, within his own life. The rationalist in Ambedkar never hesitated to change his opinions and behaviour if the facts so warranted. They appear to be inconsistencies to the ones who see it sans context. His distance from the focus of control in his socio-political environment, the vastly varying target audience (ranging from the Englishmen to the illiterate dalits) to whom he had to communicate, the exigency to respond to the dynamics of communities set in motion by the pre- independence politics, his anxiety to accomplish as many gains for dalits as he could in his life time, the exigencies for 'short' actions at the expense of 'long' vision inevitably led to mark patterns that could support array of behaviours. The first to take advantage of it were his own lieutenants for serving their personal ambitions that set the trends of distortion of Ambedkar in the minds of gullible dalit masses.

The ruling classes that always look for the grounds to divide masses had severally reinforced this distortion and accelerated fragmentation of dalits in every field. They, along with willing collaboration of dalit politicians and emerging elite, promoted and sustained the particular icons of Ambedkar that would prevent political coalescence of dalits and suck them into the vortex of parliamentary politics in order to bring the establishment much needed legitimacy. Dalits failed to note this cunning and let themselves flow in the currents of confusion the ruling classes deliberately created. Today, with increasing political crises the ruling classes seem vying with each other in co-opting Ambedkar, as though that may be their last chance of survival. If dalits stood their grounds well, that might have proved to be their last act. But, unfortunately dalits are giving them new leases of life by blinding themselves to the reality. Not only that they have not resisted these ruling class machinations but on the contrary they are curiously seen to swell the cadres of these castiest, communalist and anti-poor groups and parties. These parties who openly profess the ideology of Hindu revivalism and represent all that is decadent in Indian tradition show the temerity to project Ambedkar among their ideologues. Apart from the reasons of security that propel dalit youth into their fold, the compradore behaviour of dalit elite certainly has influenced the phenomenon. What is common in all the attempts by the ruling classes is to sap 'Ambedkar' of its rebellious content.

It is advantageous for them to show that he was the chief architect of the Indian Constitution, committed to parliamentary democracy and opposed to any ideology that propagates violence or revolution. He is projected to favour gradual change implying that dalits should patiently wait and strive persuasively to better their own lives. He is projected as the Bodhisatva that inspires *nirvana* - the State of total detachment from worldly matters. All these images have caused significant damage to the emancipatory struggles of dalits. Some of these images might be the purposeful and blatant disfiguring of Ambedkar but some of them represent genuine dilemma arising from Ambedkar's own stands on various issues. From the viewpoint of the comprehensive pro-people change in the present historical phase a democratic revolution is an imperative. The motive force for this revolution ought to sprout from dalits. The history provides a strong testimony that any radical movement in the country could be sustained by dalits and tribals at its base.

Ambedkar as a symbol for dalit aspirations holds a key to the barrage that has so far bound the revolutionary upsurge in India below the alarming levels. If one concedes that Ambedkar's framework is going to haunt revolutionary commitment till the Indian Democratic Revolution actually happens and that Ambedkar represents the ideological weaponry in the hands of dalits who along with other oppressed people are going to be the axis of this revolution, then one would clearly see the need to redefine Ambedkar in radical terms commensurate with this purpose. Many aspects of confusion with regard to the facts could be cleared with rational interpretation of his thoughts. But much might need the logical extrapolation of his basic thinking which for some reason appears to have settled in erroneous forms. As he himself showed the way in the case of his redefinition of Buddha's Dhamma, dalits will have to undertake this task, for giving themselves a powerful ideology. Their future as a social group almost hinges on this task.

There are enough clues left behind by Ambedkar himself that point to this need. There is no doubt that he was frustrated at the end of his life seeing the undesired aftermath of his lifelong struggle. He had to lament over the betrayal of the educated dalits in whom he had seen the crusaders of his mission. He had to weep with remorse that he could not do anything for his people in the villages. He had to disown the Constitution for working on which he had cut short his life at least by a few years. He had to swallow the frustration of not being able to pilot the Constitution of his conception (States and Minorities). He had to regret the anti-people State that emerged in republican India. He obviously lacked the analytical tools to see through the reasons for these happenings. His excessive religiosity and spirituality at the fag end of his life perhaps could be taken as the manifestation of this frustration. The social engineer could only be busy with problems; he is unlikely to come to grip with the design defects in the system. Almost every thing that Ambedkar pinned his hopes on can be found today in antithetical shambles. His educational society, his vision of Buddhism, the political party of his conception, the social reforms could be some of the examples. These tragic aftermaths also would denote the necessity of a critical review of Ambedkar's thoughts if they were to be used as the ideology to further the dalit movement towards its logical end. If this process is sincerely followed, there cannot be any doubt that this 'redefined Ambedkar' would be a revolutionary icon, organically linking the dalit struggle to the revolutionary struggle in the world. It will truly globalise the dalit struggle.

Bibliography

Abbe, D.: *Hindu Manners, Customs and Ceremonies*, AES, New Delhi, 1983.

Agarwal, S. P., and Aggarwal, J. C.: *Educational and Social Uplift of Backward Classes: At What Cost and How? Mandal Commission and After,* Concept Publishing Co., New Delhi, 1979.

Ahir, D.C.: *Dr. Ambedkar, Buddhism and Social Change*, BR Publishing, Delhi, 1993.

Ambedkar, B. R.: *Annihilation of Caste: An Undelivered Speech,* Arnold Publishers, New Delhi, 1990.

Asghar Ali.: *Mandal Commission Controversy*, Ajanta Publications, Delhi, 1991.

Bakshi, S. R.: B.R. *Ambedkar: His Political and Social Ideology*. New Delhi: Deep & deep publications, 2000.

Barill, C.: *Social and Political Ideas of B.R. Ambedkar*, Aalekh Publishers, Jaipur, 1977.

Bhagat Ram: *Educating Harijans*, Academic Press, Haryana, 1981.

Bhatia, K.L.: *Dr. B.R. Ambedkar: Social Justice and the Indian Constitution,* Deep & Deep, New Delhi, 1994.

Chanchreek, K.L., Prasad, S. & Kumar, R.: *Dr. Ambedkar. Social Justice and Political Safeguards for Depressed Classes,* Shree, New Delhi, 1991.

Danda, A.K.: *Weaker Sections in Indian Villages*, Inter-India, New Delhi, 1993.

Deshpande, Vasant: *Towards Social Intergration: Problems of Adjustment of SC Elites*, Shubhada- Saraswat, Pune, 1978.

Epstein, T. S.: *Economic Development and Social Change in South India*, Manchester University Press, Manchester, 1962.

Gawali, P.A.: *Society and Social Disabilities under the Peshwas*, National, New Delhi, 1988.

Ishwaran, K.: *Shivpur: A South Indian Village*, Routledge, London, 1968.

Jaffrelot, Christophe: *Dr. Ambedkar and Untouchability: Fighting the Indian Caste System*, New York, Columbia University Press, 2005.

Johnson, Glen and Bose, Sipra: *Social Mobility Among Untouchables,* Cohesion and Conflict in Modern India, New Delhi, 1978.

Johnson, S. B.: *Social Mobility Among Untouchables*, Vikas, New Delhi, 1979.

Jose, K.: *Constitutional Provisions for the Scheduled Castes*, Indian Social Institute, New Delhi, 1984.

Joshi, B.R.: *Untouchable! Voices of the Dalit Liberation Movement*, Zed and MRG, London, 1986.

Juergensmeyer, Mark: *Religion as Social Vision: The Movement Against Untouchability in 20th Century Punjab*, University of California Press, Berkeley, 1979.

Khare, R. S.: *The Untouchable as Himself: Ideology, Identity and Pragmatism Among the Lucknow Chamars*, Cambridge University Press, London, 1984.

Kshirsagar, R. K.: *Dalit Movement in India and Its Leaders (1857-1956)*, MD Pub. Pvt. Ltd., New Delhi, 1994.

Lal, Shyam: *Caste and Political Mobilisation: The Bhangis*, Panchsheel Prakashan, Jaipur, 1981.

Majumdar, D. N.: *Caste and Communication in an Indian Village*, Asia Publishing House, Bombay, 1958.

Mann, K.: *Tribal Women in a Changing Society*, Mittal Publications, Delhi, 1987.

Marriott, Mckim: *Village India: Studies in the Little Community*, The University of Chicago Press, Chicago, 1955.

Meyer, Mark J.: *Religion as Social Vision: The Movement Against Untouchability in 20th Century in Punjab*, University of California Press, Berkeley, 1982.

Michael J.: *The Untouchables in Contemporary India*, University of Arizona Press, Arizona, 1972.

Mohan, P.E.: *Scheduled Castes: History of Elevation, Tamil Nadu, 1900-1955*. New Era Pub., Madras, 1993.

Mumtaz Ali: *Human Rights and the Dalits*, Uppal Publishing House, New Delhi, 1995.

Naidu, Ch. M.: *Salt Satyagraha in the Coastal Andhra*, Mittal Publications, Delhi, 1986.

Nath, Trilok: *Politics of the Depressed Classes*, Deputy Publications, Delhi, 1987.

Nim, H.L.: *Thoughts on Dr. Ambedkar*, Siddhartha Educational and Cultural Society, Agra, 1969.

O'Malley, L. S. S.: *Indian Caste Customs*, Vikas Publishing House, Delhi, 1974.

Pantavane, G.: *Patrikar Dr. Babasaheb Ambedkar*, Abhijit, Nagpur, 1987.

Parmaji, S.: *Caste Reservations and Performance*, Mamata Publications, Warangal, 1985.

Partha, C.: *Caste and Subaltern Consciousness*, Oxford University Press, Delhi, 1994.

Pradhan, A. C.: *The Emergence of the Depressed Classes*, Bookland International, Bhubaneshwar, 1986.

Prahlad G.: *Dalit Movement in Maharashtra*, Kanak Publications, New Delhi, 1991.

Rajasekharaiah, A.M.: *B.R. Ambedkar: the Politics of Emancipation*, Sindhu Publications, Bombay, 1971.

Ram, Jagivan: *Caste Challenge in India*, Vision Books, New Delhi, 1980.

Robb, Peter: *Dalit Movements and the Meanings of Labour in India*, Oxford University Press, New Delhi, 1993.

Sarkar, J.: *Caste, Occupation and Change*, B. R. Publishing Co., Delhi, 1984.

Shah, Ghanshyam: *Caste Association and Political Processes in Gujarat*, Popular Prakashan, Bombay, 1975.

Sharma, Kusum: *Ambedkar and Indian Constitution*, New Delhi, Ashish Pub. House, 1992.

Shashi B.R.: *Ambedkar and Human Rights*, KK Publishers, New Delhi, 1981.

Shetty, V. T. Rajshekar: *Dalit Movement in Karnataka*, Christian Literature Society, Madras, 1978.

Silverberg, James: *Social Mobility in the Caste System in India*, Mouton Publishers, The Hague, 1968.

Singh, S. N.: *Reservation: Problems and Prospects*, Uppal Publishing House, New Delhi, 1987.

Tope, T.K.: *Dr. B.R. Ambedkar, A Symbol of Social Revolt*, Maharashtra Information Centre, New Delhi, 1964.

Varale, B.H.: *Dr. Babasaheb Ambedkarrancha Sangaki*, Shrividya Prakashan, Pune, 1988.

Wolf, G.: *Re-inventing Tradition,* Indian Institute of Advanced Studies, Shimla, 1992.

Yogesh, A.: *The Changing Frontiers of Caste*, National Publishing House, Delhi, 1968.

Index

□□□